COINCIDENCES

COINCIDENCES

Scott B. Smith

Living Business Press
Aptos, California

PRINTED IN THE UNITED STATES OF AMERICA

FIRST EDITION

Library of Congress Cataloging-in-Publication Data

Smith, Scott B., 1940-
Coincidences.

1. Smith, Scott B., 1940- . 2. Alcoholics—United States—Biography. 3. Journalists—United States—Biography. 4. Alcoholics—Rehabilitation—United States—Case studies. I. Title.
HV5293.S63A3 1987 362.2'92'0924 [B] 87-17264
ISBN 0-942294-75-0

Acknowledgment is made for permission to reprint excerpts from the following:

Portions of "A Vision of the Aquarian Age" by George Trevelyan are quoted by permission of Stillpoint International Publishing.

Portions of "Journeys Out of the Body" by Robert A. Monroe are quoted with permission of Doubleday Anchor Press.

Lyrics from the song "Winners" by Joe Raposo are quoted with permission of Sergeant Music Co., copyright 1973.

To Don, Laura, Ann, Al and "A", who endured it.

A Note from the Author:

This is how my life was, what changed, and how it is now. I've changed very few circumstances or names. In a few instances, I have omitted reference to persons who were involved but whose roles were not necessary to the telling. In each case, I have done that in their interest.

As you'll see, Chapter 17 brings a change in content and tone. It was necessary to the accurate portrayal of what had happened to date. In fact, my only intent throughout has been to give you, the reader, a clear picture of the evolving events and emotions in my experience to date.

My heart is singing with gratitude to those who saw me through this process, including the writing of this book. I could name dozens, but I'll hold it to these: Mike Russell, Bill Worley and Armon Mills, who gave me the opportunity; Bob Kieve and Bob Keady, who were true friends; Donna Wilson, whose integrity and inspiration kept me going; Charlie Seib, who helped immensely with the copy and tone; Dodie Gust and Bill Worthington, for their steady love; Dick Ray and his cohorts, who packaged the book; and the wonderful friends who put up with me during the writing, especially Dick Holland, Jerry Kelly and many individuals in the San Jose area.

First and finally, my life's Thank You to Bill Wilson, Bob Smith, Ed Schmidt and Harry Phillips.

April 1987

1

1975

Tucson, Arizona,
September 1975:

Boyd picked me up about 9 a.m. I'd packed for 28 days. A wornout suit, two sports coats, a few ties, some casual stuff.

Boyd grinned incredulously: "All this for a hospital?"

"Did you bring a bottle?"

"We can stop up at the corner, and you can get whatever you want."

I got a quart of vodka and some soda, and guzzled it as Boyd drove us through East Tucson, the university area, and then north to Phoenix. In two hours I'd almost finished my bottle.

The hospital people seemed nice enough. They led me to a room and had me undress. I was wobbly but okay.

Then a nurse came with a long syringe.

As she inserted the needle, I demanded: "What're you putting in me?"

"Valium."

"What for? I'm already boozed up."

"Yes, I know. But we think you ought to sleep it off now."

"How much?," I asked.

"How much what?"

"Valium."

"Fifty milligrams."

"Is that very much? I know about booze, not about drugs."

"It'll be just fine."

When I drifted back up out of the haze, it was close to evening. The realization hit me: I was in an alcoholic recovery unit in a hospital.

I can't drink in here!

I found the call button.

"Well. You're awake!"

"I want my clothes."

"You won't need them tonight. We have this robe for you." She was opening a dresser drawer.

"No, no—I'm leaving. I want a . . ."

"You can't leave."

"Wanna bet?"

I couldn't stand up straight for more than a few seconds and my arms and legs felt strangely weary . . . but I got my clothes out of the dresser and got them on.

The nurse reluctantly agreed that I had the right to leave.

I summoned a wheelchair. It took forever.

I got to the elevator and down to the front desk. I signed a release form.

Haze.

I waited in the lobby, and watched the front driveway.

Finally a cab dropped someone off. I rolled the wheelchair out to the curb.

"Get me to the airport. Fast."

I lifted up out of the wheelchair, found I could stand, even look the driver in the eyes and not sway too obviously.

He got me to the airport. I paid him with a rubber check.

There were no more scheduled flights to Tucson. But someone said there was a seat available on a charter. I wrote another rubber check.

A vice president of the university was on board—the cabin held maybe 12 people—so I turned my face to the window for most of the flight. I doubted that he'd remember me, but figured I'd better not risk the entry he might make later in their personnel files.

A friend I had phoned from Phoenix picked me up at the airport.

The haze was lifting. I was back in Tucson! Now, I thought, for just a little . . .

My wallet contained three ones. I said I was almost out of cigarettes, although my suitcase held several cartons, and asked if he could pull into that liquor store over there. I'd be right back.

I wobbled in, straightened, gathered myself as best I could—I knew I didn't look too stable—and, mumbling something about a party at a buddy's, asked the clerk what would be the most booze I could get for three dollars.

"That stuff." He pointed. "It's worse than rot-gut."

"I'll take it."

He put it in a brown bag. I went back to the car and—nonchalantly, I hoped—put the bag on the back seat.

My friend got me back out to Bear Canyon. The sky spread out, bright and cold. The house sat dark, empty.

"Well, thanks again. Sure appreciate it." I opened the back door to get my paper bag.

It was gone.

"What happened to my . . ."

"I threw it out, tossed it in the desert. You don't need any more of that stuff tonight."

"Jesus Christ!" I slammed the door as if trying to throw it through the car. "Damn it!"

He pulled away. The desert dust clouded up around me in the night . . .

I awakened, still dressed, in my big chair in the living room.

Remmmemememememberrr? Therrre mst be shom shomwherrre herrre!

Guldammm sheap shotch. Jus wanderr arrround an ish gonna show up

shomwherrrre arrroun herrre . . .

I awakened again on my bed, still dressed, my head throbbing. My lips were cracked. The clock said 2:11. My mind said I was coming off the booze and the valium, maybe was already off . . .

Ohmygawd!, I thought, the stores and bars are all closed and I haven't got a car. Where the hell is my car anyway? And there isn't any . . .

I searched the kitchen and the den, then the yard and the cabana.

No booze. Not even an empty. Someone must've cleaned up after I left.

I got back on the bed, pulled my knees up to my chin. It was so cold. I was shivering.

Images whirled in the light. Colors circling, whirling, spinning, whirling, purple spinning and orange on blue. The clock said 2:39. Was that sunlight?

No, it was my head. But—God!—look at that weird turquoise—I'm in withdrawal orange. Ohgawd ohgawdohgawdoh-

I decided to pace the floor, work it off. What did I do to deserve this?

I was shaking inside and it was coming to my outside and what the hell would I do? What would happen? Would my body sort of unravel?

Just three years ago I was running the metropolitan staff of a big newspaper—The Washington Star, for chrissake—and now I'm . . .

My pulse. It scared me. It sounded like a snare drum in my ear. Maybe I could hum to it, drown it out.

Good Eastern college and then Stanford, and . . .

Smarter than any of those dumb . . .

Purple whirling, spinning blue and red, and now orange, and ohmygawd get back on the bed!

The night whirled whether my eyes were opened or closed—did I see the same colors either way? I guessed not.

There was no rest, no sleep. Just changing, whirling colors, and my body whirling with the purples and the spinning and the terror thudding inside me, down through my chest and . . .

nightmare screams—muffled, meaningless.
I'm meaningless.
kathud kathud kathud. That's my heart I hear.
Keep going heart.
Keep going, baby. Don't quit now, baby. We'll get some relief very
soon now, buddy.
kathud
Smarter than any of those . . .

Were my eyes bulging out of me? I wanted to look in a mirror, but I couldn't get past the purples and the kathudding. In a minute, I thought, I'll be okay . . .

Stark raving terror, and no one would ever know what it was like at the End.

Ohmygawd—and the dawn lifted the dark screens and brought gray backgrounds to the subsiding purples and oranges.

I phoned the hospital in Phoenix and got an assistant something director on the line and said, maybe for the first time in my life, that I'd made a dumb mistake. He checked some records, then said I could come back, if I would not drink before I got there. I assured him I wouldn't, no way.

My hands shook so much I couldn't get the pieces of the percolator apart. Who needed coffee anyway?

I took a long hot shower, braced against the gray tiled wall, head in the crook of my arm, my mind jerking and spinning with images of my kid's faces. I dressed slowly, deciding not to risk shaving.

I called a cab, paced, sipped water, paced, discovered that my suitcase was still on the front step from the night before.

> *You'll make it, Scott. You'll survive. Just a few minutes more*
> *and we'll get what we need.*

First, a cab to the bank. I shakily signed a $20 savings withdrawal, tore it up and tried to write more steadily. On the third attempt my signature was almost readable.

I got in the busiest line, where I'd attract the least attention. I kept the breathing shallow, hands in pockets whenever possible, avoided looking at anyone.

> *So . . . if I do dry out and get through all this, is there life*
> *Afterward? Why not just keep on drinking 'til I die?*

The teller didn't question me.

I paid the cab, got the suitcase, and tried to look nonchalant walking along the Tanque Verde/Catalina Highway to the country music bar. The suitcase was heavy. I was sweating, and my knees felt as though they'd just fold under me.

A woman was behind the bar, polishing glasses, gearing up for a Monday lunchtime crowd. All those normal people, I thought.

There was one man at the bar. He looked alcoholic, shaky and grubby.

"Help you?"

"Gin and tonic, please."

I looked down, avoiding her eyes. She obviously was looking me over. I hadn't shaved and my eyes burned. Did she know me? From church? From the university? From the big spending evenings in here?

Narrow clear glass five inches high. Gilbey's gin from a bottle beside the sink. What a beautiful label. She made it heavy on the gin, squirted a little splash of tonic on the top.

Careful, lady! Don't spill that gin. Precious stuff.

I picked it up and knew she could see that I was shaking as I lifted the glass. The gin slopped against my lips, slid down into the throat. So good. So good. Hmmmm.

Was it always like this, I wondered, with the early drinkers? The shakes and the shame?

I knew she would see it in my eyes. But this was no time for pride. This was emergency medical treatment. I'd spill that precious gin if I put the glass down. I'd just have to let her see how badly I was shaking.

Warm in the gut. Warm, oh so warm in my gut and heart and throat.

"That's one dollar."

"M'father died."

It was my joke. So what if he'd died 33 years earlier?

"A dollar. You want another one?"

"Yep, he just died. Just like that. There's nev . . ."

She pulled the Gilbey's up from below and filled the glass, not bothering with the tonic this time.

I put my $10 bill on the bar.

I didn't die last night!
I'd been so sure I would die.

I slurped it down, pulled the glass away from my lips, looked her in the eye.

"Another, but a double."

"No doubles at this hour, pal."

"But . . ."

She was pouring.

Warmth inside! And the
pain and weight falling off me,
like a lead blanket off my shoulders.

I got through three drinks and, when she was talking to the other drinker, the one who looked alcoholic, I held my arm out as if I was checking the time. The shakes were going away!

A couple came in and sat in a back corner, whispering low, smiling at each other.

Trysting. M'gawd they were trysting! Isn't that the damnest thing? I grinned at the man. The world felt better. Even a smile felt okay now.

Got up, went to a phone and dialed a friend. I needed to get to the airport, no questions asked, okay? He said he'd pull up out front in 20 minutes.

Breathing slowly, walking erect and straight, I went back to my stool.

I waited forever until the male bartender, who'd just arrived, asked if I'd like another.

"Oh, I guess I might—just waiting for one of my employees to pick me up."

He was pouring. "What sorta business you in?"

"Engineering. Space program." I kept a straight face.

He poured only an inch of the Gilbey's, reached for the tonic hose.

"Isn't that a little light on the good stuff?"

"Sorta early for a heavy one, ain't it?"

"Not early for me, pal. I've been up all night. And I'm afraid this is the last one I'll get for a long while-"

He smiled at me. Did he know where I was bound?

I guzzled it, grinned.

His eyes were clear blue, icy. He stared at me as he poured more Gilbey's into the glass purposely, letting it flow over the top.

Mean son of a bitch, I thought, pulling the glass away and back up to my mouth. Screw him: I won't leave any tip.

Two hours later I was in Phoenix, and stopped at the airport bar for what I knew would be the last drink of my life. It was a bloody mary.

The hospital looked no different than it had the day before, but I felt worse. I wasn't quite drunk enough.

This time they gave me just a valium pill—a 5 milligram thing the nurse said wouldn't even affect me.

She told me not to sleep, just to change into pajamas and wait. A doctor wanted to see me.

Who could sleep feeling like this?

That was Monday afternoon. I do not remember anything about the next 48 hours.

Wednesday night, they wheeled me to a patients' meeting in a big garden style room. The people seemed pleasant enough. They were dressed in street clothes and drank a lot of coffee. They'd only give me a third of a cup so I wouldn't spill it on my blue hospital robe.

There was a sign on the table in front, but the letters blurred before me.

Someone told me that my hands were shaking so badly that they could see them moving from all the way down the corridor. I just nodded.

My chest was shaking and thudding and my head was throbbing mercilessly, the brain swimming in impulses. Great truths half formed before the next impulses swept the thoughts away.

Someone jabbed my ribcage with his elbow and told me to say that I was a patient and was there for treatment as an alcoholic.

I wanted to tell someone my life story, how I didn't deserve to be here, to be like this, how I wasn't really an alcoholic but had had such terrible pressure all my life . . .

I said my name was Scott and I thought they were treating me for alcoholic something.

Someone sniggered.

It felt like an eternity before their meeting ended and I could get back to my room.

I knew I had to do whatever the nurses told me to do. They controlled the relaxant pills and the anticonvulsion pills and the sleeping pills, and I wanted all of them and more. Anything.

For two more days, I could barely think, could not eat, could not vomit, could not stop shaking, could not even get up and walk out. A nurse said I would feel better on Friday.

My roommate was named Fred, and by Thursday night he was coming into focus. He was old and nervous. I told the nurse I wanted a private room.

She said I was in an alcoholism recovery unit and there weren't any private rooms. In fact, she said, a movie star had stayed in the room across the hall from mine—and he and his roommate had both gotten sober.

I smiled wanly at her, knowing what she wanted me to say: "if he can do it, I can."

It was hell, I thought, being cooped up like this.

I wanted to leave after a week. Their goal was to keep me for 28 days or more.

The doctor said I was suffering from acute chronic terminal alcoholism. I had liver damage. It could be terminal. I had hepatitus—that's why my skin and eyeballs were yellow. Instead of my old 170 pounds, I weighed 128 (I had weighted my pants pockets with change the day they weighed me) and I suffered from malnutrition and imbalances of the blood.

"Drink again and you'll get much worse, and probably die."

I had to spend my days listening to lectures to patients about alcoholism. They needed it. But I knew I was different. Smarter, more sensitive. More complicated.

I read everything they gave me, mostly out of boredom. I memorized certain phrases that would show the staff that I had repented and would never, never drink again.

The third week, they had my son Don and my daughter Laura come to the hospital to see their father.

I was excited by the idea of a joyful reunion. I didn't care about much these days, but I did care—very much—about Don and Laura.

The meeting wasn't joyful. The staff put us in chairs facing each other, told me to shut up, and prompted my children to tell me how selfish and unloving and unpredictable and irresponsible I'd been.

I listened. The blood pounding in my ears and throat, I tried to say that I'd been a damn good father, that they would never understand, that they'd drink too if they . . .

The staff told me to shut up and listen. I stuck my jaw out and listened.

After they left, I closed a bathroom door behind me and sobbed uncontrollably.

Oh dear God-
how?
How could I do this
to my little Donny
and sweet dear Laura?
How the hell did I come to this?
Oh God get me out of this!
I promise, God, I promise.
Listen:
Just get me out of this, and I'll do anything.

Two weeks later, thinking I'd been through the worst in my life, I picked up a 16 ounce can of beer. I had just begun.

THE PRICE OF ADMISSION

2

ELEVEN YEARS EARLIER

July 4, 1964:

They didn't search me. That bothered me. Here I was, obviously nervous, maybe lost, and they acted as though I was just another reporter. I wasn't just a reporter. I was an editor. And since a president had been killed less than a year before, how come I could walk through that guard gate? Suppose I had carried a hidden weapon?

Through the gate and up the sidewalk along the wide, curving driveway. My concern was replaced by awe. The building was white and huge and stately. It had a magic—the magic of history, of the momentous decisions that had been made there.

I grinned to myself. If the folks back in Medina, Ohio, could see me now. Just eight years earlier I was editing the "Medinamite," our high school newspaper.

Jack Horner, the Washington Evening Star's longtime White House reporter, spotted me as I wandered into the press room. He was greeting me as if I were his editor. Oh, I thought, I am his editor.

"You've seen this before, haven't you, Scott?"

"Been here once, with Ben Ruhe on a day when The Man (Ben had so knowingly called him that) was out of town."

"I thought you'd been here more often. Well, when I call you after the morning briefing, I'm usually at that desk right there." He pointed to a clutter of press releases and phone wires and notepads.

I could feel sweat pouring down my sides beneath the armpits, wondered if he knew how keyed-up I was.

"Isn't it difficult sometimes, Jack, to think straight when you're in such a wild place—not just wild but exciting?"

"That's why I've got editors, Scott." He winked, turned and disappeared to my left, a rumpled reporter/Santa Claus in a chaos of booths and desks, phones and people.

Was this a dream? No, today was the real thing. Lyndon Baines Johnson would sign the Civil Rights Act of 1964. Scott Bennett Smith, newly hired copy editor at the Washington Evening Star, the grand old lady of Washington journalism, would be there. At age 24.

I saw a notepad with the name "Pomfret" and figured it would belong to John Pomfret, a New York Times' guy at the White House. It didn't take long to get to know the right names in Washington. I no longer read the Times just for content.

Was that ruddy guy with glasses James Reston? Hell, I wouldn't know Scotty Reston—that's what he was called—if I tripped over him. What the hell am I doing here, with the Washington bureau chief of the Times? My grandfather H.R. would be reading Reston's stuff tomorrow morning over grapefruit in the kitchen of his home in Douglaston, Long Island . . .

"In a while, they'll open those doors and we'll go on down to the East Room." Jack was back at my elbow—how'd he get there? Obviously he sensed how I felt, and somehow managed not to laugh.

What if these people realized I had no idea what to do here? What if they knew I wasn't actually covering this, but just getting the feel of the White House? What if they looked for a byline in the Star? I'm an editor, and editors don't get bylines. And what if I'd carried a weapon with me through that gate? Just eight months before this, Jack Kennedy had been killed. And what if some of the older people at the Star said it was crazy for this kid to be here and it became an issue in the newsroom, just weeks after I'd started work?

Remember how it felt back there in front of the big brown radio, listening to reporters report from the White House? Remember 1950, when we thought Uncle Bennett, my father figure fresh from Harvard undergraduate, would have to go get killed in Truman's Korea?

Bet Ann never thought her kid would get here. Hope she's watching television today. This ought to show her something about her son.

A voice came in from a loudspeaker and the press moved like a herd out through the west wing and onto the driveway. I felt insignificant, 30 inches tall.

M'gawd but the windows beside the front door were so high.

The reporters seemed so casual, maybe too casual. I was amazed that some were dressed so poorly. Some of them didn't even have buttondown collars—what were they, bumpkins? If you're going to cover the President, I thought, you ought to at least wear buttondown collars.

And then in the front door. Its grace and elegance—the whole place had it—hit me. It was the first "house" I'd ever known more stately than my grandfather's home in Douglaston. I wondered if H.R. would be watching this day's history on TV.

This was better than a movie, or being head acolyte when the bishop came to town. Watch it, kid—don't let people see you staring up in awe. Cool, kid, cool.

Just inside the door, a guy who looked exactly like Bobby Kennedy was talking with someone in a pinstriped blue suit whose face was—was that Rostow? Did Bobby wear a buttondown?

My armpits were drenched, but somehow I had to assume a Press Corps Casual bearing. I had to seem not to notice the men in the corner. I had to wear my best studied frown, the one I had adopted at about age 10 when I went to Uncle Bennett's Harvard graduation. I was too busy wearing The Look to check Bobby Kennedy's shirt collar.

In the East Room, I sensed that I should whisper. It was already full of people, milling around using those same hushed tones I'd heard when our reporter Allen Drury gave me a tour of the Senate. That looked like McNamara over there. The room seemed big enough to be a basketball court, but majestic in its yellow and white and mirrors. I wished my pulse would slow down.

"Over here, Scott." Jack Horner was a kind man. I liked him, even if he was a reporter. He wasn't like some of the other, younger reporters.

"Since you haven't done these things very often yet"—mygawd, he said *yet*—"we'll get you a seat up front here." I nodded numbly.

I didn't try to talk. I just wanted to act as though I knew what I was doing, and appear as blase as the others here in the East Room of the White House, waiting for the most important person in the world to walk in for a ceremony of historic importance. On national TV, live. I hoped Lynn and the kids remembered to watch. We'd sure have something to talk about tonight.

TV everywhere. A bank of cameras in the middle of the center aisle to face the President's desk. Cameras to his left, to his right.

Why would the President of the United States put up with this? He had important things to do.

There was even a camera behind me, raised three feet on a wooden box so it would angle out across the tops of heads to the President.

The desk awaiting the President was just to my right. He'd be here, and I'd be here, and TV would be going and I was glad I didn't have to write anything about it.

Sure beats life at the Allentown Morning Call. Wonder if my old boss, George Nehrbas, will see me. I suppose he's in the newsroom in Allentown now—watching? Opening his mail? He might be proud if he saw one of his proteges here.

"Ladies and gentlemen," came a voice from off to my left, "please be seated. Because we will be live, it is essential that everyone be seated and quiet please!"

The black guy—yes, it is Martin Luther King! He's shorter than I'd thought, and so formal. He's nothing like I'd imagined.

Bobby sat down in a row across from me. He'd be to the President's right. Wonder if he ever wonders whether this man had his brother shot. He was talking vociferously. He looked tired, and very tough. Maybe even mean.

> *Holy shit!, this is for real. Keep cool—no one can hear your heartbeat. Bobby Kennedy for chrissake looks mean and these guys really are here, and I am here. This isn't some picture in Life or Time. This is it.*
> *I have made it. And I have a job to do. They're just human beings like me. And I'll know how to deal with these guys. I'll be up to it.*

King sat down. Strom Thurmond sat not far away. I wondered why they weren't arguing, Strom and Bobby and Martin Luther King, all within spitting distance of each other. Everyone seemed so nonchalant. Didn't they realize history was being made, or that the President of the United States would be here in just a few seconds?

Bobby kept on talking, jabbing the air, eyes almost wild. Yes, maybe 'mean.' Definitely very tough, like a fighter in an alley.

I felt panic in my throat.

"Ladies and gentlemen—"

I looked to my left. There he was. Lyndon Baines Johnson stood in the doorway, winking at someone to his left.

I hadn't realized he was so tall—and sort of gangly and portly at the same time. His ears were huge.

There was something so unpresidential about our President. He looked just a touch mangy.

Someone's arm came down across his path—a TV cue?—and he walked forward.

My gawd!

"My feller Muricans . . ."

That evening, as I told and retold it to Lynn across empty dinner plates in the dining room, it all seemed long ago and a great distance away. She didn't seem excited, didn't seem to have any sense of where I'd been that day, or what I'd been part of.

". . . So Johnson had been using these plastic pens and would go another maybe sixteenth of an inch with his signature—like this, see?—the signature that made it law, and he'd hand each pen to another one of the members of Congress standing around him, like this. Must've been 20 people in line to get those little plastic pens!"

She looked bored. Impossible—who could be bored about her husband being with the president?

"A guy standing there told me that Johnson, the President of the United States, had given his good pen—a gold pen the guy said had been given to him by Bobby Baker, who'd been the center of all that controversy—LBJ may have given that pen to one of the congressmen by mistake!"

Lynn didn't laugh.

"See: He had this gold pen and he was using these plastic pens to sign the legislation—real ceremonial thing to do—and he must've mistakenly given one of those guys the good pen out of his pocket . . ."

Lynn still wasn't laughing. The kids were coming back in through the porch door and she reached out to them. She was a wonderful, warm mother. They needed love, she needed love. But I had to get Lynn to appreciate what I'd experienced.

I pushed on.

"You know what else? I heard someone—I thought it was Johnson—I heard someone at a civil rights ceremony for chrissake referring to 'Chinamen'! Can you imagine? Here's this ceremony to help the Negroes, and he's using a word like 'Chinamen'?"

For the first time, I wondered whether Lynn was interested in the adventures I was living.

We'd both grown up in northern Ohio, had met on a blind date when we were 16. We married three weeks after graduating from high school and took a trip to look at colleges for me.

We visited Lehigh, in Bethlehem, Pa., where my natural father had gone. I hated it immediately. But someone there, undoubtedly with a twinkle in his eye, had suggested we look at Lehigh's great rival, Lafayette, just 20 miles east. We did. I loved it immediately and was admitted there about three days later.

By the time I graduated with a major in English, and having served as editor of the Lafayette newspaper, I had a fulltime job as a reporter. We had two children, though we were just 21 and 20, and we were ready to buy a house.

There had been no chance for Lynn to go to college. That seemed okay, since the people in her family hadn't anyway. I hadn't thought much about it. She was a good mother and housewife.

I'd gone to work during college as a reporter for the Allentown Morning Call, and I had continued there after graduation, first as a reporter, then as assistant wire editor. It was known as a much better than average paper, a good "farm club." My friend Ben Ruhe, the wire editor, took a job on the Washington Evening Star, and a few months later, in the spring of 1964, I was interviewed, tested and hired there. We bought a house in Chevy Chase—our second house, when I was age 24.

Don and Laura had grabbed a bat and baseball and were waiting for me in the yard. I wondered if I had enough energy, but went out and joined them. Soon I was playing as hard as they, and we were all laughing.

Don teased Laura about not being a good batter. Her defense would be to "accidentally" throw the ball over his head, making him chase across the yard after it. I finally announced that I'd do the batting—just hitting grounders to them. It worked. They loved it.

I hadn't had a father when I was their age. I reveled at the joy of kids and their father at play.

This seemed a lot more right than trying to keep up with the LBJs and Bobby Kennedys.

Later in that July 4th evening, as firecrackers crackled outside, the phone rang. It was my mother, Ann, calling from Medina. She had seen it on TV. She said she'd never been prouder of me.

So I had Ann's approval. Now I wanted the next step. I wanted to move ahead on the Star staff, to become a slot man, the top position on the copy desk. Then she could be even prouder. And after that, maybe within a year, I could move up another notch—to a spot on the national desk.

3

Summer 1966:

After two years and several promotions, I was getting it down pat. Even the headlines I wrote by hand had the look of Burt Hoffman's printing—small, crisp, clean, block letters.

It didn't bother me to know that I was imitating his hand. It was professional to produce such clean letters. I often wrote catchier heads than Burt did—which he freely acknowledged. It even seemed to please him.

The important thing was that I was inheriting Burt's job. And Burt ran the national staff. John Cassady was above him, but John's job was different. Burt ran the national operation day by day, edition by edition, crisis by crisis.

I knew, however, it would take years to get the rapport Burt and Charlie Seib had developed with the reporters on the national staff.

Burt had been the principal assistant national editor of the Star. He'd been brought along in that job by Seib, who was becoming managing editor. He was the man who'd hired me. Burt was taking over the job Seib was leaving—assistant managing editor for news.

Both had been brought along by Newbold Noyes, the editor of the Star, and a member of one of three families that had started the Star more than 100 years earlier. Newbold was, therefore, an inheritor of some of the Star's oh so private stock.

The Star's management was loaded with members of those families. Newbold stood out among them. He was bright, tough, experienced, hardworking. Many of the others were not.

So at age 26 I was getting the No. 2 slot on the national desk. I would be the man making the spot decisions on how the Star handled major national news.

It was not enough, though. Something kept driving me. And something inside me felt hollow.

I wanted to get this position right so I could get the next promotion. That one, I was sure, would satisfy me.

We were working with a fabulous staff—people like David Broder and Mary McGrory on politics, Robert Walters and Walter Pincus doing special projects and investigations, Bernie Gwertzman on foreign affairs, Jack Horner at the White House, Cecil Holland and Bob Walsh on the Hill, Bill Hines on space shots and science, Jerry O'Leary doing Latin America, Richard Critchfield in Vietnam, Henry Bradsher in Europe, Dana Bullen at the Supreme Court, Lee Cohn on economics, Lyle Denniston and Steve Aug on the business and regulatory beats.

How could a 26-year-old be their boss?

In my two years in Washington, I'd begun to understand the media, and even though the Post was overtaking the Star in advertising and circulation, the Star was still the Establishment paper, more cautious and conservative—and respected.

The only other Washington paper was the Daily News, an afternoon tabloid that made no attempt to be a serious national paper, but often gave our city desk fits on local crime stories.

Most of the city's television and radio reporters were just Shinola—not very bright, not very careful. Only two stood out to me among the TV people we'd competed with: John Chancellor and Barbara Walters. Most of the rest were not people we'd ever hire at the Star.

The Star had maybe 150 reporters and editors. The newsroom, on the third floor of the Star's building in Southeast Washington, was large by most standards. But reporters were packed in, and the stars among them got the windows.

Editors handling the news floor would have needed binoculars to see out the windows. But there wasn't much to see anyway—the elevated Southwest Freeway went past the windows at eye level.

I came to understand why the best reporters got the windows: They were the squeaky wheels. And smart editors hired reporters who had a bit of the squeaky wheel in them.

Editors were paid to be people-handlers. I used to say editors should get combat pay.

One reporter, an excellent investigator named Miriam Ottenberg, was a newsroom legend in her own time. One Saturday night she turned in what she considered a hot page 1 story for the Sunday paper and then left for dinner. A few hours later, she returned to the newsroom and looked at the freshly printed Sunday page 1. When she saw that her story didn't get the prominence she thought it deserved, and when Phil Price, the news editor, didn't pay proper attention to her complaint, Ottenberg whipped off her belt, flailing it across the desk at Price. Phil just leaned back and smiled as he watched the belt whistle past his nose.

The good reporters who'd 'made it'—and who delivered—could get away with occasional ego displays.

But when young reporters got too hard to handle, they didn't make it. In my time there I saw some good reporters go down the elevator. Carl Bernstein, of later Watergate fame, was one.

The national reporters were true professionals. Maybe that was because they'd made it to national and weren't full of resentment. Or maybe that's why they had gotten national assignments in the first place.

David Broder and Lee Cohn were always easy to work with—a joy, in fact.

Broder, while covering the 1966 congressional campaigns, would come in about 6:15 a.m. to help me go over the overnight wire material and see what the Post and Times were reporting overnight. Then he'd sit down and pull it all together in a wrap-up for our afternoon/evening readers. He didn't have to do that, but he did it.

Cohn, small, bright and industrious, was the same way. In many ways, he was my favorite.

Lee Cohn could write about such things as the implications in a new bill affecting Treasury bonds and make it understandable and interesting. That was miraculous to me. And he was always smiling, always helpful.

It wasn't easy to get a reporting job on the Star. Some brilliant young Ivy Leaguers started as dictationists taking stories from reporters by phone, or as copyboys/girls. Some started as summer interns. They included Lance Morrow, John Stacks, Warren Hoge, Sheila Kast—"kids" who later worked their way up or out to bigger jobs elsewhere (Morrow and Stacks with Time, Hoge with the New York Post, Kast with ABC/Washington).

I'd worked my way up too—faster than most. I believed I was the best of the younger editors. I know now I sometimes was arrogant. But inside something else was going on: I felt woefully inadequate. And I felt I couldn't let anyone else realize it. I had to be able to handle our reporters.

Burt Hoffman 'set me straight' one day. He said we needed to have a little chat about tact.

Burt was about 40 and it seemed incongruous that he was so liberal yet still kept his wavy brown-black hair in a crewcut. Most 'liberals' wore their hair long these days. It was, I thought, a signal that no matter what your job, people could be assured that you were a caring, virtuous person. A liberal with a crewcut. Part of his tidiness, I supposed.

For our chat, I sat on the old red leather couch in Burt's new office.

He was less delicate with me than he wanted me to be with our staff. I took that as a compliment.

He said my arrogance had offended some of the reporters. They all knew I was young and inexperienced, he said, but very good—a good editor with good ideas. Just too blunt.

It hurt. But if I wanted to become a Burt Hoffman or a Charlie Seib I would have to learn what he called tact. I had never even thought about anyone, especially me or my family, having "tact."

As Burt went on, I fought hard to keep the anger down. But he was my elder—my mentor in a way—and far more experienced. Certainly he knew what I'd need to do.

"I agree, Burt—I've always been like that. Too damned direct."

"That's right, Scott. The reporters get . . ."

"I mean, these people are my elders. Like Lee Cohn—I like Lee, and I can't imagine ever changing a word he writes. It's the cleanest copy I have ever . . ."

"He's not the problem, Scott."

Burt's face was drawn into tight lines. I thought it would take effort to get your face that tight. Burt did it when he was really serious about something. "You've gotten some other people sort of, uh—well, they wonder who the hell you think you are, when you yell across the newsroom that you're going to rewrite their leads, and everyone on the whole floor can hear it.

"You've got to understand something here, Scott. Someone's lead (the first paragraph of a news story) may be all fouled up—right? That's what you see every morning—right?"

I nodded appreciatively.

"Some of them can't write worth a shit, Scott. But that doesn't mean they aren't good reporters."

He does understand!

"That's a lesson Charlie taught me, long time before you ever got here. A good reporter is someone who gets information first and gets it right—not necessarily a good writer.

"Guys like Broder and Cohn, they're the exceptions. They can report and write. Obviously, some of our people—and it would be the same at the Times or the Post or Wall Street Journal—some of them just don't have a gift, a knack, for writing.

"Well, their egos are on the line out there in the newsroom—other reporters and editors are around. In probably every case, you're doing the right thing. It's just that their egos are—well, they wrote those leads because they thought they were good leads.

"Anyway, you just don't ever announce that you're rewriting them—not to them, and definitely not to the whole goddam newsroom."

"Well, I don't mean to 'announce' it, Burt. I just . . ."

"I know, I know. I had to learn some of these things myself. It's just a difference in how you do things. You want to put out the best paper possible. You want the stuff to read well. Right stuff in the lead, tight writing, good grammar—all that.

"The thing is, Scott, you've got to learn to just go ahead and do it, without yelling about it. And then, if there's a question of fact, you just quietly go ask the reporter, or ask the reporter to come up to the desk and you just ask them your questions there—so no one else can hear you, not even Belmont Faries."

Faries, the news editor, usually sat to my immediate right, wearing an old green eyeshade that reminded everyone of the '20s. He was one sharp cookie and yet I suspected that some of the national staff reporters didn't like him. In some cases, he probably knew as much about the stories they were covering as they did. I thought he was great; he wanted to put out a good newspaper.

"What if Bel's the one who's spotted the problem, Burt?"

"That's not the issue. You're usually the one who spots the problem. Belmont has to trust that you're getting it right. Anyway, the point is that you, Scott Smith, have to cut out all this yelling, this arrogant stuff of yours."

Silence. Burt let it sink in.

All I wanted was for Burt to like me, and to promote me, and then I could tell my mother . . .

"Arrogant? I hope I'm not . . ."

"It's not that you mean to be, Scott. It's just the way you come across sometimes. Maybe inside you're not feeling superior at all, but sometimes the way you say things it seems like you feel superior, and the staff just can't stomach that."

I came off the couch.

"Jesus Christ, Burt! I'm just trying to put out the best paper possible, and they're worried about their goddam egos?"

"Yep."

"They're so arrogant themselves—how can they accuse me of . . ."

"Yep. That's just the way it is, Scott."

I couldn't get over it. And here was Burt now, his face in a sudden smile, warm, almost perplexed, a smile that seemed to say "that's how it is and I don't know why either."

"So, Burt: What the hell am I supposed to do when reporters screw up?"

Burt was still smiling, his hands palm-up. He shrugged. "That's what it means to be a good editor, Scott—to clean that crap up and still make the reporter feel like he, or she, had it right all the time. You can rewrite these people all day long—hell, all week long—and they won't complain—at least most of them won't—unless you make a mistake or make 'em feel small. They're really pretty insecure people, you know."

Driving home through Rock Creek Park late that afternoon, I resolved to learn tact, to be a cushion for reporters, a safety net, to learn how to smile during crises, keep my voice low, to never get excited, to never show my feelings. I'd be a superior editor.

And that way, no one would see how I felt inside, no one would pick up that terrible gnawing hole down deep, where I really lived.

Not only did I feel inadequate. I was terrified.

Our two-story brick house on a corner lot near East-West Highway felt more like Silver Spring, but had a Chevy Chase address, and the neighborhood had a heavily Jewish population.

I had noticed that the Jewish neighborhoods generally seemed to have much better schools. And they were quieter neighborhoods.

The kids went to Rock Creek Elementary, and across the street from it was the Parkway Deli. On Sunday mornings we'd get kosher stuff for brunch at home, or on Sunday evenings I'd buy rye bread, corned beef, cole slaw and beer. It was a good neighborhood, and I was only 25 minutes from the Star's building just to the south of Capitol Hill.

We played bridge on Saturday nights with the couple across the street. Otherwise, we stayed to ourselves. I worked long hours, was seldom home.

Late that evening, Lynn and I sat in our wicker chairs on the porch and I told her about my conversation with Burt.

She didn't say much, but she had a strange look on her face. She left and soon after, I heard her going upstairs to bed.

I got another beer. The streetlights sent long shadows of the tall oaks across the yard.

My mother Ann had wondered when I'd "get serious and go to law school." Why not? She was a lawyer. My uncle Bennett was a lawyer. My grandfather Carl had been a lawyer, and a judge in his semiretirement. Why not be a lawyer?

Ann had said that if I got a law degree—lawyers knew more about intellectual thoroughness, she said—I could run for Congress and be someone instead of just reporting from the sidelines.

But: I didn't want to be a lawyer.

Suppose I went to law school—I'd have to get a scholarship—and then ran for Congress from Maryland. I'd have to locate in a district where someone was retiring or where I could beat an incumbent.

So suppose I did that, and I got elected. After two years or maybe four, when the time was just right, I could swing around and run for the Senate.

"Senator Scott B. Smith, R, Md., said today . . ."

Hmmm.

I heard the shower upstairs.

Okay: So I get through law school and a couple of terms in the House, and I become a senator. Then what?

Ann had implied it.

The Senate, she'd said, would be marvelous training.

And magically, there it was: The image.

We were sitting in the Oval Office in front of the fireplace. I was sitting forward, elbows on knees, on the offwhite couch. Ann was on the couch to my right, leaning back, head slightly cocked, asking: "Now when are you going to be a good president?"

Time for another beer.

I was pacing the porch.

My 'potential,' my goddam 'potential' . . . ever since I was maybe four, they'd told me about my goddam 'potential.' So unless someday I was a *good* president . . .

Time for one more beer? Why not?

I'd been trying to please my mother and my family so I could get—could get what, Scott? What was it you were after?

Never mind whatever it was I'd been looking for. At least now I had an answer: Maybe I could never please them completely.

I was doing pretty damned well anyway. They ought to be proud of what I was doing. Principal assistant national editor of the best paper in Washington, D.C. Nothing shabby about that at age 27.

I went inside, slammed the door, and flew up the stairs to our bedroom. I hoped she'd be wearing that white gown I could almost see through.

"Lynn? . . .Honey, I've just figured out the whole thing about . . ."

There was no answer from the mound on the bed.

How the hell could she fall asleep so soon?

Back down the stairs. It was 12:35. Maybe one more beer.

The porch was so nice this time of the night. The trees were so tall, the streetlight at the corner so suggestive of the romantic quality of H.R.'s neighborhood on Long Island.

Such a great place to just sit and think. And the beer's just right and I feel warm inside. I don't feel small now. In fact, I feel like I'm loved or something.

Feeling like that would be my secret. And sitting out there in the dark, I thought, no one would know if I drank the whole damned six-pack.

Hell, I could just sit there for a couple more hours, do or say or think anything I felt like, and just be warm and secure.

I have never had one friend, not one woman even, who's made me feel like this. Like the

> *world's warm and I am loved and I'm okay, not some inadequate kid trying to keep up and keep all the normal people faked out.*

I got up and took the last can of beer from the refrigerator. God I felt good!

As taught, I loved our institutions. They were full of such wonderful promises. And here I was, walking through the West Wing, young, rising rapidly in the capital of the world, with the institutions all around me.

The East Coast was the heart of the universe. It was here, I thought, mostly Washington and New York, where the institutions came together.

Someday, I figured, LBJ's picture might smile down from 11x14 frames in countless school rooms across the land, another human institution within our heritage, another hero in the Washington-Adams-Jefferson-Lincoln chain.

"Birrrd? Birrrd! Where are ya?"

The voice boomed. It had authority. It was our president calling his wife.

He was standing in a doorway in the West Wing, and I guess Lady Bird was somewhere down the hall.

I was just passing by with a couple of reporters. They were babbling on about politics. I didn't listen. We walked on toward the press room, which was humming with speculation about the latest U.S. statements about our victory in Vietnam.

Later I mentioned my consternation about this Texan-president's style to Burt Hoffman. Burt loaded up his pipe with that knowing smile he'd get, chuckled and told me the latest that was going around the party circuits: the story about Douglas Dillon quitting as secretary of the Treasury.

Dillon was pure Blue Blood. He'd supposedly been recruited, massaged and nurtured by the Kennedys, who certainly were not true Blue but had the bucks and clout to act as if they were.

The story was that Dillon had quit after being in a conversation with LBJ during which the president had stepped into a bathroom, sat down and continued the conversation without missing a syllable or closing the door.

". . . So there's your president, Scott."

I shook my head, feeling confusion, even some sadness.

"It has nothing to do with being an effective president," Burt said.

"Well, I guess it does, if he can't hang onto smart people because he's so . . or, Burt, is it possible that Johnson's so smart that he knew exactly what he was doing, that he was trying to get Dillon to quit?"

"You're catching on quick now, Scott. We'll never know the answer."

The East Coast media people were abuzz with LBJ stories. Birds chasing birds from one power line to the next, a chorus of group glee: LBJ was gauche, Texas tasteless, didn't belong in the White House.

"Camelot" was gone. Oh the tragedy.

The media boasted of objectivity, fairness. I knew, however, there was no way LBJ would be allowed to be their kind of leader.

The whole Camelot mystique was phony, a media mirage, but it was the East Coast Establishment's perception. It did not matter whether the Kennedys or the media, or both, had created it. It was myth becoming legend. Perception becoming reality.

Our Mary McGrory, a Bostonian, had been quoted by Author William Manchester as saying when Kennedy was killed and then Ruby shot Oswald: "The Republic is finished. We'll never be the same. It's all over."

With that kind of horror in their hearts, how could the Elitist Establishment ever put up with a clumsy Texan?

I knew better than to talk about it. Probably there was no way LBJ could get a fair shake in the media; I was part of the media and doing well.

I presumed I could not get ahead if some media people thought I saw through what they were unknowingly (I hoped) turning into "history."

Even Lynn wouldn't realize that I was part of the very sham I detested so.

But I knew it, and it was gnawing at me.

Mid-1967:

Scott Smith was getting "smarter" everyday, getting better each day at hiding whatever political principles he'd learned, whatever he felt was right. I was in a job in which I wasn't supposed to show my politics.

The Washington Post, the New York Times, the three network news teams—were they really all the same? Was each being put together, day to day, by people who either thought alike or else acted as if they did, perhaps so they wouldn't be ostracized?

The Washington world was buzzing with closed-minded people calling themselves liberal. I had never known there could be so many wealthy, pampered people who claimed to know so much about poverty.

I was proud I worked for The Star; it clearly made a sincere effort to report objectively, to hide whatever biases the reporters or editors held toward the news (except for McGrory, whose stuff was labeled "Point of View").

The Post and Times seemed to be hell-bent on "reforming" rather than "reporting," but always in the guise of being great objective, omniscient institutions.

Sometimes, their slanting was so subtle that you would never know it unless you worked for the opposition.

I wondered how often reporters or editors at the Times and Post were the victims of their own biases. News stories or facts that ran against the Establishment's beliefs sometimes would be omitted, or worded in insidious ways that supported an underlying point of view.

Despite our personal political preferences, Burt and Charlie and I shared a conviction that if all the information was available to the American public, right decisions would emerge.

When I said the Post seemed so intent on deciding which information the public should get, Burt would nod and grimace knowingly. We were with the right paper, and we were the right guys to keep it fair and objective. We were fortunate.

That was fine, but I was drinking after work at Mr. Henry's on Pennsylvania Avenue with Star people, and some of them left me feeling sad and alone. I saw that some of them were not much different—though less arrogant—than the Post/Times/network people.

Or was it just that I was different? I felt different. All the time.

I knew that I just wanted to be respected for putting out the best national-news package possible. I wanted especially my mother's respect.

Did these people in Washington want love from everybody? Was their 'liberalism' a way to show others that they believed in the proper things and therefore should be accepted?

Or was I just so young and naive that I couldn't see their nobility?

I wondered about it, usually when driving home up Rock Creek Park after a few drinks, but I generally assumed I was in the wrong, and I never, never mentioned it to Charlie or Burt.

I knew I was part-of—part of a group that was rising to journalistic clout, part of an Elite. It was damned tough, I thought, to get into that Elite. I wanted it, and hated it.

My chest was tight with resentment. I felt trapped in a world I wanted yet couldn't criticize.

4

My father, Donald Maxwell Smith, had died when I was two years old. He'd been from Douglaston, Long Island, and had met my mother Ann on a blind date while she was at Smith College. They eloped, kept the marriage secret because Smith girls weren't allowed to be married. But then he was offered an excellent sales-management job in Indianapolis, and she left Smith College after her junior year in order to join him. I was born there, in 1940.

In the fall of 1942, he had gall bladder surgery. He developed a blood clot in his leg. The next day it occluded his heart and he was gone.

I was told my Daddy had gone to see the man in the moon.

We moved back to my mother's town, Medina, Ohio, and Ann was accepted at Western Reserve Law School. Her mother Elsie had graduated from Western Reserve, 30 miles north in Cleveland, perhaps 25 years earlier. Smith College granted Ann a diploma based on her performance in the first three years there.

Then Ann took a law position with Firestone Tire & Rubber in Akron. After ten years, she married again, to Alfred C. Meyers, who'd been a purchasing executive at Firestone.

In the meantime, I'd grown up, if you could call it that, in my grandparents' home in Medina, population then 7,000. I called my grandmother Elsie "Mom," my mother "Ann."

Ann and Al had a son—we called him "A" for Al—when I was 16.

Both Elsie and Ann were strong stock—smart, educated women whose first husbands had died while they were in their twenties.

There were two strong men in my early years: my uncle, Bennett C. Wilson, 12 years older than I, who went to Harvard, then the Air Force, then Harvard Law; and my father's father, H. Raymond Smith of Dougaston, the man I call H.R.

H.R. had been chief engineer and a director with Raymond Concrete & Pile, which later became Raymond International. His wife, an opera singer, had left him for a conductor. He had raised their three sons himself during the Depression—while maintaining a large house and several domestics—on a salary which the Depression had cut in half. He'd taken the "empty half" of his salary in penny stock.

H.R., as I saw him, was a blueblooded model of self discipline and deep spirituality. Both strengths showed in his face—the kind of face and radiance that would turn even men's heads in a restaurant.

So it was comforting to me to be in college at Lafayette, 80 miles west of New York, and then to be in the Washington area. I could get to H.R.'s for weekends and to experience the love and the graciousness I'd been shown as a child.

But the news was full of war and assassinations and attacks on people like H.R. and my family. I bit my lip, daily, hourly.

Reporters and editors and other Washington insiders—we all laughed at LBJ. Lynn didn't laugh. I loved it: she was not slick-hip. She was real, and politically/personally a mainstay for me.

Lynn saw no reason to endlessly discuss political issues. Politics was simple to her; either you understood what was right, or you didn't. She was more interested in schools or getting the couch recovered.

I'd come home and over the first two cocktails dive head-first into the complexities of a political situation. Lynn would go start the vegetables.

Sometimes, in the office or at home, and especially when discussing politics or my career, I'd feel a tight band inside my chest. It felt as though it was vibrating, making me tremble on the inside. It was sickening, frightening.

It was one of my secrets.

I would not tell anyone about it; I feared that a medical exam would show heart or lung problems—or worse yet, that I couldn't handle my responsibilities.

When the tightening would start I'd breathe deeply to see if I could get air. I'd check my vision, hearing, balance. All seemed okay.

I thought maybe Lynn was the problem. She saw no reason to split hairs or debate the finer points of national affairs—which was the very stuff I was dealing with every working day.

I knew that anyone who had a problem as unmentionable as mine needed a couple of drinks after work to ease the pressure.

And the booze worked.

One night I almost lost my temper, trailing her from room to room, asking Lynn whether she was even reading the Star, let alone the other papers or the news magazines. She said she didn't need to read in order to understand what was right and what was wrong.

She was right and I knew it. I apologized, then wondered why.

I was the one bringing home the paychecks that paid for the house and the groceries for christsake! And the issues sometimes weren't simple. I loved discussing them, and she wouldn't play. I felt frustrated and angry. Yet I loved her for it. And she knew it, enjoyed it, even when I got insistent or resentful.

I slurred to her one night that bourbon was the best conversationalist I could find: No matter what I said, it always agreed with me. I didn't tell her, or anyone, that it also eased that band across my chest.

Early 1968:

We'd visited some close friends, Sam and Mary Seiler, in their new home north of Silver Spring, in a woodsy-horsey area of big houses and sprawling wooded lawns. Wonderful neighborhood, I said, in spite of its name—Quaint Acres.

We saw a "for sale" sign. End of a long dead-end street. Square brick columns on each side of the driveway. Tall trees everywhere, a state park to our right. The house was three stories, but built into a slope so that from the street it looked low, nestled into the earth.

Swimming pool. Three fireplaces. Recreation room with fireplace and pool table, plus room for a ping pong table. The living room looked into the tops of trees rising from the canyon that slid off to the right of the house.

We couldn't afford it. We bought it. We'd be happy there.

H.R. came to visit, loved the house and went to work installing a light above the garage to illuminate the driveway. And he drilled holes in the tops of the garbage cans and bought elastic straps so I could keep the raccoons out of them at night. And he took me to Sears to buy yard tools. I was going to be a homebody.

We'd sold stock he had given us in order to buy the house. He seemed to approve. It would, he said, be a good use of the stock if we stayed in the house for a long time.

Wednesday morning, November 6, 1968:

The newsroom clock said 8:09 a.m. I'd been in that chair, the national "slot," since 10 the night before. I felt less tired now that we were coming down to the wire. The deadline for first-edition copy for page 1 would be 8:50 at the latest.

A phone at my left hand. Two more straight in front of me. One on each side of the portable TV. John Cassady sitting across from me. The news desk to my right. The whole newsroom was a cacophony.

The wire service copy was being sifted by others. I was getting the state-by-state vote-count summaries, the AP's "A wire" wrap-up stories, and our staff copy, which I would read, scan against what television and the wires said, then farm out for editing.

Phones were ringing: Reporters at various sites in the city and around the country phoning with the latest on House races (the Democrats were looking better than 2-to-1 in the new makeup of House of Representatives), and the Senate races (it looked as though we'd have 18 new Democratic senators, 15 new Republicans).

Compiling the congressional results was nightmarish because you couldn't make mistakes in a Washington paper. Maybe a Toledo paper could get something wrong and get away with it, but we couldn't, not here where jobs, contracts and the future hinged on seemingly obscure races in South Dakota or Georgia.

The presidential race was close, unbelievably close. We all knew that in less than an hour, one of us would have to make the decision: Would Washington's most cautious paper declare Hubert Humphrey or Richard Nixon the next President?

The Post and Times and networks had gone through hell the night before, trying to figure a winner. They'd generally said Nixon probably would win, but it was more in doubt now than it had been in the early hours of the morning.

Burt was saying that Humphrey could pull it off, that this "could be another Truman and the Chicago Tribune," a reference to how that newspaper had declared the wrong man president.

We all knew how delightful it would be to have the world remember that the Post and Times had been wrong, that the Washington Star had gotten the presidential-elections story right.

I was the one person reading all the numbers from every source from every state. And it was looking to me as though Nixon had won, although I wasn't saying so yet.

I saw that the popular vote could even be a toss-up, but Nixon was looking stronger now in electoral votes. And it was the electoral result that would determine which man's name went in our banner.

I noticed that Charlie Seib had diddled with an 84-point banner headline for page 1 that would say it was "too close to call." I shuddered; I'd almost rather go on the street with the wrong winner than with a pansy of a headline.

By 8:35, Newby Noyes, the editor, was making a relatively rare appearance at the national desk, conferring with Burt and Charlie. They all looked over at me.

I handed them my latest numbers, showing Nixon ahead by less than 100,000 popular votes out of roughly 60 million cast for either Nixon or Humphrey. My electoral count showed Nixon by a clear margin, but still not quite over the 270 needed.

There was silence in our little circle. Beyond us the newsroom sounded like a stadium.

Belmont Faries, the news editor, said it was time for a decision.

I spoke up: "Let's just give ourselves a few more minutes. It's worth it."

Newby looked at me, and I thought I'd overspoken my bounds.

"That's right," said Newby. "Give it a few more minutes."

This moment—this was the heart of my job: Deciphering a very tight, tough situation. Staying cool in the midst of pandemonium.

I went back to the numbers, a phone to my left ear, conferring quietly with a reporter. The TV in front of me, its little earplug in my right ear, my left hand switching the dial back and forth among the networks, checking their numbers. I sorted through the latest summaries from the Associated Press, United Press International, the New

York Times Wire Service, and Dow Jones. Of them all, I trusted AP the most.

As I stared at our numbers and AP's, I knew what the truth was to me.

"Humphrey won't win it. He can't win. Nixon hasn't won it yet, but we should go with Nixon because there is no other possible outcome. It may be another hour before the numbers put him over, but Humphrey can't get the electoral votes, even if he pulls ahead in the popular vote."

For a moment Newby, Charlie and Burt stared at me. Then Newby nodded: "Which may very well happen . . ." He looked at me absently, as if listening to his own mind racing through logical sequences.

There was nothing more I could say. No more screaming, no more sweating over where the numbers looked right or wrong. Burt knew more than I did, I always felt, but I had the numbers here in my hands and had said exactly how it looked to me. Burt was silent, pulling on his pipe.

I felt that I might have just made the biggest mistake of my career. There was nothing I could do.

"You have nothing more from Missouri, Scott?", asked Burt.

"Just what you see right here. Same numbers as the networks."

"Alaska? Has Alaska changed at all?," asked Charlie.

Newby interrupted:

"Go with Nixon."

I felt the air flooding back up my throat. In just a few more hours, I could let down, relax, have a few drinks.

Mid-November, 1968:

We'd gone to H.R.'s for a New York weekend.

Sunday morning, he took me aside and opened a small gray box. Inside I saw a set of spoons—very, very old spoons. The silver was soft. There was an "S" on the handles.

"I am giving these to you. Someday you'll understand exactly what they are, where they came from."

I stammered a thank you, knowing I should not ask questions.

November 20, 1968:

I'd gotten back to the newsroom from lunch when it began. The band across my chest pressed in so tight I wondered if I could breathe.

A heart attack? Would the band tighten? Would it strangle my heart or arteries?

I stood with my buttocks against the rim of the copy desk, trying to get my breath.

> *I don't want to die! My father died young! My mother's father died young! God help me! I don't want to die! Oh, help me! I can't get my breath! I don't want to die. . .*

There seemed to be a thin wall of air or space between my skull and my brain. My hands were sweating. My feet were sweating.

I knew I had to tell someone what was happening before I dropped.

Who? Who could I trust?

I saw Ray Dick, chief of the copy desk and a friend. Between gasps for air, I told him.

"Let's get you to the medical office." Ray's face registered concern.

The medical office was on the second floor. We took the back staircase and I wondered whether I'd collapse and tumble headfirst to my end. I gasped. Good!, I could still breathe.

I sat down and a doctor looked over at me. "You're right on time," he said.

"Huh?"

He peered at the biographical and medical data on me, then came over to put a stethoscope on my chest.

"I'll be right back." He went into the anteroom, came back with a small white paper bag.

"Here: Breathe into this."

"Huh?"

"You're hyperventilating."

"Huh?

"Anxiety attack." He was listening to my heart.

"Huh?"

"Relax, the bag won't hurt you. Just breathe in, and out, and in."

I had to know: "Is my heart—is it okay?"

"No problem."

I breathed heavily into the bag, felt the air push back at me. What the hell was this about? Some kind of doctor he was, having me breathe into a paper bag!

He went on about the oxygen mixture in my bloodstream. I didn't care. I just wanted him to let me out of there. . .

". . . too young for your responsibilities."

". . . too young for your responsibilities."

Whoa. I asked what he meant.

"You're awfully young to have this much responsibility, so you feel very insecure and anxious."

"Well, I. . ."

He pulled out a prescription pad.

"No," I said. "I don't want any tranquilizers—they're habit-forming. I don't really need them."

"You have some liquor at home, don't you?"

"Yeah. . ."

The prescription was pretty clear: A stiff drink followed by sex, whether Lynn was home or not, followed by a nap.

I followed the script exactly. When I awakened, I was fresh, ready for the cocktail hour and our party. It was Donny's tenth birthday.

The best deal on bourbon was at the big liquor store at Georgia Avenue and the District line in Silver Spring. I'd gotten into the habit, two nights a week, of driving over there after dinner and stocking up, and sometimes stopping for a little extra at the bar across the street.

A Friday night in December:

I turned on the bar stool and caught another look at the tall woman. She was sitting back against her chair, listening to some sort of gossipy chatter about the staff at Walter Reed hospital, which was nearby.

Her white sweater showed promise. Her thighs were spread and I could see the bulging V in the crotch in her pink slacks. I looked at it, and at her, and she caught my eye.

She smiled. I turned away. I figured she could tell that I was married and had two kids at home.

I stirred my drink. I knew I should go home soon, but I was tempted to stay and see what would happen. What the hell, I thought: I never got the chance to 'date' when I was in high school or college.

Neither did Lynn.

Oh no! The thought hit me hard. What if she ever felt like this, tempted to try a little something some night—or maybe some day when she knew I'd be at work?

My heart pounded. I'd kill her!, that's what I'd do. She is mine!, the best looking, sweetest woman I'll ever know.

I went home.

Lynn was sitting up in bed.

"Stopped for a little drink over there."

"You coming to bed now?"

"Want me to?"

"What do you think?" Her eyes were sparkling.

An hour or so later, staring at the ceiling and smoking a cigarette, I asked myself what the hell I'd felt so guilty about—I hadn't done anything wrong.

As I drifted toward sleep, my tongue was huge, as if inflated, inside my mouth. Damnedest thing.

I could remember how, in childhood in Medina, when I was three or four, after my father's death, I'd get this feeling that my tongue was so huge.

There was something locked in my memory from way back then, something way down deep inside me, something very important. What the hell was it?

> *It's something about how or why I exist, about where I came from. Something, maybe, about God.*

I turned over. Forget that sort of stuff, Scott—you've got important things to think about, like LBJ's press conference tomorrow night. I was a newspaperman, not a spiritual type.

(A few weeks later.)

Lynn insisted that we "do something together" for a Sunday. I'd been studying the Sunday papers and suggested a movie. There was an interesting new French thing showing in downtown Silver Spring. She said okay.

It wasn't what I'd hoped. I had thought from the title, "A Man and a Woman," that the film might break through a few sexual taboos. But I wasn't disappointed. It was sex at a deeper level, and I was not prepared for what I would feel—nor the effects it would have on me years after.

As the theme poured out, and the opening scenes—a man, his child, his car, a beach, a dog, playful joyous wonderment—filled my senses, I began to cry there in the dark.

What was it? Was it that I'd never had my Daddy when I was a kid? No, there was more than just that.

As the love story rolled across the screen, I hoped that no one would see me—although I secretly wished Lynn would see my tears and and ask what was wrong.

How could I tell anyone? The film was putting my own dreams in front of my senses, and down deep into my psyche. There was no escaping the truth: As much as I loved my stepfather, Al, and my grandfather, they were not My

Daddy. And as much as I loved Lynn, she was not the Right Woman I'd expected somehow, somewhere.

I clutched her hand. It was damp, limp.

I got up and went to the men's room, where I could have the familiar reality of a cigarette.

Back in my seat, the tears came quickly again. I turned my head away from Lynn, gripping my own left hand firmly in my right.

We walked to our car.

"Lynn—that's how it supposed to be."

"What do you mean?"

"That film is about romance, Lynn—real romance."

"Yeah?"

"Well, didn't you just love it?"

"It was okay I guess."

"Just 'okay'?"

"Let's stop at the deli and get some corned beef for sandwiches for dinner, okay?"

I knew I would buy the soundtrack, and knew it would be a secret.

January 20, 1969:

Lynn had never looked as formal, and I loved it. We danced, wandered through the huge halls of the Smithsonian arm in arm, carrying champagne glasses. A trumpet blared an old Sinatra song through the history on the walls.

Magic.

"Lynn—remember that night I took you to Baltimore to hear Sinatra and he looked right into your eyes when he was singing?"

She squeezed my arm joyfully.

The whole town was a party. There were separate Inaugural Balls in five locations. Our new President would visit each. We'd chosen the Smithsonian.

"Look—the Secret Service is getting ready!"

She turned and put her lips up to be kissed. "Do I really look so good tonight?"

A trumpet was leading a danceband through "If Ever I Could Leave You" from Camelot.

"Hmm . . hear that song? . . . Hmm you look wonderful, honey." I kissed her lightly. "C'mon, I want you to see Nixon in person!"

She was warm, beautiful, sexy, the mother of two bright and beautiful children with me. Nothing could pull us apart.

July 20, 1969:

This was even better than an election night. And more historic.

I'd done nothing for eight weeks but work on stories and pictures—even a "Star Magazine special report"—on this day's events.

Two guys were going to land on the moon, get out and walk around on it.

That moon, where my Daddy had gone. That sphere up there, 237,000 miles from here!

I knew that my mind wanted ways to dramatize what my heart felt. This was more important to me than to most people, I was sure.

A lot of reporters and editors seemed so nonchalant about it. Many of the "liberals" were bitter about it: All that money on a silly space program when there were poor folk out there starving because this monster Nixon was cutting back on the Great Society.

I resented the bastards. Phony, phony, phony, I thought. For one thing, the welfare programs hadn't worked. For another, the "liberals" were acting like spoiled brats. But there was no way I'd tell anyone I felt that way. I just avoided and ignored them. Stay cool, kid—professional, objective, and successful.

Here, I thought, was the biggest historical event in the history of man since Jesus' death. Man was leaving his planet, stepping out onto another body spinning through space!

How long would it be before man encountered other beings out there? How long before man radioed back a description of another civilization? In historical perspective, it would not be very long now.

I'd felt the events themselves as they unfolded on television that afternoon: The Lunar Module touching down, the historic "The Eagle has landed!", then Neil Armstrong and Buzz Aldrin climbing down a little ladder onto the powdery surface of the moon, staying out there for more than two hours, while another astronaut, Michael Collins, circled above them, waiting to rendezvous and take them back to Mother Earth.

As the historic night wore on, I went to the office. We would put out that historic Monday-morning edition and then I'd be on vacation for three weeks!

I'd left Don and Laura and Lynn at my parent's summer place at Quogue, Long Island, a week earlier. I had worked long hours, and had enjoyed having the house—and the city—to myself.

And all I had to do now was make sure those two guys got safely off the lunar surface, make sure our paper was the best it could be, and see it reach the street. Then I'd be in my car and on a long vacation. Someone else could edit the stuff about the return to Earth and the welcoming and fanfare. I was tired; it was time for me to celebrate.

Adrenalin charged me as I settled into the slot—"my slot" at the national desk—to edit and write and rewrite. I hoped I had shaken off the martinis I'd been sipping during the day. I sifted through the early wire copy, got the TV focused, dialed Bill Hines, our reporter at the Space Center in Houston. No answer; he'd call back soon.

This was sheer joy—putting together the definitive package on history as it happened. And Hines was the best and the brightest in the space-reporting business.

TV in front of me, phones arranged to my front and right.

Something stopped me. I stood up, almost alone in the still-empty newsroom, and I heard my own voice inside my skull.

Memorize this moment, kid.
There'll never be another moment like it.

August 1969:

I'd never known a simpler, more graceful grandeur, than the small New England town. Quogue was all of that—plus the ocean. I found my own magic there, the way youthful things often are—magic, beyond words because they glimmer in the heart and imagination as much as in physical reality.

I was an Ocean Person. Sometimes I wondered why, but decided there was no way to explain that, either.

The town was hidden along the south shore of Long Island, in the Hamptons. Ann and Al had bought a low-slung gray ranch house along the wide main street. It was good south-shore summer living: A sheltered home, near the wide beaches but "in town," weathered shingles, a parched sandy green-tan yard, a few trees, a small pond behind the house.

The beach was about half a mile away, across a bridge spanning the narrow inland waterway between beach and town.

Charlie Seib had suggested I take my whole three weeks of vacation in one shot each August. It went against my nature to use up all of something good—I'd noticed that I never finished the last bottle of booze, never smoked the last cigarette. But I said okay. And he was right. Especially after all the hours and emotion I'd spent on the space shot.

I'd been away now for seven days. No deadlines. No reporters. No phones. No traffic jams. And I was out of that hideous Washington humidity.

At 7:30 a.m., I got in my Chevy convertible and headed down Dune Road.

I'd learned about "getting the papers before breakfast" from an old family friend, Gene Willson. Gene was a past master at "getting the papers." He could take an hour at it.

A New York station was playing "A Man and a Woman." I wondered if I'd see that Right Woman in the little newspaper store.

How often had I looked for her? And what would I do if I ever saw her, met her? A married man with two kids and a big job!

Got back to the house and read the Times while my mother and Lynn cooked bacon and eggs and the children cleaned up their tent in the backyard.

We got to the Surf Club at 10:05, right after it opened.

I loved the post-weekend feeling—Monday-morning routines—garbage men and gardeners were back at their tasks, the weekend revelers gone, the beach town returned to its real residents.

Some day, I'd live in a little seaside town like this.

We'd changed into swimsuits and I met my mother at our beach. The sand was already hot in the August morning.

She sat in a canvas beach chair, her pencil poised over a Times Double-Crostic. I pulled a chair over beside her and sat looking at the deep-blue water, wishing the surf were bigger.

"Lynn and the kids went walking."

Ann nodded absently. "You ought to get this definition, Scott. You're always so good at these. Who was Sir Osbert Sitwell?"

"Annie, what do you believe about . . . about death?"

"Oblivion."

There was silence. I stared at the ocean. Why was my heart pounding?

"Oblivion?", I asked.

"Yes."

"But. . ."

"It's our reward."

I didn't want to debate it; I, after all, had no idea what I believed, if anything. And this was my mother, who had survived my father's death, who now had worked so hard with her husband Al to provide these summer vacations. So why get into it with her?

I got up and walked. The sand felt oddly harsh. I wanted to not feel anything.

Suddenly, my own voice was screaming into the wind: "Gawdamnit!"

The bubbling dazzling white surf, the shades of blue, the white-yellow of the sand, the deep warmth of the sun on my shoulders and face.

Purity. That's what it was! Purity! Look at it! Too brilliant to be a goddam practical joke on us!

Oblivion?

My head was screaming.

What I feel inside is more real than my own flesh.
How could the conscious me not exist after death?

Was my father lost in oblivion? Could he not feel now? What an awful thought! But that's what the woman who loved him thought—that my Daddy, Don Smith, had gone off into nothingness.

If so, why? Why would all of this beauty exist? Why? It's all so meaningless if we're just here for a flick of time and then we're off into nothingness, not even knowing we're in oblivion.

I was so alive! I knew I at least existed.

It was maddening. I'd grown up in the Episcopal Church and I'd taken quite a few hours of religion and philosophy at Lafayette, and here I was, stupified and angry. I was 29 and knew this was the great issue of my life: Was I here for a purpose? Would I live on?

I walked half a mile, turned, walked back.

That hollow feeling was there, that dread hole in the center of the chest. Damn!

"Ann . . . sorry to interrupt you."

She looked up over her sunglasses, still intent on her Double-Crostic.

"I'm gonna see if the bluefish are running down the inlet. I'll be back in the afternoon. If you need to find me for anything, I'll be standing on those rocks along the jetty."

"Have fun, dear."

I knew what I needed: Long casts into the deep still tide running through the inlet, and a good cold can of beer beside me.

The guy four fishermen to my left had hit a striped bass about two hours ago, they said. He'd lost it. But no blues so far.

I was using a 9-foot Daiwa rod and heavy Daiwa reel with just 20-pound test line, to give the fish a better chance. The wind was to my right, sweeping in from the ocean, and I could cast a two-ounce lure about 80 yards.

Cast with a grunt, watch the lure fly like a missle, then let it sink for a slow count of three, then bring it back in fast spurts, always ready to jerk the rod if there was a hit on the line.

The year before, at about this time of day, I'd hit three big blues, and they'd been the highlight of my vacation. Annie loved to cook them, but the great joy to me was the fight—and it was a pretty fair fight—to pull that incredibly fast, strong, wildly jerking, angry five or ten pounds of bluefish up out of those fast currents and onto the rocks.

After an hour and a half, and no hits, it was time for another Budweiser. I put my rod and gear on a big boulder and picked my way across the rocks back to the ramshack store, back at the road.

The place was always so open, the ocean winds whipping through it, yet it always smelled of ocean vacation—fish, and engine oil, and grease from the hamburgers and french fries.

I sat on a stool and gulped down a beer. This was vacation!

I stayed right there. It was working.

Five beers and I was losing that hollow feeling, and the tight band across my chest was loosening.

I asked for another Budweiser, opened a fresh pack of cigarettes.

Who knows?, I thought, maybe H.R. has a better answer about death. I know he believes in God and acts as if he'll see his deceased son, my father, again.

Sometimes I wondered about how I used the word "gawd", which I distinguished from "God". But even when I was swearing using "gawd", did I mean "God"?

And if He, It, existed, could It really hear me? And was it really so evil to use His, Its, name so profanely? Hell, it was just the way we all spoke—just semantics. I seldom meant "God"—I meant "gawd" as a semantic catch-all.

It didn't matter. I took two more Budweisers back to the rocks. It didn't look like anyone was getting anything, but what the hell? I always got some thinking done there, and no one knew how good all that beer felt in my brain . . .

What was it with me? In almost anyone's book, I had it all—the fast, glamorous, tough job in the news capital of the world; the lovely wife and two adorable kids; the big suburban house. Yet I was endlessly, restlessly searching.

I felt that I had to earn each day's happiness. I did not naturally deserve it.

Searching.

For relief.

For freedom.

For joy.

Not only was I somehow vaguely uncomfortable and dissatisfied, but my best friend came in a glass. Something wasn't right.

And there was the hollow feeling so much of the time, and also the tight band around the chest.

Now it was almost midnight and that Right Girl still hadn't come in.

We'd walked here about 10, Lynn and I, and after half an hour, I'd walked Lynn back to the house; she had a headache. I excused myself, said I wanted to hear at least one more set of songs from the pianist, since it was the last Friday night of our vacation.

Nando's Mirimar—a blue-light name, I thought, for a nice little bar/restaurant in Quogue. The place was done in blues and silvers and perfectly tanned faces, mostly either Mc-Something or Jewish, although the town population was mostly Protestant. Cocktail piano and hefty drinks.

"Oblivion!" Imagine that! My mother thought we'd get the "reward" of not even knowing we existed! And we wouldn't exist to know we didn't even exist.

So where's that Right Girl anyway? I've only got two more days—about 60 hours, to be exact—before I have to drive back to Washington and work.

Let's see: Three weeks ago this hour, we'd just arrived and we were all sitting in the living room having drinks. Two weeks ago this hour—what? Oh yeah, Lynn and I had gone to Dune Deck and she'd been so lovely in that dress. And so good afterward. And one week ago this hour? Oh yeah, the Willsons were over and we were playing bridge.

And 24 hours from now? Maybe I'll be walking down the beach in the moonlight with that Right Girl, finding out her name and where she lives, and . . .

"Excuse me."

It was a soft voice. I turned and saw the long streaked blond hair, tanned high cheekbones, blue eyes.

"That's okay—have this seat." I motioned to the barstool in front of me.

"Thank you, kind sir," she grinned.

Had I ever seen such beauty in all my life?

A tall deeply tanned man in a white jacket elbowed between the woman and me. Muscular, maybe 45, slightly graying, well dressed.

Aw shit. I'm going home.

The next day, an old family friend and her daughter, both from Roslyn, Long Island, joined us at our bench.

The daughter was about 25, a woman most men would have thought rather plain. But her face struck me immediately, and she helped me notice her body.

She'd been lying on her back in a two-piece suit and I'd been swimming. As often happened when I surfed in cold water on a hot-sun day, I had an erection. I wondered if anyone had noticed it before I could get to my towel, cover up and sit down on one of the beach chairs.

She shifted her knee, spreading her thighs slightly. The top of her head faced me and my view was as if I were above her.

A moment later, she was brushing sand off her flat stomach—I couldn't see one particle of sand, try as I might. Then she raised the elastic band on her suit bottom to brush sand off the red line the elastic had left on her skin. It gave me a quick view of the flat abdomen and the wisps of pubic hair before she snapped the elastic shut and sighed as if something had just gone through her mind.

M'gawd, Smith, you're married, sitting here with your mother
beside you, and-
Ohmygawd! Look at her!
She was single and living on the upper East Side.

We flirted subtly and by the time I drove Lynn and the kids back to Washington, I felt intrigued—almost compulsively intrigued.

The job and career were going well. And I had won first place in a national contest for highway-safety writing—for a magazine piece about the hazards of Washington's Beltway.

I bought a red Fiat convertible with the money I'd won. The car said something to me. I didn't know what.

I stopped after work at the Shoreham hotel for a couple more drinks, discovered that Tony Bennett was singing out on the patio. He did "I Left My Heart in San Francisco," and I wondered if or when I would ever see San Francisco.

Didn't want a table, was booze-loose enough to walk up to Bennett's left and stand along a wall, sipping my Tanquerey.

The small orchestra started a new song. A waiter brought me another drink without being asked.

Tony Bennett. A head full of Tanquerey gin. The Shoreham. Evening breezes. And now he slid into the new song. I'd never heard it.

For once in my life
I have someone who needs me
someone I've needed so long

Microphone in his left hand, brow furled, he had turned and was singing straight at me.

The spotlight swung around. I didn't care if people saw that I was crying. Tony Bennett was singing this to me.

For once I can say
'this is mine you can't take it'. . .
For once I can touch
What my heart used to dream of,
Long before I knew
Someone warm like you
would make my dream come true.
For once in my life
I won't let sorrow hurt me,
not like it's hurt me before.
For once I have something
I know won't desert me—
I'm not alone anymore

He finished and the crowd applauded.

I sped out of the patio, through the lobby, to the other bar, gulped down another Tanquerey, and drove home. Lynn was in bed asleep. She was, in fact, snoring.

A September Saturday, 1969:

Lynn had that look on her face and she knew it infuriated me.

"Goddamnit all to hell 'n' back, Lynn!" I was almost shouting, yet holding back. "If you can't live the way I live, then I'm going to have to find other ways of getting along!"

She just stared at me. "You're drunk!"

"If—if you're not interested in the stuff I'm interested in. . ." I took a deep swig of the Scotch. ". . .I'll go elsewhere."

"And what does that mean?"

"Figure it out for yourself!"

"Honey, I don't even know why you're so mad. One minute you're working in the yard, the next minute you're in here slamming things all over the kitchen when there is absolutely nothing wrong around here, and now screaming and swearing at me."

Oh damnit, she couldn't understand, I thought. I stormed out through the porch, jumped into the Fiat, backed out, drove away.

It was so damn difficult to pinpoint. There was just something. . .

And that look on her face.

B'gawd, if I went somewhere else to live, I'll bet I wouldn't drink as much.

But anyone, anywhere, I thought, anyone who had my wife, my mother, my job—anyone would have to drink like I did. It was the only way.

"Lynn," I said aloud, "you'll just never understand!"

The car skidded on the gravel as I pulled into the parking lot at the little liquor store. I'd do whatever I damned well felt like!

A Tuesday in November:

My buddy Rob called me at the Star at 9:35. We'd just cleaned up page 1. Rob wanted to get together right away. He was going out of his gourd. And no, he couldn't discuss it over the phone.

We met at a restaurant/bar near his office. He was a high-level economist with the government. We each had a beer.

The problem, said Rob, was his wife Candy again. He couldn't take it anymore.

Rob was about 35, good-looking, very Midwestern. Candy was about the same in each category.

He broke down, and for the first time since I'd known him, explained what was troubling him so deeply.

They lived in a nice little subdivision in the Bethesda area, had three kids in public school there. They'd had a party about a year previously and late in the evening, Rob had needed more beer. As he walked down the basement steps to get it, he had seen Candy kneeling on the basement floor, giving oral sex to the guy from across the street.

My heart sank as he told it.

We ordered another round as Rob tried to list all the remedies he and Candy had tried.

Another round. "No menus, thanks, we've got to get back to our office."

We switched to scotch around 2.

By 6:30, I called Lynn, said I'd get home when I goddamn well felt like it.

We wandered out of the bar around 10 and I said I'd follow Rob home just to make sure he made it okay. He seemed pretty drunk.

We made it and Rob offered me a nightcap.

We sat at the kitchen table. Candy soon joined us, unaware that Rob had told me all about it—the affair with the neighbor, the marriage counseling, Rob's own attempts at affairs, his impotency with any other than Candy, and about the marathon negotiating they'd tried.

Two drinks later, I decided to phone Lynn. I was just fine, would be home shortly.

I hung up, turned, and fell face-down, flat on my nose.

"You alright?"

"Sure, sure," I said as I got back up onto my knees, pulled myself back onto the chair.

I finished my scotch, kissed them both, got into the Fiat, backed out of their driveway, slammed into first gear, hit the accelerator and swung out down their quiet street—and straight into a tree.

My head hit the steering wheel. Blood on my shirt.

The front of my prized car was crumpled in front of me. I strained to see over it. A strange sound: the engine was still running.

Head spinning, vision doubled, blood dribbling onto my clothes, I cranked the wheel and got my little red spider to pull back from the tree, swung the wheel enough to get it headed back across the yard toward the street.

The front fenders were bent so badly that I could get no more than maybe a 10 degree turn without backing and repeating the maneuver.

I made it home. I calculated later that I had made at least fifteen 90-degree turns and gone about five miles. I didn't see one other car. Nor a cop. I'd gotten away with it.

Early December 1969:

Amid the normal schedules and announcements, someone had put a flyer about sabbatical fellowships from Stanford on the newsroom bulletin board.

As I jotted down the address in California, Bill Basham wandered up, his long heavy arms draped across his wide chest, the laughing eyes sparkling out beneath his freckled forehead and red hair.

"Time for the sun to slide right over it, I think, Scotty."

"Right over the yardarm?"

"See ya there?"

"Four minutes, Bill."

I arrived at Mr. Henry's a little later than the city desk crowd, pulled an extra chair over and just listened.

John McKelway, a Scotsman whose father had been editor of the Star and whose uncle had written for the New Yorker, was brooding at me. We stared each other down while Basham and Woody West argued about judges in D.C. Superior Court.

I liked each of them. I liked them as a group. But I never felt quite at home with them.

One of the city desk's better reporters was at another table with one of the dictationists, a woman with bright red hair. Both had gone to Ivy schools. Their eyes, leaping into each other, oblivious to the office crowd just 15 feet away, told me they were quickly overcoming the fact that he was married and had a family.

Part of me snickered at him. But most of me was envious as hell. She was quite a woman—bright, saucy, good-looking, my kind of crazy.

I went to the bar and got another double Tanquerey, slid quietly back into my seat and leaned back. To hell with getting home on time, I thought. I'll say I was waiting for the traffic to let up.

I wondered whether some more of the staff women might come up to Mr. Henry's. Especially that girl whose face, hair, body, voice, eyes, education, attitudes and sly smiles were really getting to me. An unspoken rapport.

She never comes up here, I thought. Wonder if there's a place where she goes. Probably in Georgetown. I think her father's in the CIA and they live in Georgetown, to the right of M and Wisconsin. Maybe she goes to that quiet little bar up there on the corner.

One more drink and I'm heading for Georgetown.

Lynn announced the next morning that things were so tough with us that she didn't think she ought to go to Ohio with me for Christmas, this 1969.

I was stunned. I said I didn't understand. She said it was better not to let the families see us like this.

So she'd taken my threats seriously. I was surprised. Here she had it made, being married to a successful editor, and she was saying things that could encourage me toward singleness.

Did she know how crazy I was feeling? Maybe, I thought, I ought to tell her that I'd mailed off that application to that Stanford program, not that I'd stand a chance of getting it, but just that it would make her see that unless she changes, like I want her to, she's in deep trouble.

Well, I thought, at least if we split up, I could drink without her giving me those depressing looks.

Mid-December 1969:

I'd arrived ahead of Burt, and chose a table to the rear. I loved Chadwick's. They took good care of me—my glass, ice and Tanquerey gin were usually on the table by the time I got to it. Best place on Pennsylvania Avenue.

What the hell was wrong with me?

There was nothing wrong with Lynn.

I knew that.

Nothing wrong with her, yet I had this inexplicable, wordless yen to get away from her.

The stuff I'd told her the night before had been true. Well, mostly true. We were growing in different directions, I'd said. She wanted family, I wanted romance; she liked meat 'n' potatoes, and I liked oysters on the half shell. She said that didn't make any sense. It made sense to me.

There was nothing wrong with Lynn, I decided, but I was growing.

Ten minutes later, Burt sat down and ordered a beer.

"Why beer?"

"I just can't drink the other stuff, Scott."

"Why not? It doesn't fill you up like beer," I said.

"I just shouldn't drink it. It can get you drunk."

"Burt, did I tell you enough so you understand what I'm feeling—I mean, it's like I could fall in love with that redhead in New York."

"I could, I'm sure."

"But you never met her."

"I know." His eyes twinkled. "But you told me about her, and I could fall in love with, say, any one-third of a group of any 100 women."

I could not believe he said that.

"What do you mean?"

"Just that. I could fall in love with 33, or anyway 10 out of every 100 women, aged 20 to 40. I could just walk in a room, look around and fall in love with any one out of 10 of them."

"Burt. There is only a limited little number of women who would be right for you—or for me. I mean, like, hell, I don't know—maybe 10 on this whole planet."

"Wrong, Scott."

He ordered another beer, as though he hadn't said about the most preposterous thing I'd ever heard. I guessed he just wouldn't ever understand about love and women.

I'd been yelling at her, and finally she'd stormed off to bed.

Just as well, I thought. Now I can get some peace and quiet.

I pulled my new bottle of cognac off the shelf, put some ice in the icebucket, got a glass and a fresh pack of cigarettes. And I got it all into the den and closed the doors without anyone seeing or hearing me. I locked the doors and cranked up the stereo.

Tonight I'd conduct "Promises, Promises." No matter that I'd done it last night. It was good therapy.

I put the glass and bucket on the shelf in front of the turntable, grabbed a broken pencil, took the evening's first swig of cognac, and began.

I tensed my arms, the pencil clasped between the thumb and index finger of the right hand, just the way I'd been taught in the music theory and composition courses in high school.

It was always tough to get the downstroke exactly in time with the start of the recording, but I'd done this one so often I got it nearly right.

Relief. Bacharach for president! I settled into my conducting. It would be perhaps an hour and a half tonight. Enough to finish half the bottle. I kept on conducting, pencil in right hand, drink in left hand.

It had bothered me the night before that I'd apparently finished the whole bottle, thrown it in the garbage and gone to bed and couldn't quite remember it. Tonight, half the bottle.

> *I was wearing a tux, the spotlight on my back. President and Mrs. President—let's see, would it be Nixon tonight?—were in the third row center, right behind me. My mother and brother and grandmother were to their right, and H.R. was to the left of the President, as erect and attentive as ever. And farther to the left was that Right Girl, her eyes adoring as she watched her right man drawing just the right tone and tempo from the pit orchestra, and. . .*

I was half-way through the bottle, had done the entire music score twice, and my arms were aching. But I kept going. Creative geniuses can't stop.

Sometime early in January I made the decision.

January 20, 1970:

The alarm went off at 5:05 a.m.

I showered and shaved, trying my best to be quiet and to not-think about what I was doing. Just do it, Scott. Just do it. Lynn never even stirred.

I made sure my mind didn't wander to the kids. No use making myself feel any guiltier.

I went out the door, suitcase in hand, aware of the drama of what I was doing.

Here I come—a little New York trip, then apartment-living on Capitol Hill, singlehood and women and fun.

The suitcase barely fit in the back seat of the little red Fiat. At 5:35 I sped away, the kids and the house and Lynn behind me.

As I crossed the district line on Georgia Avenue, I remembered that just a year earlier, to the day, Lynn and I had such fun at the Inaugural Ball. It had felt so right! And now. . .

I was amazed: WMAL was playing "Leaving on a Jet Plane." What a perfect thing to play for me this morning . . . was it really for me? Did someone know?

I felt shaky and guilty. Propelled as if I was driven by some predestined force. I had no idea why, knew my rationalizations were just that—my mind trying to justify or explain acts which I didn't begin to understand.

February 1970:

I found a one bedroom basement apartment close to work and the Capitol. Lots of beams and bricks, and a fold-down serving bar in the door between the kitchen and the livingroom. No garage, but I figured my Fiat would be safe; most of the neighborhood people drove old Cadillacs.

Ann and Al announced that they were headed east and would visit me. It took me two days to realize that they were checking up on the older son, who had left a fine house and good wife and two wonderful children to live in a basement apartment.

On the day they arrived, about two weeks after I'd moved in, an old black man was murdered on the sidewalk in front of the house. A neighbor told me that the man had been accosted by a group of young black boys in daylight and when he said he had no money, they beat him to death.

That evening after Ann and Al arrived, a female friend just "happened by" during cocktails, and the four of us went to a restaurant. I was relieved because I sensed that Ann and Al were reassured by the whole evening. Scott was okay.

Everyone thought Scott was okay.

The routine came easily: Up at 5:15, to the office by 6:30, finish late in the afternoon.

Don and Laura came for weekends and the female friend often helped me entertain them.

And she drank.

Harry Bacas, city editor, friend and a sensitive man, had gotten me increasingly excited about auto-crossing, which I explained to "outsiders" was slaloming in a car. I got good at it and won a divisional championship. I noticed that I wasn't drinking quite as much on Saturday nights, because I wanted to be in better shape on Sundays for auto-crossing.

Most weekday evenings, I'd drink at one of the bars until I felt Just Right, then go home, put on one of the two Bacharach albums I loved so, fix a drink, and conduct for maybe half an hour. Then I'd decide whether to eat, work, go looking for a woman or conduct some more.

The switchboard operator had a call for me.

"Mary who?"

"Mary Blessed."

The switchboard was only 20 feet from the national desk, and when I looked over she threw up her hands to indicate she didn't believe it either.

"Hello, this is Scott Smith—can I help you?"

"You guys sure have a system to screen phone calls!" The voice was young, educated, exuberant, unimpressed with the acting national editor of the Washington Star.

"Not good enough for me, somedays. What can I do for you Mary uh. . ."

"Your switchboard girl got it wrong. But it's—everybody laughs anyway—it's Breasted, B-r-e-a-s-t-e-d."

"I'm not laughing."

"Wellll. I'm working for the Village Voice and I thought you might want a few pieces now and then about the peace marches and other activities up here. I'll be in Washington next Tuesday. Can I come meet you?"

"Three-thirty Tuesday."

I wondered what the hell I was doing, to agree to see someone from a radical paper, much too chic for me, about covering a radical cause from the inside. How could someone like that meet the Star's standards for objectivity, let alone writing?

Mary Breasted was standing in front of me at the desk, trying to introduce herself even though I was involved on the phone. I asked her to sit in the news editor's office; I'd be right in. Her eyes were bright, open. She spun and walked through the newsroom as if her daddy had just bought the paper. Tall, long stringy brown hair. Leggy and bright. Maybe 26.

I sat in the small office—Harry Bacas, the city editor, Belmont Faries, the news editor, and I shared it—and listened as Mary sat in the old overstuffed chair and told me her background.

Radcliffe, although she'd never gotten hung up on the boys in the Yard. Except one, David it was. New York, yes, but mostly Connecticut suburban. Daddy's crazy, bright, not right-wing like so many of his neighbors. She'd worked hard to get into the village, and now she truly lived there, on Christopher Street, and breathed, drank, smoked, slept and ate the village. She generally liked her editor and wouldn't think of leaving the Voice although several people had suggested she ask the Star for a fulltime reporter's job. She really wasn't involved in the peace stuff, just covering it. But the people around her were very plugged-in and she had observed some very interesting planning sessions. It wouldn't fit into her normal stuff for the Voice, and besides she needed an outlet on a daily paper, and, well, she had written a book about sex education in Orange County, and all she had to do was just report what people had said and done and it was absolutely hilarious, but maybe I wouldn't really think so, and anyway it was called "Oh! Sex Education" like "Oh! Calcutta!" as if there was something shocking in showing little kids how mommy and daddy fuck late at night when they can hear the bed jiggling, and she would want to write another book some day but right now she just wanted to report what was going on in the peace movement and obviously Washington readers needed to know about it, and. . .

I liked everything about her.

She was not just bright. She was outrageous and knew it. Unpredictable and knowledgeable, innocent and brilliant and profane.

She dealt in specifics, which I liked. And she had a great sense of humor, especially about herself.

The wide-set eyes had a glimmer that told me she wasn't really listening to her own babbling. She was a wisp of clouds drifting across a blue distance, yet in a strange way professional.

I guessed that she knew damn well that with her feet about 18 inches apart and no slip under her full skirt, wonderfully loose, she was giving me a good look straight up her thighs—good thighs, firm and smooth.

Smart. A writer. And sexy. Scott, it's Jackpot time!

I suggested that we would need to discuss all this when I had some free time. She smiled, nodded, said she'd be back in Washington the following Wednesday. I invited her to go sailing with Burt and Bruce Hopkins and me out of Annapolis that afternoon.

We sailed at eight and she slept on my daybed that night.

Ten days later, I was with her—really with her—in Greenwich Village.

It was impossible to know what or how Lynn was feeling. Hurt and angry, I was sure.

That had been part of the problem, I thought. She'd always hidden her feelings.

The kids were hurt and missing me, I knew.

And I knew that no matter what I did with them, I couldn't ever really explain what had happened.

I also knew that I was so caught up fighting for my own survival that I had to avoid sensing what Lynn, Don and Laura felt.

I couldn't handle my own feelings, let alone theirs.

When they visited me, the pained questions in Donny's eyes would send me into drunken nights. The frown on Laura's face was a nightmare, and again I'd spin into the booze.

Lynn was deeply and visibly hurt. I felt guilty and remorseful—and helpless.

Alcohol was getting me through.

In Washington, the guys at Chadwick's on Pennsylvania Avenue would put a bottle of Tanquerey on the table before seating me for lunch. Then they'd ask my guest if he or she wanted a drink.

In New York, the tall thin guy behind the bar at the Lion's Head recognized me and remembered that I wanted a Ballantine's scotch.

I was making an impression . . .

In April, when I went to New York to see Mary, I visited H.R. in Douglaston.

He was sitting in his rocker in the dining room, wearing the usual brown cardigan and white shirt. Engineering

News Records were piled high on the table; a book was in his lap. He looked great. He said he was going to do some weeding, then we'd have a cocktail and then go to Lorraine Murphy's in Great Neck for dinner.

A little later we met in the kitchen. He was standing in his familiar fashion, a manhattan in his hand, shirtsleeves rolled up to his elbows, the brown cancer-looking marks dark against the tan on his arms. He looked 65, not 80.

"Watch this stuff, Scott." He swirled his drink. "It's hard on the liver."

"I do watch it, H.R."

H.R. only drank two a day, and on a very special occasion three. He'd had his one now, and he'd wait until dinner to have another.

He went up to shower and dress, and I wandered about the house and yard. I stopped at the refrigerator to refill my glass. I loved having my cocktail with me in the bathroom while getting ready, whether I was heading for Manhattan and the theater or just to a restaurant.

H.R. and his home were home for my heart and I knew it.

At dinner, H.R. had two more and I asked what the occasion was. He said he thought it was damn fine I had applied for a fellowship at Stanford. Also he had something special for the waiter, who, I gathered, had been serving H.R. for several years.

H.R. summoned him after the entree, handed him an envelope. I could see what was in it: 200 shares of AT&T.

The waiter, a Filipino man in his 60s, didn't understand what the official-looking papers meant. H.R. explained what the stock was, what the stock was worth, what the waiter's options were: sell it now or hold onto it and collect dividends.

The waiter's eyes were moist. He only nodded and said thank you.

H.R.'s eyes were bright, dazzling.

What an example.

It was the last time I saw him.

5

Late April 1970:

I was flying to New York for dinner again. I loved the feeling.

Here I was, a kid from a small midwestern town, now hopping airlines like it was old hat. I was no longer watching the Big Boys play the game; I was legitimately part of the game.

The week before when I'd done this, I'd crossed paths with Henry Kissinger in the Eastern shuttle wing at National. The secretary of state had said "Good evening, Mister Smith." I'd been equally impressed by his personal genius and by my own importance. Imagine, Henry Kissinger remembering me! It had convinced me that commuting to New York for dinner was smart.

But something was very wrong. I only sensed it at first.

On this Thursday-afternoon flight, I was sitting staring out the airliner window at the Cheasapeake Bay Bridge when I noticed the strange little hair-like spot. I assumed it was on the window, but when I moved my focus, the spot moved too.

I started testing it.

Everywhere I looked, the spot went along.

Eye damage! It's from the drinking.

The very thought made my chest feel tight. I downed my martini, buzzed for the stewardess to bring me another.

M'gawd it was Saturday! I didn't need to get up now.

I stared blankly at the family photograph on the wall. Someone was snoring!

Ohgeezus. Judy.

She'd arrived about 9 at night. It was now 8:05 a.m. What the hell had happened? It was going to be my "hot Friday night." She was a leggy blond I'd met on Capitol Hill, and she'd suggested we "get together."

I'd been really keyed up about it, I remembered, and had stopped at Mr. Henry's in the late afternoon, picked up some groceries, tossed down a few more Tanquereys at the apartment while awaiting her.

She'd thought it would be hot, too. Trouble was, by midnight, we'd gone to one too many bars. I could vaguely remember that she had to sleep on my daybed because I didn't dare try driving and I'd also been too drunk to get anywhere with her.

So how the hell do I get her out of here?

I tiptoed out to the bathroom, then to the kitchen. She was still snoring. I saw the dregs of one of the night's Tanquereys, swished it around, unscrewed the bottle lid and added to the languid gin left from the night before, closed my eyes and downed it in one long draw on the glass.

No, Judy hadn't awakened.

I tiptoed past the daybed, closed my bedroom door behind me and slid back under the covers, pulling them over my eyes.

Billie was an old family friend. We'd grown up together, yet never known each other closely.

Now she was a New York social worker, still single. We'd each been back in Medina to visit our families—our parents were very close longtime friends—and I'd been gently, wonderfully surprised when we eagerly drifted toward each other at a Christmas Eve party.

Lovely face. Bright good eyes. Comfortable and intelligent, not out to prove that she was either liberal or liberated. What a relief. And she wore good clothes, not the hippie stuff that was considered fashionable.

By March we'd met for a quick weekend in Washington, and agreed to go somewhere—anywhere—for a "getaway weekend."

We went to her old stomping ground instead of mine—Nags Head, N.C. I loved all of it—every old shingle house along the dunes, even the little grocery we adopted as our own.

And I adored the simple sight of Billie on her knees in a yellow swimsuit, her head tilted slightly as she lost herself in a book while I sat in the sand with a beer and a wish that I had more.

More what? I knew that I didn't know. There was a song in Bacharach's "Promises, Promises" about it. About a guy who was an absolute cad who always wanted more. I hated the song.

Our lovemaking was tender. We were very, very fond of each other.

It delighted me. I had no idea how much it scared me.

That spring, there was Billie, and there was Mary, both in New York, and there was Linda in Washington, and I sensed a whole long line of Judys if I wanted them.

And there was usually a Playboy magazine beneath my bed. The fantasies were often better than the realities. At least with the Judys.

Billie was getting to me.

But Linda was always around, ever ready to go have a drink with me, or to pour for us at home.

Somehow Linda was the safest, the least threatening to my conscience or my heart. She drank with me.

My heart died every Sunday night that I had to drive the kids back to Maryland.

I could usually handle seeing Lynn, even wondering whether she'd started messing around yet. But I could not handle saying goodbye to the children and driving away.

It was my own personal horror movie, a waking nightmare. Kissing Don and Laura goodbye, usually under a scowling look from Lynn, then getting in the Fiat, heading up the driveway, not wanting to look the neighbors in the eye—they always acted as if there was something wrong with me.

I would sob, driving back down Colesville Road, then duck into a bar called the Pub at Colesville and University for two or three quick ones, trying to get interested in whatever was on the bar's television set. But I'd see families eating there together, and even alcohol couldn't stop that pain.

I learned that it wasn't quite as difficult if I took someone along.

The woman who felt the most right with me, and with the kids, was Billie. But Billie was usually in New York.

I had to get away from the pain. It was just too damned much. And I knew that my performance on the national desk was going to slip unless something changed.

Billie and I rented a cottage south of Nags Head for the first week of June. It stood on stilts, had a deck and kitchen, bedroom, living room, plenty of salt air and surf sounds.

I told her I wanted to live this way all the time.

We had dinner almost every night at a gracious Old World hotel. Sat by the window with pressed table linen, wonderful old black waiters, fresh local lobster and fine wines.

Billie would put her hair up in a bun because I loved that. I'd sit and stare and melt, then help her out of her embarrassment by getting myself going on yet another political issue. With another drink, of course.

We were comfortable, loving, joyous.

We'd been there five days when I got the news.

We came up from the beach about 3, happy, hot and tired. There was a message taped to our screen door, obviously left by the woman who owned the cottage:

"Call John Cassady."

I grabbed a beer, jumped into the Fiat and roared up the road to a phone booth. If there was tragedy in my family, Cass would be chosen to call me.

"Hi, Cass. Scott."

"Hello Scott! How's that ocean living?"

"Wonderful. Just came up from the beach and found a note to call you."

"Well, I probably shouldn't have called, but I thought you might want to know . . ."

"Know what?

"Actually, I don't know."

I lit a cigarette. He didn't sound as though it was bad news. I had assumed it would be.

"There is a letter here for you. It's from Stanford."

My heart leapt. Oh, bless him for calling!

"If you'd like, I'll open it."

"Yes. Please."

"Okay." I couldn't hear anything for long seconds.

"You've got a fellowship, Scott. The letter says you have been accepted!"

I thanked him and rushed back to our cottage, grabbed a cold beer and looked around for Billie.

"In here."

She was curled up on the bed with her book, a towel

wrapped around her head, another around her body. She'd obviously taken a shower.

"I . . ."

"What is it? You look so . . ."

"I'm going to Stanford University for a year on a fellowship!"

She glowed up into my eyes with joy.

"I don't deserve it, Billie."

"Come here, Scott."

The drive back to Washington was quiet. Billie read, and I tried to envision what Stanford would be like—would there be palm trees on a northern California campus? Would the women be California-beautiful like you see in magazines? How close is the ocean to Stanford?

The steamy heat of late-afternoon on Capitol Hill was oppressive as I drove down the ramp at 3rd S.E., past the Star's building to our right. Billie broke her silence:

"This has been the most wonderful . . ."

"Hasn't it?" I looked at her. Her eyes bore back into me.

"I hate to have it end—almost a whole week in my favorite place, with a man I have fallen in love with."

It stabbed my heart.

Suddenly the air was thin, my pulse raced wildly, erratically. Panic grew down inside me.

> *Oh no, Billie, no. You deserve a good, decent guy. Not me. Can't you see? I'm on my way down, not up?*
> *I have this secret, about how I feel,*
> *why I drink like I do,*
> *why I have this spot in my eye.*
> *Can't you see, Billie?*
> *There is something very very wrong with Scott now.*
> *The way I drink . . .*
> *Can't you see it, Billie?*
> *No, no, no, no, Billie.*
> *I can't—I couldn't do it to you, Billie.*

The silence lasted until I got six blocks north, turning right onto Pennsylvania Avenue. "How about a beer?"

She nodded. I parked in front of Mr. Henry's, led her to a table near other people, went into the men's room and stared in the mirror.

I threw it away, threw it away with my silence.
The best thing that could happen to me.
Ohgawd, Scott, what the hell is so wrong?
And why would you, this one time,
be the noble man
you've always just pretended to be?

By the time I got back to the table, we were able to look each other in the eyes without showing the terrible sadness. My beer was waiting, but she'd decided to have a Coke.

I drank quickly, ordered a double Tanquerey, then another, and another and . . .

The last Monday morning in June:

It was dead time on a Monday morning, but the news was so slow that we'd finished work on the first edition early. Belmont Faries was bubbly, Bruce Hopkins was handling the slot, and I was having an easier-than-usual day, one of those Mondays when I could work with reporters and editors on projects.

I answered the phone the moment it rang.

"National desk. Smith."

"Hi Scott—it's your mother."

"Hi Ann."

"I have some bad news."

I knew. She didn't need to say it. My heart knew. She said it anyhow.

"H.R. died this morning."

"Oh God, Ann."

There was a long okay silence. We had both loved him so.

"He did it just like he said he would, too."

"You mean-?"

"The doctors said he had water on the chest. Nothing they could do. It would be slow. So he got up in the middle of the night, shaved and put on a suit and tie, went down to the garage, started the engines in both cars, sat down in his favorite, and just went to sleep. With a smile on his face."

The details droned on. Each pushed a knife deeper into me.

H. Raymond Smith, father of my father. He had been my father.

They were both gone now.

I drank from 5 until 7 that evening, while I packed and talked with friends, all the while barely hearing my own voice or theirs. Then I headed for Long Island, stopping first at a liquor store on East Capitol Street for a six-pack.

This was, I knew, a crisis of something way down in me. Of the heart.

I knew I could not handle it.

Aloneness. I am alone.

It was the best reason in the world to get drunk. Anyone would understand.

Booze, whether beer or hard stuff, was the best friend I had ever found.

Life's not the same now.

I didn't even make it to New Jersey. Midway through Delaware, I pulled into a motel and phoned my mother. I told her not to worry, that I was just tired. Hung up, pulled up the covers and passed out.

The morning was too bright, too real. I drove from the motel to a liquor store, then back up onto the highway and north toward Long Island. And I kept noticing that damned spot in my eye. Was it really from the booze?

By the time I reached metropolitan New York, I felt alive and human again. There were six empties on the floor. It was 10:40 a.m.

The funeral was awful. I thanked Ann that she had protected me from one last look, and that she and my uncles had decided upon a closed casket.

As a minister rattled along, doing the best he could when he hadn't really known H.R., I sat within my own subconscious, shutting off the voices and the faces and the casket, trying to picture H.R. smiling, trying to see him standing there in his shirtsleeves in his kitchen, telling me one more time, as he had just two months earlier, that when his body started to go, he would end it quickly himself.

And what was it he'd said? There was "no doubt," he'd said, about living on.

Well, I had doubt. That was certain.

The philosphy professor at Lafayette had drilled it into me: You might as well be an optimist about it, because either you live on or you won't know that you didn't.

Was H.R. just an optimist?, or did he know something?

My brain said the professor was right. My heart said something else.

Or was I just a softie?

I was 30 years old and starting to sense that this issue was vital to me. My father had died when I was two, and now my father-figure had died. And I would die.

Was this why I had loved the English Romantic poets so much in college? Because they'd addressed the issue so directly? I'd grown up around people who seldom discussed it—except H.R.

The next evening, back at our house in Quogue, I tried to get my mother to talk about death. She wouldn't.

I kept having one experience all evening: I could still see the dazzle in H.R.'s bright, clear eyes that last night I'd seen him, right after he gave the waiter the 200 shares of AT&T.

But meanwhile, I kept noticing the hair-like spot in my eye, kept associating it with my drinking—kept trying to get it to go away. It didn't. I was missing Billie—Billie might understand, yet I just could not stick her with a guy like me. I hoped she was happy.

The next day I headed back to Washington. At least I had Stanford coming up—something new so far away from all this.

In August, after seven month's separation, Lynn and I decided we needed to talk seriously about my forthcoming trip. We went to the lounge at the Sheraton-Silver Spring. And we danced. She felt so good.

The next weekend she visited my apartment. I sauteed fresh scallops and afterward we lounged on the daybed/couch, our legs casually touching.

My heart pounded as she announced that she didn't want to get her dress wrinkled. Who was seducing whom? It had been so long since . . .

"This is gonna be so good," she breathed, "that you'll never ever want any other woman again."

Maybe we weren't compatible day to day, but I loved her.

I left in September, wondering whether Lynn and I could put our marriage back together. If we did, I thought, Billie would be okay, she'd meet someone who'd be good for her.

September 1970:

The long days on Route 280, rolling westward into sights new and enthralling. I noticed that there were a couple of songs I would switch off. "Lara's Theme" from Dr. Zhivago was one. It told me how sad my love for Lynn was. And

Bacharach's "Alfie" seemed to warn me of what I was becoming—a coward running from the first woman he'd known who felt deeply right to him, afraid to love Billie and be loved by Billie.

Newscasts were great because I knew, to the mile, how far I was from the origins of the news. I was alone in new country, with no one knowing where I was, with no responsibility. It felt wonderful.

I had a routine and I was proud of it. I'd buy a package of lemonade mix, drink it until 4 in the afternoon, then stop and add gin for the last hour of driving before checking in to another motel.

It was the least I'd had to drink, morning to evening, in several years. It meant I could cut loose at night.

I'd stopped overnight at the Holiday Inn at Grand Island, Nebraska, and said farewell to the Midwest with a drunken attempt to pick up a waitress. Then on a sun-filled Thursday afternoon, I started to ascend the foothills, the little Fiat lugging slightly with the weight of its load: My KLH stereo and speakers, my old Royal typewriter, two suitcases, a pile of sweaters and slacks, a two-gallon cooler, and me.

As I first saw the rise of the Rockies through the little windshield, I felt a chill.

As if I've lived here before.
Long ago.
I died out here, tragically. Long ago.

I wouldn't let my mind pursue the feeling. Booze and song were the answer. Except "Lara's Theme" or "Alfie".

I stopped in Cheyenne, parked near the railroad tracks, and just walked, soaking up my first sense of The West.

I'm right at home.

I stayed at the Holiday Inn in Laramie that night, and again felt completely at home. It was the happiest drinking and the best sleep I'd had in weeks.

There was snow on my car in the morning and for some reason it told me not to think about H.R. unless they were happy thoughts. That seemed impossible, to have happy thoughts about him.

He's dead, Scott. Gone.

Just keep driving, Scott. And don't worry about that spot on your eye!

The Salt Lake City area was postcard beauty. I'd never realized such places were real.

I knew about the Mormons. They didn't drink. So what? Who cared? But what if I lost my booze somehow, and couldn't find any place to buy it?

I stopped at the airport Holiday Inn, checked in, and noticed a lounge. Huh? A lounge?

I heard a yell and saw a beer bottle flying toward me. It missed. The folks in the lounge were having fun. I sat down on a stool, tried to look casual. Ordered one of those Coors I'd heard about.

Someone had put a portable radio on the bar. Streisand was singing "Stoney End."

Boy, that Coors was good. I bought five more for the room. I'd have gotten more, but I wasn't too sure this Mormon motel would have an ice machine, even if it did have such a bar.

I ate in the motel dining room and returned to my room about 8. The phone was ringing as I turned the key. I hurried in, noting that my Tanquerey and part of a Coors were sitting beside the phone on the table between the beds.

"Hello, Scott." M'gawd it was Elsie!, my grandmother.

"Hi, Mom! How'd you get me?"

"You gave your mother your schedule, remember?"

"How're things back in Medina?"

Someone was in the doorway.

"The weather's been too rainy, and you know how humid it gets here. How is your trip, dear?"

"Great!"

It was a woman, leaning on the doorjamb. Blue jeans, tight white tee shirt. Blonde, slightly pudgy, maybe 30.

"I love the West, Mom. Especially this place. You should see the mountains here! They're so high, so majestic."

"Yes, Scott, we saw them from the train when your uncles and I went to San Francisco a few years ago. I envy you."

"Mom? Can you hold on just a minute?"

Drink in hand, I went to the door.

"Can I help you?", I asked.

Blue eyes—glazed, laughing eyes. "Are you the Mr. uh Gray who wanted a girl?"

"For what?"

"For an hour."

I stared at her.

My grandmother's on the phone, some pudgy blonde whore's leering at me, and I'm in a Mormon town 2,000 miles from home.

"No, no, my name's Smith."

"Oh sure!"

"Just a minute."

"Okay." She took the glass out of my hand.

I went back to the phone. "Hi. Sorry, Someone came to the door and-"

"Is your car running all right? I worry about you so in that tiny little foreign thing."

"Just fine, Mom."

The girl had poured herself some of my gin, and sat down on the bed across from me, her legs spread, eyes laughing.

"Well, I won't hold you, dear. I know you want to go sight-seeing. Have a good trip, and please call me some night. I get so lonely just sitting here by myself."

"Thank you for calling, Mom. And I will call you. Love you."

"Goodnight, Scott dear."

The woman held the glass to her lips, eyes running up and down my body.

"So your mother calls you every night when you're traveling? Aren't you a little old for that?"

"No, no—it was my grandmother."

"That's nice . . ."

"And I don't travel a lot, not out here."

"So you want me, sweetie?" She got up, came toward me.

I stood up quickly and walked to the doorway.

"Fifty for an hour, sweetie, all you can handle, and then some. Even . . ."

I turned, tried to smile. "No thanks. You've got the wrong room. And my name really is Smith."

"You'll regret it all night if you don't try it, sweetie. And for you, for fifty dollars, I'll even give you head and then take it up the . . ."

"Head?"

"You like head, sweets? Uh? You like?" She wore a dumb little pin on her shoulder strap. I wondered what it was. "I just love giving it."

"I don't think I uh quite know what you mean, about this uh 'head'."

"Where's your wallet? I'll show you . . ." She ran her tongue around the edge of my glass.

"No thanks, miss. Nope. No thanks. Whatever you . . ."
"Goddam you, you cheap-ass son of a bitch!" She stormed out of the room.
"Hey, wait a minute," I screamed. "You've got my glass, my Tanquerey!"

San Francisco and Palo Alto were woodsy. That was my first surprise.

There was something about the eucalyptus trees and it wasn't just the wonderful pungent smell. Something distantly familiar, something deja vu.

I rented an efficiency apartment right up against the Bayshore Freeway, started my classes and bought a dramatic Studio One print of the fog in the bay.

The Stanford program of year-long fellowships for journalists had some likable people in it. A guy from Time and I played tennis some mornings. A guy from Newsday loved ping pong, and we'd spend hours trying to beat an editor from South Vietnam.

I wasn't drinking quite as much and felt healthier. I was starting to read again.

My second Saturday, I awoke at 8:30, stopped for breakfast at the Town & Country shopping center, then headed southwest out Page Mill Road, up into the foothills, and into the mountain ridges.

I had never seen or felt anything like the redwoods. I'd drive a mile or two, then decide to stop and just stand or sit among the giants, marveling and wondering how and why I had stayed in the East for 30 years.

The road finally flattened, and there were fields of flowers left and right. Commercial growers. What a waste, I thought, people spending their whole lives just growing flowers.

Suddenly the horizon in front of the little Fiat included a wide blue horizontal line. I slowed down and gulped.
There, out of nowhere, was the Pacific Ocean!
I was at a crossroads called Pescadero. San Francisco was to my right, Santa Cruz and Monterey many miles to my left, or south.
I headed south, wondering if this "Pacific Coast Highway" was the real one, the one I had always heard about.
I felt strangely peaceful, oddly at home.
It was my first moment, first day, on the Pacific, yet . . .

Two hours later, and again, almost suddenly as I drove along, Monterey Bay opened wide before me. I pulled over to the side of the highway and sucked in the sight and the air.

The Monterey Peninsula poked gently out into the Pacific to my right, the city tucked safely into the pocket formed by the Peninsula.

There was something about the gentle slow slope of the treeline atop the peninsula, slipping to the right down to the ocean, something about the safety of the harbor, something . . .

Deja vu.

This, I said aloud, is where I want to live.

Someone had suggested 17-Mile Drive in Carmel. I spent hours stopping, getting out, marveling, wishing my mother and family could see this, driving another mile or two, stopping again.

The cypress trees get to every tourist. But I knew I was different; the trees were more special to me than to some jerk from . . .

I resented the tourists, although I was one.

I felt like a visitor yet at home.

I was exuberant, yet at peace.

I wanted to celebrate, yet didn't want a drink.

As the sun slid into the horizon, I sat at the bar in an Italian restaurant on Monterey's Fishermen's Wharf. I knew that I shouldn't think about H.R. I scribbled, feeling sheer genius, my ultimate truth on a cocktail napkin after my third double:

> *and the cypress itself was just a sad, sad poem. alone. forlorn. worn down by time. alone in this beauty.*

Great! I wondered, seriously, if I should quit the newspaper field and be a poet. Bartender, another double, please . . .

9:40 a.m. on a Thursday in October, 1970:

I'd been wandering about the Stanford bookstore because there were so many leggy blondes in short shorts there.

I hadn't meant to buy a book, but it was the quickest way to get to stand in line beside the short one in the white see-through tennis dress. I couldn't think of anything to say to her. She paid and left. I dug into my wallet and threw down $15, grabbed the receipt and tried to seem casual about chasing after her.

She sauntered out to the fountain area.

Book under arm, I did the same.

She started to read.

I sat down 20 feet to her left, opened my package, pulled out the book, wondered why in hell I'd bought this thing: "Deliverance," a novel by some poet from down south, James Dickey.

I smoked and read, and smoked and read, and suddenly it was quarter after 1. The girl must've left the fountain plaza by 10; I hadn't looked at a woman in hours. And I could not stop—Dickey's prose had me spellbound. This man was a writer!

The book's language was compelling, the story gripping. That's it, I decided—I should be a dramatic novelist. Poetry, plus novels. That's what I was meant to do. To hell with newspapering.

The next morning I enrolled in a creative writing class, taught by a gentle redhead whose husband was a novelist.

It had been a long Friday night, drinking and buying rounds at the bar, writing a long drunken letter to Lynn, fielding a phone call from a lady who wanted to visit me.

Now, Saturday morning, I figured I'd head for Big Sur.

I was shaving. The razor shook slightly.

But that didn't bother me.

What got to me was that I had unwittingly shaved off the right half of the moustache I'd been growing.

I went to the Tresidder cafeteria on campus almost every morning because there were so many leggy blondes there. Great way to wake up, watching legs, looking for panty lines, trying to catch an eye, a smile.

And I hadn't asked one girl for a date.

On this morning, I sat down at a circular table along the wall. A tall broad-shouldered, student sat down across from me, alone, with two glasses of juice. I had bought the San Francisco Chronicle. He asked if he could borrow the sports pages. Later, we chatted briefly and introduced ourselves. His name was Jim.

The following Sunday morning, I sat at the counter at Bob's Big Boy in Mountain View staring at the sports page. There was a picture of the guy from that morning in the cafeteria: Jim Plunkett, it said, the Stanford quarterback, perhaps the best in the nation.

The following Tuesday, I spotted him, again alone, at the same table at Tresidder. I sat down, offered him the sports pages. He said no, he'd already read it, he had to get to class. I said okay but I'd like to chat sometime—I was a newspaper editor in Washington, D.C. He said okay, smiled and left for class.

We'd chat occasionally and it made a mark. The kid was a quarterback, a star, yet quiet and self-effacing. And he was saving his money so he could help his blind Mexican-born parents.

My eyes were opening.

I spent hours, night after night, working on a very long short story about a cripple who was trying to survive violence in an insane world. I couldn't understand why I was writing it, but I felt that it had to get written.

Once it was done, I put it in a box and never read it again.

Palo Alto was pure college town and I felt out of place.

I got to talking with a professor, at the Stanford Inn during my almost-nightly drinking bouts there, and told him I felt like an outsider. He pushed the topic and I heard myself announcing that I felt out of place in the world. I felt that everyone had a secret about how to live, I said, and I didn't have it.

He got up and left.

The classes were a delight. And I did not have to perform, wasn't allowed to take anything for credit, wasn't expected to take any examinations.

I spent my work hours—it sure didn't feel like "work"—on music theory and composition, fiction writing, Victorian humor, current economic issues, some environmental concerns, and even sat in on some neurology classes with premed students who dissected cats' brains.

I read and listened and marveled at how far off Washington was. Washington, my longtime power and news capital of the world, was getting closer to the west coast of Europe than the heart of America, it seemed. Going the way of Atlantis?

Big Sur commanded me.

I'd get surges of compulsion to be there, and I'd jump in the Fiat, pick up a cold six-pack or a bottle of Tanquerey, and head south. I didn't know why.

I'd push down 101 to Route 17, through San Jose—I didn't like San Jose—then up over the Santa Cruz Mountains, then swing south down Route 1, Pacific Coast Highway. That entrance ramp, from 17 onto 1 in Santa Cruz, became important to me: There I could start breathing again!

It was irrational. I didn't care; it was how I felt. I had no idea what it would mean later in my life.

I'd discovered the Bixby Creek area of Big Sur. I'd park along the dangerously narrow roadway, wander out into the meadows above the surf, glass or bottle in hand, stretch out in the field and listen and drink and dream and drink and . . .

It was a Sunday afternoon in October, and there was a young couple wandering around the meadow holding hands. I approached the guy, plastic glass in my left hand, right hand outstretched: "Hi—how ya doin?—I'm lookin for a little help. Would you just hold my ankles for a moment while I hang out over that bluff?"

We walked over to the edge and I got down on my stomach, set my glass in the grass beside me, and inched forward. "Now—just hold onto my ankles, okay?"

The bluff was about 300 feet directly above the surf. I spit and watched it fall, bending in the coastal wind, plopping into the water just behind the breakers.

If I'd jump, I thought, I'd fall 300 feet and land either in the soaring, surging surf or on the rocks. There was no doubt I would die.

The blue-green-azure transluscence of the churning water was spellbinding, hypnotic, the colors flashing and rolling up at me like whales' eyes, inviting, knowing.

"Hey uh, bud, uh—how long ya gonna do this?"

I edged back, stood up, got my drink.

"Thank you! That was quite a thrill, something I like to do about once a month." It was a boldface lie, but I hoped it made my behavior somehow seem less bizarre to them.

The girl stared at me with some sort of knowing. Then they spun and left me standing there, glad I had done it. B'gawd, I would do it monthly!

I flew back to Washington for Thanksgiving and decided to stay through the holidays. I wanted to do anything possible to put the marriage and family back together.

Just after Christmas, I suggested that Lynn, Don and Laura go back to Palo Alto with me for the winter/spring term. Lynn finally agreed.

The first several weeks felt idyllic for me, having my children and wife, and Stanford and Big Sur. But it was more important to me to go get another six-pack. Which I did at least twice a day—plus the gin and the bourbon and the cognac.

I couldn't understand why it was more important to get the booze, but it was and I certainly didn't think I had a choice.

Then Stanford was over. We returned on a southern route, through Tucson and San Antonio, Galveston and New Orleans.

Shortly after we got back and I went back to work, Lynn and I got into yet another argument. My lid blew. I moved back to Capitol Hill.

It was March 1971, the last time the four of us were really together.

Summer, 1971:

Charlie Seib, the managing editor, came out to the national desk, smiling, long arms dangling in a care-free style.

"Scott—Newby'd like to see you."

My heart froze.

Newbold Noyes, the editor. Inheritor of Star stock. Brilliant, genteel, tough. What the hell had I done wrong? And why was Charlie, who said he would join us, smiling?

Newby was waiting, also smiling, gesturing us to choose where we'd sit. Sweat was rolling down my ribcages. I lit a cigarette.

There was small talk about my Stanford experience, about politics. But he didn't delay long.

"Scott, do you understand what kind of shape we're in?"

"You mean as a company?" I was wondering how Newby could keep his shirts so neatly pressed all day.

"Losing money. You're aware of that?"

"Yes, but . . ." I wondered if he or Charlie could smell the sweat. My shirt was drenched.

Newby frowned. He got up and paced.

"It's getting worse not better, Scott. You know that. We've tried this and that, circulation gimmicks and real stuff. Advertising campaigns. Expensive.

"My argument's been that we should improve the product with that money. We've spent a lot of money. But revenues keep getting worse, not better.

"No matter what we've done, it's all been Bandaids." He peered at me. "The Star, Scott, is in trouble."

What the hell is going on here?
He's being too friendly to be firing me.

"Scott, Charlie and I have talked hard about this. I—we think you ought to become our first metropolitan editor."

"Huh?"

"Metropolitan editor. We'd change the title of city editor to metropolitan editor. You'd be running all of the city and state staffs."

No. Don't do it.
You came here to work on national stuff.
You don't even care about local stuff.

I looked at Charlie. He looked comfortable with the whole screwy idea. Newby was waiting expectantly.

"I uh . . ."

"I know it, Scott. You came to Washington because you wanted to be a national guy. I don't blame you. You know, that was my national desk before you ever got here. I loved it, just like you do. Same with Charlie. We know. But the fact is, this paper is in red ink. Deep. Jack (Jack Kauffmann, the publisher) has me convinced that Editorial has got to help. What we've been doing hasn't worked. It's that simple—not that we're doing anything 'wrong', just that it hasn't . . ."

I relit my cigarette, leaned back, closed my eyes for a moment.

Newby was giving a speech! The new corporate strategy was simple and I had become part of it. The Post had outstripped the Star in circulation and advertising revenue and the situation was getting worse. We were an afternoon newspaper. They were in trouble everywhere. Unless we changed, we'd die.

The Star's strategy would be to throw its editorial muscle into local coverage, become better grounded with the permanent population in the Washington suburbs. Scott Smith would revamp the local coverage, make it deeper and brighter at the same time.

His voice trailed on. I watched Charlie. Charlie watched me. I smoked two more cigarettes. I became, very slowly, comfortable sitting there.

And when I left Newby's office, I was the first metropolitan editor in the history of the Washington Evening Star. I was 31 years old, would have 110 reporters and editors and dictationists under me—many of them absolutely impossible to work with—and my first decision was where I'd go to celebrate.

6

May 1973:

I was sitting in a right-hand window seat, bloody mary in hand, blinking in amazement at the barren brown of southeastern Arizona below. I'd forgotten just how bleak yet gentle-lovely it could be.

Would I want to live out here, so far from all the years I'd spent on the East Coast? So far from the south shore of Long Island, so far from my parents, so far from the Star and the White House, so far from the center of world power? So far from Lynn? So far from . . .

Hell yes!

The jet was passing high mountains to our right. I gazed down at the melange of roofs and pools and, yes, yes—there were palm trees. Amazing how palms can mean "away" to the traveler from the East Coast.

Perfect, I thought. I need palm trees.

Yes. I wanted the job. It would only pay half of what I'd been making, but I wouldn't have to work umpteen hours a day, and would have the summers free. And teaching might be just fine. And I'd pay less in taxes. And housing in Tucson would cost so much less. And what the hell, anyway—I wanted to do this.

I sighed. I didn't care as much about teaching as I cared about getting away from Washington and the mess there.

In Tucson, no one would be able to reach me. No one would be bugging me.

They'd finally gotten to me in Washington.

Newby had called me into his office in April. He said they needed a more flamboyant metropolian editor. They were concerned about how I was "reacting to pressure," he said.

I'd said it was Lynn's fault.

Newby had ignored that and suggested I become "special assistant" to Jack Kauffmann, the publisher.

I'd sensed that Kauffmann thought I drank too much. I told Newby I wanted time to think.

I'd gone home, gone swimming in vodka and confusion for a week, then decided I'd resign if I could move west. I'd heard that the University of Arizona's journalism faculty was tough-minded—not "communications theory".

So I applied for a job there, and they'd asked me to visit.

Yes, yes, yes. I decided to get a rental car, find the Plaza International hotel, have a drink or two in my room, meet the faculty members at 4, then drive around Tucson and get to bed early. The interviewing tomorrow would be crucial.

The town looked just perfect. It was nowhere.

I'd only been through Tucson once before, on my way back from Stanford in '71. Lynn and the kids and I had stayed at some starlit motel on the edge of town and she'd felt good so we'd gotten two rooms and let the kids go swimming while we drank cocktails in our room at sunset. I remembered too well.

Just shut the brain down when that stuff starts, kid.

This would be so different: Living out here in the desert, sipping gin and tonics by a pool, watching the sun go down, knowing the phone wouldn't ring. Ahh.

The eggs were cold, the orange juice warm, and breakfast at the Plaza International the next morning was dreary. But no matter. I wasn't hungry. I was enthused—I'd liked the guys in Tucson. And the morning paper was reporting news from back in Washington that made me glad not to be involved.

"Paging Scott Smith, paging Scott Smith."

Who could that be? Maybe the Star wanted me to go back, as executive something or other. Maybe American Airlines had found my silver cigarette lighter. Gee, people were looking at me!

It was Phil, the retiring chairman of the journalism department. He said the president of the university wanted to meet me. Nothing to worry about. It was routine in hiring situations. Last step. Could I meet Phil at 8:20 —less than a hour—in his office?

Damn! In the walk from my table to the hotel's tiny lobby, I felt the old band tightening around my chest. Nerves.

I got on the elevator deciding that I'd figure out two broad, vague, philosophical questions for the interview. Any university president undoubtedly would take up the entire time, when he was supposed to be interviewing me, answering my questions instead and talking about himself—and he'd think it was a good interview and approve the hiring.

The only trouble was my hands. The band around the chest wasn't visible, but the hands were trembling again.

No wonder, I thought. Anyone's hands would shake if they got summoned to be interviewed by the president of a university that had 30,000 students.

The vodka was on the dressing table just inside the door. Three inches of vodka in a short 7Up would quiet those hands, and loosen the band around my chest. Oh thankgawd for it. This interview was crucial—what the hell would I do if it didn't go well?

Even though they say no one can smell vodka, I thought, I'd better take the toothpaste with me on the drive over to the campus. No problem. The timing was tight, though: It was 7:55 a.m. I wasn't worried about choosing my tie. I was concerned about the rapid gulping I'd have to do.

In fact, I decided, maybe I'd better get two of those drinks down.

The teaching job was mine, and my world was suddenly upside-down—which felt fine to me.

I had previously left Capitol Hill and gotten another house in suburban Maryland.*

Now Don and Laura wanted to go West with their father. The house would have to be sold quickly if we were going to enjoy the move, I said. I'd suggested we make the trip by camping across the country.

I packed in the glow of a Washington springtime, loading books into boxes, listening to the Watergate hearings on television during the days, drinking beer and creating new Double Crostics at night.

It felt strange, not working, not getting up at 4:30 or 5:15, not fighting traffic and deadlines and angry reporters. I

*Footnote: While writing this book, in 1986, I decided it would be best for everyone if I omitted references to a woman who was involved during this period of time.

searched for a good quotation about the dangers of the Puritan work ethic to make into a Double Crostic.

While running the metropolitan staff, my "hobby" had been the creation of a weekly Double Crostic for the Star's Sunday magazine.

I would miss my window above the back yard. It was second-floor-level, up where the robins and bluejays and sparrows would sit, just across from my table and the pile of books and pencils and erasers and papers that went into creating the Double Crostics.

I kept telling Sam and Mary Seiler that I was so glad to be out of the news flow. Watergate was the biggest day-after-day scandal in televised news history, and as I listened, whether packing books or clothes or pouring another bloody mary, it became more like a soap opera every day. And a couple of the cleaner-cut Nixon guys I'd known were starting to look like future prison residents . . .

Hot sun and fresh faces were so much cleaner, healthier. Who'd want to be editing that Watergate stuff, calling the shots on something that tacky?

The house didn't sell. No matter; it would. I lowered the price by a thousand and held a big garage sale. We'd leave anyway, let the realtor sell the house.

No more winters, no more snow, no more prima donna reporters or dumb parties. Nope. Going West!

Late in June we set out for seven and a half weeks of cross-country camping: the Black Hills of South Dakota, the land around Cody, Wyo., and then Jackson Hole, the near-wilderness of northern Idaho, then down along the cold, windy beaches of northern California.

I wondered whether Don and Laura could appreciate such a trip.

I wore a red-orange long-sleeved shirt and white checkered bermudas, day after day. We had routines: Good hearty breakfasts and lots of coffee. Day excursions in the hills or fishing or into the towns. And I had beer at midday, gin and tonics starting about 4, until whenever Daddy snored off.

There were mornings when the mountain chill just wouldn't break. But I learned to slip a little Gilbey's into my coffee. I felt free to do what I wanted.

On arrival in Tucson in August 1973, I rented a furnished bedroom apartment for the period we'd be house-hunting. We waited for word that the house in Washington had sold.

We found a couple of cheap restaurants we liked, discovered that the Walgreens at El Rancho on Speedway

Boulevard had the best prices on hootch. The kids hoped we could get a house with a pool, and many of the places we inspected did have pools.

The summer-long vacation was coming to an end. The mail one Tuesday made that all too clear.

The faculty would have a champagne brunch to celebrate the start of the school year.

I rumbled around the apartment, wondering whether I had to go. It was just the sort of obligatory stuff that had helped me decide to quit Washington and go teach in Tucson. Maybe I should tell these people right now that I do not care to go to their idiotic little faculty gatherings.

I went.

It was politely conducted at fellow professor Jim Lamb's east Tucson home, one of the thousands of pleasant, middle-class, single-story places out east of the older downtown neighborhoods.

Jim had been with the Associated Press in Philadelphia when I was in Allentown and later editing wire copy in Washington, so we had mutual friends in the business and something to talk about other than the Wildcats football team or the intricacies of the university phone system.

Everybody stood about talking as if they were having a fine time. But my mind was on something else: Jim and his wife were serving, and I knew that Jim noticed that my hand was trembling.

Then, over eggs, I thought that his wife, a practicing psychologist, had noticed also. A shrink! She might be able to see how I felt inside. Damn—I'd liked her until this.

And how I felt inside was worse than trembling hands. I had that familiar tight band across my chest. Had I felt it so long that I almost didn't notice it anymore? Thank God for booze; it was the one thing that made me feel okay.

Over crepes and coffee, I casually mentioned how my shoulders ached from lifting (boxes—we were moving into a house) and swimming. Nancy Lamb nodded. Sure—the shaking was from stiffness, not booze. She didn't know about it after all, I thought in relief.

But as I drove back to the apartment, I wondered whether in fact the whole Western world knew that something was very wrong down deep in Scott Smith, the guy who took a 50-percent cut in pay to get out of Washington and teach in Tucson. One of these days, I thought, I'm gonna let another shrink take a shot at me.

For about the same price as a tiny place in Washington, we'd bought a four-bedroom, two-bath house, a rambling, makeshift sort of middle-class place with a large pool, a toolshed for a cabana, a cowboy-sounding name for the dusty road in the Bear Canyon area.

The house was all on one concrete floor (covered with new carpeting) and from the living room window we could see Elephant Head, a hump in the mountains near Green Valley, 40 miles to the south. On a clear day, we could see ridges that surrounded Nogales, Mexico, maybe 65 miles south of us.

I tried to explain to Laura that it was pretty incredible to be able to see so far. She wondered how many boys would be in her class.

To our north, beyond the pool, we could see Thimble Peak, a jutting little knob 5,400 feet above sea level, strikingly three-dimensional against the majestic sweep of the Catalina Mountains, which rose to 9,000 feet, with dark pines at higher elevations.

Our road was a winding dirt path, two cars wide, through good but tract housing. It was great for a return address—see, Ma, we're cowboys!—but the dust settled in the back of the throat like old very-thin sandpaper, and I was soon asking neighbors what it would take to get the road paved.

One, an older man who died of bronchial problems soon afterward, said it would take a joint decision by God and Conrad Joyner, a county politician. God would be all for it, my neighbor said, but Joyner was too smart to try to get any more taxes out of us.

Another neighbor showed up in September. Bob Linder. He had an oldshoe smile and a Santa Claus belly and was in his late 30s. Tall yet pudgy, he looked comfortable in his pastor's collar. He explained that he'd been sent to Tucson by the Lutheran Church in America to establish a mission church in the fast-growing sprawl of east Tucson. He needed help.

I told Linder I liked him even if he was "a goddam minister asking for goddam contributions." Something about the man was comfortable and upbeat.

I got up and poured us both a gin and tonic. The gin was good against the desert dust. He stopped after just one.

An hour and two drinks later, I volunteered to help with any writing the mission church might need, and one drink after that agreed to go door-knocking for his mission.

The classrooms were in the basement of the social sciences building. My tiny, windowless office had been a janitors' closet until the journalism department expanded.

I taped a wide poster of the cockpit controls of a 747 jet across the wall behind my chair, and tried to make people, or me, believe I thought my office was funny. I hated it, yet somehow sensed that it was appropriate.

I was teaching basic news writing, feature writing, and overseeing the state's only journalism review.

The beginners in the basic class were my favorites. I'd wear bermuda shorts in class, make them get things right, tell the truth about Washington and about the business, and most of them understood. We'd walk and write and drink and laugh and write and drink together. We were teacher and students yet friends. They were the best escape I'd found. Some of them knew it.

I knew I wasn't conforming; it was fine by me.

On a Friday afternoon in late fall, I went doorbell-ringing. I'd promised Bob Linder I would do it, and I was feeling just right—and what the hell, maybe I'd meet someone I'd like.

About 4:30, I returned to the house for a break.

"Hi, Dad." It was Laura. "Where you been? The car was here, but you weren't."

"I've been out knocking on doors, asking people if they'd like to help start up a church."

Laura was laughing.

After a good cold, stiff drink, I headed back out into the desert dust, feeling resolved to find at least one taker.

A woman in her 50s peered at me from the cool dark of her foyer and asked if I believed in God.

"Of course, ma'am. "

"Then you wouldn't be drinking like that," she said.

As I stomped across the sparse grass she'd been trying to grow, I wondered whether I really believed in anything.

Did I believe in God? Obviously. I was working for a church, wasn't I?

After all, I thought, something created those mountains up there. And something took care of our country and the president.

Maybe that something didn't need to know that I existed, but it took care of the human race and I believed in it, whatever it was!

Didn't I?

At 5:40 I braved a front yard that seemed to be teeming with dogs, and knocked.

A very short woman with small black eyes peered out at me. "Yes?"

"Hello! My name's Scott Smith and I live down on Twilight Trail, and I'm asking our neighbors if anyone would like to help this guy Bob Linder, who's trying to start up a new church out here in the desert."

Her nose twitched and the little black eyes seemed to be grinning at me.

I pushed another dog away.

"We have seven mutts—hope you'll excuse them," she said.

"I love dogs, ma'am. Good thing, huh?" I smiled to her, and the eyes smiled back.

"Well—my husband and I were just having a little cocktail. Would you like to come in?"

"Why sure, ma'am. Thank you!"

She led me past the living room to a sort of family room that looked out on a fenced area—more dogs—and the ravine where I knew the creek and the coyotes ran.

Her husband stood up, pipe in one hand, glass in the other.

"Brownie, this is—what'd you say your name was?"

"Smith. Scott Smith."

"Brown. Lionel Brown," said the husband.

He was maybe 50, tall, thinning blond bair, friendly blue eyes.

"Mr. Smith here is canvassing for a new church, Brownie."

"Well, we're not very interested in churches," he said.

"Are you from New England, Mr. Brown?'"

"New Hampshire, long time ago. Would you like something to drink?"

"I'd love something. Gets pretty dry out there."

"When did you move here?"

"This year. Came from Washington, D.C."

"How about a martini—that's what I'm having."

"That sounds good."

"Artie, fix this gentleman a martini, would you?" He sat back down in his overstuffed rocker and put the pipe back in his mouth. I guessed he was through talking.

"So you're starting up a church."

"Well, I'm not—I'm just doing sort of some survey work to see how many people might want to be founders."

"Brownie," said Mrs. Brown, handing me a martini, "that might be interesting—to be founders of a church."

I stayed for an hour and the Browns, more like old friends every minute, agreed to come to an organizational meeting two weeks later.

As I pushed back the dogs on my way out—Artie Brown took care of dogs that otherwise would be killed at the pound—I noticed a set of golf clubs in the Browns' garage.

"You play, Brownie?" I nodded toward the clubs.

"Yes. Not well, but once a week"

There was a silence.

"Great game. I love it."

"You play, do you?" He was still at the door.

"Sure do! Maybe we can get out together some afternoon."

"We'll see," said Lionel Brown, closing the door.

Over the months, I found a good way to take the pressure off. It was called lunch. Lunch had nothing to do with food. Lunch meant getting away from the pressures of campus life and being able to relax.

I boiled it down to two menus: Vodka on the rocks in the bar at the Plaza International, because it was seldom used by university types; or vodka with 7Up while driving around any neighborhood to the north of campus, or a respite in the park.

The park was in a barrio area, and very few white people were around. I knew that the chance of seeing someone from the journalism department —rather, of their seeing me—was remote.

There was some chance of getting robbed, I supposed, but I had no sense of danger. In fact, I felt relief every time I went there. There was no way university people would spot me.

I'd leave campus about 11, drive to a Circle K convenience store, buy two cold cans of soda, drive to an alley beside the park, empty half of each can and refill each with vodka from a quart bottle I kept in the trunk of my old silver Toyota (I kept another bottle under the front seat, in case someone rear-ended me and broke the bottle in the trunk).

With two cans of 50-50 soda and vodka, I'd walk over to a picnic table and sit on it.

Ahhh, relief. Alone. Anonymous. I could think and drink freely, watch the clouds wander in the Arizona sky, watch the birds. I'd usually stay for an hour and a half.

I'd noticed a mailman who also went to the park for lunch. He too was white, in his 30s.

He troubled me greatly. He'd sit at a bench maybe 20 yards away, just quietly having his lunch. What troubled me was that the guy actually ate food for lunch: a sandwich from a sack, and a quart bottle of milk. Same routine every time I saw him.

I'd be sitting there with my soda and vodka and this mailman would be eating a sandwich and drinking milk.

Sometimes, I turned so I didn't face him.

I never said hello or looked him in the eye.

One day I saw him throw his lunch sack in the garbage, then start walking toward my bench. I froze. He never walked in my direction!

Sweat popped out on my brow. I looked away quickly, as though I didn't notice him. He'd walk right by.

"Hi."

I looked up. "Hi," I said weakly.

"Hot day, huh?"

"Sure is," I said. Be casual.

"Mind if I have a little of that soda?"

Ohgawd. What the hell was I going to do? The "soda" was now hot vodka!

"Wel-l-l, it's, uh, sort of hot and flat at this point. Sorry."

"Oh that's okay." He grinned and picked up the can.

Ohgawd.

He took a hefty swig. I expected him to gag.

He didn't react.

I looked at him and he looked at me. My eyes asked the question. His voice broke the silence with his answer. With a silly-ass grin, he asked: "Want some of my milk?"

The guy had been drinking vodka all this time! He had spray-painted a glass milk bottle with white paint so it always looked like milk.

In spite of this new bond, I didn't go back to the park. Something was too shameful about it.

The Tanque Verde Lutheran Church Mission. It sounded sort of pioneering. I started to get excited about it after the organizational meeting. About a dozen people had shown up, and almost all of them had one or two drinks with, I assumed, booze in them. I volunteered to do more for the church.

They didn't even notice my drinking!

It was a man's campus. The blondes were ample, the brunettes superb. The bookstore was good. I learned how to hang out.

After one longer than usual "lunch" at the Plaza, I sauntered over to the bookstore, and casually picked up a book and bought it.

"Gawd, Brownie," I exclaimed over cocktails the following evening, "I'm reading the best damned thing."

I wondered why his eyes were moist yet twinkling.

"It's about—it's called something like 'I Ain't Much, Baby, But I'm All I've Got', and it's about the sort of stuff I think we all need." I tossed down the rest of the Tanquerey. "Want another?"

"No thank you."

Why was Brownie always so damned stiff? Damned New Englander. I walked around the pool and into the kitchen for a refill.

Brownie had followed me. "Afraid I'd better get home, Scott. Artie's making enchiladas tonight."

"Brownie, you ought to get this book!"

"Glad you got something you're so interested in."

After he left, I grabbed the paperback and plopped down again in the huge 1930s chair I'd bought at a garage sale for $40.

This guy, the author, Jess Lair, had had a heart attack and it had made him realize that he'd better get his life right. I loved his philosophy.

It was built upon the principles of the Alcoholics Anonymous program. I thought the principles were solid, despite their origin.

Something was wrong in me and I knew it.

I knew I wouldn't drink as much if people would just leave me alone.

I knew that anyone who had my background would have to drink a lot to overcome it.

Anyone who'd had my job in Washington would have to drink a lot.

Anyone who'd had my wife or my mother or . . .

Why wouldn't the world just leave me alone?

The pressure was getting bad. I'd slip out of bed about 2:30 a.m., quietly make a short drink—just vodka and ice—and sit in the living room, usually with no lights on.

I could see the lights twinkling from the desert floor of the Tucson area sprawled out, sleeping. No one would call me at this hour. The mountains in Mexico shimmered in the moonlight.

Sometimes I'd sit near the pool. No one would bother me there. Freedom, until the sun started tiptoeing up behind the mountains to the east again.

I dreaded the daytime. I didn't know why.

We made friends with the Cantwell family. Their daughters would spend time in our pool, and I liked to be around the mother, Penny, who always had a secretive sort of twinkle in her smile.

Sometimes I'd fantasize that Penny had a crush on me. She clearly didn't. In fact, I had a sense that she looked right through me.

> *Did everyone look right through me? Did I exist?*
> *Time for another drinkie-poo.*

One night John Cantwell and I went drinking. John was a U2 pilot and liked beer. Not enough to keep up with me, but he liked beer.

We piled into his pickup and made a funny turn, I thought, at Tanque Verde Highway and Wrightstown Road. It was 11 at night, and John turned left, toward the desert.

We found a shack of a bar a few miles out, sauntered in and ordered beers.

"John," I whispered. "We're the only white guys in here."

He just shrugged and swilled his beer. John wore cowboy boots and his jeans fit him.

I was in my baggy bermuda shorts and a button-down oxford cloth shirt.

Nothing happened. Until I went in the men's room.

I was standing at the urinal when I felt an odd poke in the small of my back.

"Don't move, shitface." The voice was Mexican.

"What do you want?"

"I want to see you sweat, shitface." He chuckled.

I sighed and pulled the zipper up.

The object in my back was pulled away. I turned slowly, hands high in front of my chest. Where the hell was John, my buddy?

The face behind the gun was cracked with years of sun and hatred. Age indistinguishable, the body squat. The small silver gun in his right hand pointed at my belt.

"Wh-what do you want?"

"We want you to buy us some beer, white boy."

That was the night I bought two rounds of beer for the house.

I was standing alone on the 12th green at the El Dorado course. It was 1:55 and the temperature was 106. I was playing alone. No one else braved the midday heat, so I always had the course to myself.

I stared at the shimmering magnificence of the Catalina Mountains, and spoke to myself, aloud:

"Something like that didn't just happen. That's why I go to church, why I do these things. God created those mountains.

"If I were those mountains, God would have created me, too.

"That stuff in church goes too far. God can't be everywhere, and there's no reason for Him even to pay attention to Tucson, let alone a professor on summer vacation playing golf."

"I'm completely free. No one can see me, and God doesn't care. I can do anything I damn well want to."

Winter and coursework and Christmas came and went. The church grew, I stopped even trying to have sex, the kids seemed okay.

And then came a Sunday we'd all awaited—Elsie, my grandmother—"Mom" was flying in.

Her plane was due about 2. So I invited Bob Linder over after the morning service, for a bloody mary, since I had an hour to kill.

We sat talking about church problems and I went through three hefty drinks while Bob sipped one medium one. I felt unbearably tired. Must be the "valley fever" they'd warned me about, I thought.

The kids said it was time to go to the airport. One more drink, guys.

They came back 10 minutes later. I told them to go ahead, I'd take a nap since I was so tired. Besides, she was my grandmother and she'd understand.

"Dad!"

"You all just go, Laura. I'll be ready when you get back."

"But Dad!"

"Just go."

My grandmother never said a word about my drinking. We spent five days seeing Tucson, and even when I took a drink in the car for our visit to her brother Homer in Green Valley, she never said a word.

That was a relief—or was it? It seemed as though a grandmother should be more concerned.

Her third day she asked me if I had ever gotten the book she'd sent me.

"You mean that thing about the seagull?" It was by some guy named Richard Bach and I'd tried to read it late one evening.

"You didn't like it?"

"I thought that book was so corny I couldn't believe it. Just awful!"

Her face fell. "That's too bad. I had thought you, of all people, would love it."

"Thanks for it, Mom, but it just didn't—how about a drink?"

"No thanks, dear, it's a little early for me." Her face was impenetrable, granite.

The five days flew past in a fuzz. But no problem. She was Mom to me. She'd always be there.

Bob Linder said he needed to chat. Could he come in?

It was a sunny, warm 9:20 and I had not a thing to do all day. Maybe golf later.

"And what's with this business of asking whether you can come in? You're here twice a week, and just about my closest friend. Hell—you almost live here some days, Robert."

"Thank you, Scott." He seemed troubled.

I fixed coffee and we carried our cups out to the chairs by the pool.

Bob was talking, uncharacteristically, about his wife's tough times with her first husband. I tried to act interested. It was boring. Was there something wrong in Bob's marriage?

" . . . and she watched your hands shaking during the service, when you were supposed to read that Lesson aloud, and after the service, Scott, when we got home, she told me you're an alcoholic."

Ohhhhgawd.

I sucked in my breath and waited for Bob to continue. He didn't. He just sat there, a calm and loving look in his eye.

"No way, Bob. I just . . . I mean, look, Bob—if you had this life I've had, and all that pressure from your family, and after all those years in the Washington rat race, and . . .

"No way, Bob. Not me!"

I shrugged as if it were just a passing remark he'd made.

"She's convinced, Scott." His voice was so quiet, gentle. "And I think she's right."

I went in and pretended to make coffee, all the while pouring vodka into my cup. I was soaked in sweat.

After some small talk, he left, a sad but loving half-smile on his face.

Knowing what they thought about me, I figured I'd better make sure I was around the Linders quite a bit. They'd see I wasn't defensive about my drinking. I also could tone it down a bit around them. Not too much, but a bit.

Also: There didn't need to be so much booze so visible in the kitchen cabinet. They probably thought that three half-gallons of vodka, replaced every two or three days, was 'alcoholic'.

The next morning, I bought seven quarts.

One in the trunk, under the mat on the left.

One behind the box of old bedspreads in the toolshed/cabana.

One under my sweaters in the bedroom closet.

One behind the least-looked-at books in the den—the history books.

And the other three could go in the back of the cupboard underneath the stove.

The system would be very simple. I would be seen pouring myself a vodka martini or two before dinner. Otherwise, people would just see me drinking Lipton's powdered iced tea mix.

The recipe was so simple: Ice, six inches of vodka, add water, then dump some tea powder on the top and stir gently so the vodka doesn't rise; use a tall blue plastic glass so one can't see through the sides clearly. What the hell? I carried my glass with me all the time anyway. So no one would get it by mistake.

People didn't understand. I could control my drinking! And, as a concession to their over-sensitivity, I wouldn't be quite so obvious—or generous—with it.

I was on my way to work about 9 a.m., sipping "coffee" from a blue mug, when I noticed a new fear: I couldn't make a left-hand turn in rush hour or heavy traffic. Even if no traffic was approaching, I was afraid my car would just stop and some oncoming car would slam into me, head-on.

I broke into a sweat. My brain said the fear was irrational. But I knew it was total, and that it felt irreversible. I really *was* going bonkers.

I found a shrink in one of the medical offices along Grant Road by the most anonymous method possible: The Yellow

Pages. I would not have thought he was a psychologist. He seemed so Texas, so down-home.

On my first visit, after ten minutes, he asked if I laughed much.

"No, I don't," I said seriously. "That's a good point."

"Why?"

"There's nothing to laugh about."

"That's bolesheet, son."

"Nope, it's not." I spent the rest of my session explaining how daddy had died and my mommy had gone away to law school, how I'd been successful but my ex-wife didn't understand me, how my years in Washington were such toil and heavy, heavy pressure, how a woman was driving me bonkers and she was too tall anyway, and how the university's politics stymied my ability to truly teach and inspire these fine young people.

A week later, as I sat in his parking lot gulping down enough to get me through another hour with him, I decided to change my appointments to afternoons so I could loosen up a bit beforehand.

Once inside, I asked the shrink about his background and his credentials to judge my problems. He talked for 20 minutes. I asked another question and his answer took up the rest of the hour.

A week later, with a 3 p.m. appointment, I was in a talkative mood and confided at length about Lyndon Johnson's style and how LBJ had made some $14 million in television stations back in Texas.

As the hour closed, the shrink told me three jokes and said he was glad to see me laughing. Maybe the therapy was starting to work, I said.

I decided to try bar-drinking. Maybe that would help me feel better and delay my arrival home to boot.

I stopped along Speedway at a place called the Blue Note. Inside, a 45-ish woman with baggy tits was doing a bump 'n grind behind the bartender. There was a young, well constructed brunette serving drinks at the tables, but she acted as though she didn't like either her job or the customers.

I left after two drinks. Back to commuter cocktails. I'd just start taking a different route home—up Campbell Avenue almost as far north as I could go, then east along Sunrise Highway, where there were many 7-Elevens and

Circle Ks conveniently placed along my route, then back southward on Sabino Canyon Highway down to Tanque Verde Road and back on eastward, then back northward. It added a full half-hour to the commute. That equalled one more drink. And that's all I wanted, ever. Just one more.

7

February 1975.
Tucson.

The head of the journalism department called to me as I stood at the departmental mail rack.

"Scott, you got a minute?"

I drifted into his office. He got up rather stiffly and walked around me to close the door.

There was some small talk about classes and weather. He was somber, nervous, not his normal jovial self.

Ohgawd.

I glanced at my Timex: 8:35 a.m.

"We need to talk, Scott."

"Okay. About what?"

"Well, about uh . . . uh, about how you're—vexed."

"I'm what?"

"Vexed. You know—vexed."

The guy had his door closed and it was early morning and he wanted to confront me. I knew what he wanted to talk about, but I didn't dare let on that I knew. No one was going to get at my only friend.

"Just what is going on with you, Scott?"

"Well." I got up and sat back down, as if I'd needed to shake something off my lap. "I'm just—shit, I don't know. I'm just not ver- very happy, I guess."

"That's obvious, Scott."

"My home life—it never has been . . ."

"No, Scott, it's not that. Not your home life. I wanted to talk about how Scott is vexed, and what we can do to get some change in how you're . . ."

"So it's both."

He leaned forward: "Some help for your . . ."

"Both. Both the job and at home. There! I said it." I looked him in the eye, even though I knew my eyes were my customary bleary-red. "I said it—okay?"

"Well, what are you going to do about it?"

I couldn't hear him. My mind was focused on one thing only: The pressure of the confrontation.

There was only one thing that could help me, and that thing was under the driver's seat in my Toyota, out in the parking lot.

Palms sweating heavily. Hands shaking. Bottoms of feet sweating. Short of breath. Ohgawd, help!

It didn't occur to me to ask if I could get my thoughts together and come in later. Then I would have been able to get myself prepared for this.

I needed to get to my car, get that relief, and get away from the department chairman, the building, the campus.

Nightmare. Living a nightmare.

He was still talking. I'd never helped out in preregistration in January. I'd been gone too much. There was sweat on his forehead.

I interrupted him. "Look. Why don't we just call it quits—huh?"

"Quits?"

"I'm not happy. You're not happy. I'm not vexed, but I am unhappy, very very unhappy—I, and you're right, I've missed some registration days and I've been sick, and also just hurting inside, so I'll just . . ."

"We could . . ."

"No. I'm quitting."

I stood up, my emotional focus still on the parking lot. Nothing could get me there fast enough.

"Scott—you don't . . ."

"Can I just go down to my office for a second to type up a letter of resignation?"

He stared at me. Time stopped. Finally he shrugged. I hurried down the hall, typed a one-sentence resignation, hurried back, handed it to him, said I'd be back later to discuss my schedule for the remainder of the semester.

"Okay, Scott." He looked confused.

I hurried back out, turned right, kept my head down and whisked past the students milling around the water fountain beside my office. I slammed through the back exit of the building, out to my car.

I started the engine, wheeled around the parked cars in the small lot, pulled the bottle into my lap, made a fast right turn into the street and brought the bottle to my lips.

Relief!

No one would take this away. No one!

But what the hell had I just done?

The psychologist and I met about a week after my resignation. I'd had at least half a quart of vodka so far that day.

He told a joke about Southerners. I laughed. He told several more, then he asked what was the problem. I told him I had quit my job.

He said that was okay, that I probably needed to express my anger somehow and ought to consider getting a punching bag. Also, he said, golf was good because it involved hitting an object, and hard.

He never once mentioned alcohol. Nor did I.

I got to the parking lot knowing that either I had cheated myself by not telling him about my drinking, or the guy was blind. I decided not to see him again, and not to pay his bill.

March 1975:

At spring break, I announced to Don and Laura that I was leaving for job interviews in San Francisco and they could reach me at Hunt Bennett's office there in an emergency. I packed a suitcase and left.

It was a Thursday night. I spent it with Carolla, a young, bright former student who'd said she wanted to travel with me.

When I got to her little apartment at 8:10, she was sweetly nervous and very eager. I suggested I fix us a drink and then we'd just get in bed. By 9:45 we had exhausted ourselves, and I slid off into sleep.

As usual, I awakened about 2:30. I slid out of the bed silently, went out and sat on her living room couch with a glass of vodka, no lights except the dim streetlight from under the door and along the edge of the musty old curtains.

What the hell am I doing in a rundown apartment like this in north Tucson, Arizona? Shaking and scared and a dumb bicycle parked in the kitchen, and the smell of old furniture that has gotten wet too often. What the hell's going on with me?

I padded into the kitchen, poured more vodka, decided to risk the sound of getting an ice cube out of the old refrigerator.

Downed the vodka, crawled back into her bed and sank into sleep.

We spent Friday at her place in Tucson, even though I knew my kids thought I had flown to San Francisco on Thursday night. They were all right, and it was so great to take this free time, when no one in the world really knew where I was.

Friday night I knew I had gotten too loaded, but she said it was okay since I'd been under such pressure.

It had been so gawdawful long since I'd felt a woman's arms around me. Funny, I thought, staring down into the pillow and her hair.

If I had to make a choice, I'd rather get the hugging.
The warmth means more than the sex.

Suddenly I had to call Brownie. It was 10:50 p.m.

"Guess where I am, Brownie!"

"Where?" He sounded sleepy.

"Carolla's."

"Why are you there?"

"Three guesses, Brownie." I winked over at the face in the pillow. "Anyway, I just thought you'd like to know."

"Sure. Well, thanks for calling, Scott. Goodnight now."

He hadn't understood. Damnit, this was important, that Scott was with a nice warm girl.

"Maybe I should call him back, tell him where we'll be tomorrow."

Carolla reached across my chest and pushed the phone back to its cradle, purring into my ear that there was someplace she wanted me to be now . . .

We got on our flight to San Francisco on Saturday morning. I was delighted: Not only did they serve bloody marys, but weather forced us out over the Pacific. We flew northward along the California coast, then inland across Monterey Bay.

I was by the window.

"Look," I whispered. "Look at that!" The hooked coastline of the deep blue bay was flickering in morning sunlight, the surfline a dazzling white, the buildings and homes looking tiny but secure in the gentle slopes of the towns of Monterey and Carmel.

I grabbed her arm, and took a long pull on my third drink of the morning.

"That's where I want to live someday."

"That would be nice, Scott."

" 'Nice'?"

She didn't understand. No one ever understood!

"Someday, I will! I will live along that bay."

She squeezed my arm and reached for the airline's in-flight magazine.

My favorite cousin—more than that, a friend—Huntley Bennett was waiting for me at the Newsweek office on Jackson Street. It was just the three of us, alone in the big, posh offices, and I was ready to celebrate.

But there was something in Hunt's eye. "What are you drinking, Scotty? Scotch?"

"Fine."

There was no banter, no small talk.

Something's very wrong.

Hunt was the most jovial guy in the family—in fact, the most jovial guy I'd known anywhere. Maybe he was on edge about something, or maybe it was Carolla, who had settled into the office couch, letting her skirt ride a little, her ripe young thighs so inviting.

Hunt, still silent, poured four inches of scotch into a big wide glass.

"Drink it."

He sat watching me sip it.

Something in the room was deadly.

"So how're things in San Fran . . ."

"Scotty, just drink your drink for a minute."

I looked him in the eye and saw all the masculine disciplines of the Marine Corps and Dartmouth coming right back into me. I looked down at the scotch and ice.

> *Ohmygawd, what now? Was he onto me, too?*
> *No way, b'gawd.*
> *It was my only friend and no one would take it away from me!*

He waited while I gulped, then finally interrupted the silence:

"Your Mom, your grandmother Mom, died on Thursday morning.

"Annie—your mother—has been trying to locate you for three days."

Silence.

"Mom? Died?"

"Yes."

I pulled air and scotch down into me. At least my best friend was with me, right there in my right hand where I needed it.

"Died?"

"She got sick there at home and by the time Annie or the ambulance could get to her, she was gone, Scotty. I'm sorry. She was one helluva woman, your grandmother."

"She was . . ." I tried to remember. "She was your father's sister, too, Hunt—you'll miss her too."

Long silence. I felt tiny, lost. Hunt broke the silence.

"Yeah. I wish I could get back there for the funeral. But I can't."

"What about . . . what am I . . ."

"I got you a reservation on a plane Monday morning, Scotty. You can rest up for a day before you go."

I got up and walked to his countertop bar.

Sonofabitch! I'd been drunk the whole time Mom was in Tucson. It was the last time I'd seen her and I'd been drunk.

I poured a fresh scotch. Sonofabitch!

Monday:

Elsie Bennett Wilson was dead. She was my grandmother, but she was the woman who took care of me through my pre-teen years, age 3 to 12, after my father died and while my mother was becoming a lawyer and then worked as one.

She was the woman I called Mom.

She was dead.

Dead. Dead, dead, dead. She was dead.

I reached up and buzzed for the stewardess. She came immediately.

"I'm sorry—I know I've already had two of these, but my Mom just died. I'm on my way to Cleveland to bury her. Could I just get another of these?"

"But they're doubles, sir."

"I know. But, frankly, it'll take more than these four little bottles, even more than six of them, before I'd ever feel it at all."

"I understand, sir."

Dead.

Mom was dead.

And I'd been out cavorting, escaping. She'd died and no one could reach me.

Scott, what the hell are you doing to yourself?

Screw it. Drink this stuff until I don't feel one goddam thing, and maybe with any luck I'll die. It'll be okay and there's nothing to feel so guilty about, damnit. I was taking a well-deserved holiday. There was nothing I could have done anyway.

I reached up and buzzed again.

She had compassionate brown eyes and lovely blond hair and nodded to me.

"That didn't take long."

"One more time—okay?"

"Okay—but that will probably be all, sir."

She didn't know about my briefcase. I reached in, got the half-pint out, put it in my jacket pocket and went to the lavatory.

Inside, I drank all but the last inch of the vodka, with no burning effect or aftertaste. It was just something to pour into me. Thankgawd for it, I thought. I put the pint back in my jacket, slicked my hair—gawd it had gotten so long!, I wondered what my mother would think of it—hadn't seen my mother in a couple of years, either—and went back to my seat. The stewardess had put the new miniature vodkas and a fresh can of 7Up on my seat for me. What a fine girl she was!

Dead. Elsie's dead.

Her husband, Carl, had died 13 years earlier. H.R. had died five years ago. And now Elsie was dead.

My life was flying faster than the airplane. Fast, too fast. Speeding past me, my own lifetime going faster than I could go.

Death. You're gone. It's-

It's just like the family has said: It's oblivion, that's what it is. Death is oblivion. You don't exist, therefore you don't even know you're in oblivion.

My father died and he doesn't exist. H.R. doesn't exist. And now Mom doesn't exist.

I thought about the church we were building in Tucson. Lot of good that did me. Mom was dead. Gone, her body already disintegrating. A hideous vision flashed before me, and I couldn't shake it: My grandmother's face slowly disintegrating.

Shouldn't drink too much. But it's my only relief.

I got up and walked back to the galley. She was there, and I told her about it.

"So you're saying, basically, that you'd like another double, sir?"

"That image, right in front of my eyes! It's awful."

I didn't know whether it was real or a con job. Just get the booze.

I'd had six doubles by the time I arrived Monday night, in time to go to the funeral home.

It was the first time I'd ever felt the meaning of the word surreal.

All these people standing around in the gawdawfulest dim rooms, and Mom's body there in a casket. People telling me how wonderful she was, as if they knew it better than I did.

Old Medina friends, yet we had nothing to say. They'd ask how Tucson was and I didn't know how to answer.

This funeral-home tradition is crazy, I thought. We'll all pay our tribute at the funeral, and we'll all have our private ways of mourning. What the hell is the point of standing around some stupid dark place trying to make small talk? Is that any way to mourn or honor the dead?

I tried to tell my mother how I felt. I thought she'd agree, especially because it was her mother who had died.

But Ann stayed calm, rational, explaining that Elsie had been "a real leader" in Medina and in fact in the state—and people, other people, needed a way, no matter how stupid or awkward, of showing that they mourned her.

It was true. Elsie had gotten a degree from a good college in about 1920. She'd first married a very popular lawyer who'd run for political office but who died in a flu epidemic. She'd remarried, Carl Wilson, a lawyer again. She'd been president of the library for years, even president of the state library board. Her brothers, whom she'd raised, both went to Dartmouth. Her own two daughters had gone to Smith and Carleton, her son to Harvard—not bad for a lady in a small town in Ohio.

The funeral was Tuesday at 10. I managed to stay just ever-so-steadied through it all, thanks to the new bottle in my bag, the bottles in my mother's kitchen, the leftover bottles at Mom's house.

The family gathered in Elsie's living room after the cemetery ceremony. I could not understand: it was the only time I'd seen the whole crowd together and no one had a drink. I waited a proper half-hour and left "to go driving, maybe take a walk somewhere."

I wanted a huge drink and a chance to . . . to what?—to cry?

My mind rang with the Bennett family's normal posture of steel: "You don't have to cry. Be brave, gracious, noble. There is no need for emotions."

It was, I presumed, the same armor they'd worn when I was 2 years old and my father had died suddenly at 28.

I went back to my parents' house, got out the gin, put some heavily emotional music on the stereo and sang aloud.

There was my old debate, between my ears:

Black sheep, Scott, you're the strange one in the family.
—But why? Why don't they show their emotions?
You will be strong and brave.
—I don't feel strong or brave. I hurt.
We are strong. You're acting weak.
—I want another drink.
You've been weak and irresponsible.
—I know, I know.
You missed meeting Elsie's plane in Tucson.
—I hated to let her see me drunk at 2 p.m.
Your mother couldn't find you when Elsie died.

—I was just trying to have a little love!
You arrived here drunk.
—I was trying to drown the emotions you don't want me to show.

Just before 2 that night, my mother and stepfather knocked at my door and let themselves in. I was in bed.

"Scott." My mother had a strange choked pain in her voice. "We've asked your brother to drive you up to the airport in the morning."

I waited. She was going to say something terrible.

"We've changed your flights, and you're going to land in Dayton on your way back to San Francsico."

"Dayton!"

"Yes. An old friend of your father—your father Don—a man from Douglaston, is going to meet you there."

"Huh?" I sat up, pulled a cigarette out.

"He used to have your problem, Scott."

"My problem? Dayton? What the hell is . . ."

"Your drinking, Scott. That's the problem."

Silence in the dead night.

"I think you should go see him—just for breakfast. He's driving over to the airport in Dayton to meet you, he loved your father so much. He's been dry now for about 15 years. Or is it 20?"

"Ann. I don't always drink like I have this past couple of days. I know it's been heavy, but I just have felt so . . ."

"Scott, your face was puffy when you got off the plane. One look at that puffy face and I knew what was wrong."

"What do you mean?" My voice was rising.

"You're an alcoholic, Scott."

Silence. Long dead silence.

I broke it at last: "Bullshit! That's bullshit!"

My stepfather straightened and stepped toward me, a glint in his eyes. "Don't you ever, ever use that word around your mother!"

"Oh—hell!"

"We'll get you up at 5 and you can . . ."

"Five?"

"Your plane leaves Cleveland at 6:30."

"For Dayton, Ohio? This is just insane!"

"It's for your own good, Scott."

"Well, I'm not some dumb alcoholic slob or whatever you called me."

"I said alcoholic, not a slob, Scott."

"And I don't drink all that much. I've had valley fever! You don't know about living in the desert, but I got this awful valley fever and I have had no sleep ever since Huntley told me about Mom—which is why my face looks puffy—and I do not need to go to goddam Dayton Ohio to see some guy who . . ."

"Goodnight, Scott."

My mother's voice trailed off as she closed the door behind them. It was so choked with sorrow I couldn't argue.

I still had four fingers of gin and tonic in the glass beside the bed. I gulped it down, all of it, and turned out the light.

We'll see. They'll see. I'm just an emotional wreck, that's all—not alcoholic.

My brother and my stepfather took me to the airport before dawn. The embarrassment was enormous. There wasn't much small talk.

Breakfast in Dayton, Ohio, March 1975:

The man had clear warm eyes and didn't seem to be preaching at all. I was amazed. I liked him, but I knew I didn't need his message.

"So then I started drinking even more, and I didn't realize, Scott, what was happening to me, but I . . ."

"Excuse me a moment. I've got to go the bathroom."

I hoped he didn't notice that I carried my 26-inch pullman suitcase with me to the bathroom. But if he did, he did.

No one was in the men's room, but I locked myself in a stall just in case.

I sat, pants still up, on the toilet, pulled the suitcase up to my knees before me, and unlatched it. I felt around in the dirty clothes until I found it.

Relief!

I sat guzzling, and looked at my watch. It was 7:20 in the morning and I was sneaking off to a men's room with my suitcase so I could drink vodka straight from the bottle because I was so shaky and my hands and feet were sweating. But, I remembered, I've been through a wringer—who wouldn't have a reaction?

Just enjoy the relief, I decided, and then be nice to this guy—he is a nice guy—and get on the next plane, I decided. I can get more relief on the flight to St. Louis, and then the flight to Las Vegas and on to San Francisco. Just hang in there, and don't let this guy get to you.

Another two gulps and I headed back to the coffee shop.

He'd driven a long way on six hours' notice to have breakfast with me. I thought he must be nuts.

In San Francisco I stayed with Hunt, and he got me an interview with the brass at the San Francisco Examiner. They needed a high-level editor.

The interview was at 2 p.m. I drank until 1:55. The interview lasted 15 minutes. Several days later, I got a note from the Examiner saying it was too bad I had enjoyed San Francisco so much.

A summer Sunday afternoon, Tucson, 1975:

The kids were playing at a neighbor's. Golf was out of the question today—the courses were too crowded on Sundays. I could play Monday. I could play every weekday. I didn't have anywhere to go on weekdays.

Feet up, drink in left hand, reading the Sunday paper. The doorbell rang.

Two men were standing there grinning, as if they knew me.

"Can I help you?"

"Hi Scott. I'm Boyd. And this is Luke."

"Yes?"

The one named Boyd had exceptionally straight thin brown hair and laughing blue eyes. About 45, I guessed. The other guy, Luke, was maybe 50 and must have been 220 pounds and 6 foot 2, and all muscle. And he was bald.

Boyd stuck out his hand. I shook it. Then Luke's—it was enormous and gnarled. What was this all about?

"We're here, Scott, because some friends who love you think it might be good if we talked a little."

"About what?"

Boyd stepped toward me. I backed up. He moved into the living room. Luke followed. They sat down.

Who the hell were these guys, pushing their way into my home on a Sunday afternoon? They could be thieves or kidnapers or . . .

"About our drinking, Scott."

"Huh?"

"Yeah: You see, we're both guys who are learning how to not drink, and you've obviously got a problem."

"I do?"

"Yup, you're . . ."

Suddenly my brain was on fire! "What the hell are you guys doing? Why don't you just leave now? Okay?" I gestured toward the door.

Boyd sat down and smiled.

Luke sat down and smiled.

I just stood there.

> *Scott, here's what you do: Humor these bastards,*
> *act like you're interested. But whatever they're selling*
> *isn't for you. You don't need it. You're not like them.*
> *Then get 'em out of here. Stay calm.*

"So, uh, would you guys like some uh iced tea?"

Boyd looked at my tall blue plastic glass. It was vodka on ice, but it looked like iced tea because I'd sprinkled in instant iced tea powder.

"No thank you, Scott."

"No thanks," echoed Luke.

"I used to drink like you do, Scott," said Boyd, his eyes friendly, "And I had a good job too, like you used to have." Was he rubbing it in?

I sat down and picked up my "iced tea," savoring the hot rush in my throat and gut as I "sipped." Boyd paid no attention to whatever I was doing, just kept talking.

"I flew B52s. Flew them in 'Nam and Cambodia. Not bad for an old guy like me, huh? I'm career military, retired now, at 40. Healthy and got a retirement and . . ."

"You don't seem so . . ."

"Well, that's because I've stopped drinking."

Luke, leaning forward with a big grin, finally said something: "You should've seen Boyd before. He looked terrible—old and shaky, like you look now, Scott."

Who the hell did they think they were?

Boyd kept it up: "Yeah, you look pretty sick, all right. I can see why your mother's so worried about you."

My mother! What the hell?

"Did you know that your mother has . . ."

Luke interrupted. "Wait, Boyd: not yet. Scott, I was even worse than Boyd here. I used to put down a quart a day—that's probably more than your system could handle these days—even when I was working."

No way I'd say so, but I was doing more than a quart a day.

"I'm a pipefitter. You probably don't even know what a pipefitter is, but . . ."

"What's this about my mother?"

Boyd smiled again. He irked me, looking so chipper and acting so familiar and having such a friendly smile.

Luke continued, ignoring what I'd asked. "Maybe you can handle a quart a day, maybe you can't. Some guys need a quart to keep going all day. Some guys don't. You're drinking vodka, right?"

"Uh, I . . ."

"Most of us, we end up drinking vodka because somewhere we got this notion that people couldn't smell vodka on us." They both laughed.

"Shit, Scott, I used to put down a quart of that stuff and I couldn't see straight and I was stumbling and slurring my words, and I thought no one could smell it on me!"

They both laughed. It was infectious. I sipped my "iced tea" and tried not to laugh.

"Trick is, and you probably already know this, to spread the hard stuff out with a few beers along the way. Right, Boyd?"

Boyd was still laughing. Luke continued: "You know, a little beer along the way just to spread the effects out, make a quart last all day. Of course, lots of days, what I did was, I'd run out of the vodka and I'd have a coupla cases of beer there, so I'd just put down a coupla cases of beer in an afternoon! And *then* I'd go out to the liquor store to get me some vodka." He laughed again.

Luke had a bright, wholesome look about him. I couldn't imagine him as a drunk.

"You don't figure I was down and out, huh?"

He'd read my mind!

"Boyd could tell ya. He saw me, like the time . . ."

Boyd interjected: "Oh yeah, Luke! Tell him about the car and your thigh!"

Luke slapped his knee uproariously. How come these absolute strangers were having such a fine time in my living room, and insulting me to boot?

He told how he'd once slipped out of the car seat at a liquor store parking lot, and a taxi had driven right over his thigh—without breaking it.

It was sickening, baffling. Why did these guys think it was so funny?

I got up to get some more "iced tea," hoping they wouldn't follow me. They didn't. When I got back, Boyd looked me in the eye. "Your mother has sent a thousand bucks to a hospital up in Phoenix, as a down payment for treating you."

"Treating me?"

"Relax. It's not bad. It's an alcoholism program. It's in a special section of a good hospital, and . . ."

"My mother called you?"

"Scott, you don't have a secret anymore. You could hide that stuff for a long time, but now everyone around you knows you're an alcoholic."

"Well I don't know it! If you guys, if any of these goddam people had all the problems I've been through and . . ."

"That may be."

"I grant you, I drink. Hell, everyone drinks. But anyone with the jobs I've had and then with all that pressure, and . . ."

Luke interrupted me. "Excuse me for telling you, Scott, but the truth is that we've all had problems."

"Not like I've had, and not like I've got now! So . . ."

Boyd stood up, smiling fondly now. What the right did he have to be fond of me?

"Well, Scott. You think about it. We're just telling you that if a couple of stumblebums like us can stop drinking, you can stop drinking too."

"Okay, Boyd, I got your message."

"And after we leave, sometime when you're alone, maybe you'll take a peek at this." He handed me a small blue pamphlet. "It's a test. It'll help you figure out whether you're an alcoholic."

They left and I threw the pamphlet in a desk drawer, took a hit straight from the half gallon of vodka, topped off the "iced tea," and went in to the bedroom, where I just sat blinking for a long time.

The next morning over coffee-on-vodka, I opened the pamphlet. It had 20 questions about the effects of drinking.

No one was around. I went through the questions, answered only nine of the 20 "yes."

Then I found the small print: If you had answered "yes" to just three, you "definitely" were an alcoholic.

I got up, pulled the draperies closed, locked the doors, pulled the phone cord out of the wall and poured myself a tall straight vodka.

It was late; the bartender had turned the lights on.

The woman had been referring to church that morning. Was it Sunday?

"So . . . ya wanna come take a little midnight swim?"

"With you?"

"Just me, Sally."

"Sandy's the name, and no, I'm afraid I'd better get home. Back to the grind tomorrow."

I got up, went to the men's room, then wandered out into the parking lot.

The Cow Pony bar. What a great place! I'd have to come here more often.

I had bought a new car—a mustard-colored little Datsun. It would help me feel better. And people would know I was okay.

I'd get a job selling advertising space in a magazine. They were always advertising for sales people.

I put the classified section back on the table and got up for more coffee. That was it, I thought. I'd get some experience in the commercial end of the business.

But I'm not a sales type.
I'm an editor!
No—no sales jobs for me.

I got back up again and added some vodka to the coffee. I phoned Bob Linder to see if he could play some golf today. He couldn't. Phoned Brownie, but he wasn't in his office. I'd play alone.

At least I'd settled that little illusion—I'd never get into sales. That was for people who couldn't do things like edit newspapers.

8

October 1975:

My stay at the hospital in Phoenix went the full 28 days and I was sure that I had licked alcoholism.

I'd read all the books and literature, attended meetings and lectures, written a life history, gone to group therapy, acquired a keen intellectual understanding of the whole field.

Everything would be okay now. Everyone would know that Scott was cured.

The children seemed apprehensive when I got home. Bob Linder told me it would take time, but if I would just not drink, over time they'd know I was okay.

Lionel Brown and the Cantwells and others all knew where I'd been.

I felt brave, stoic.

On my sixth day out, I had a minor emotional upset.

The old band came back, tightening around my chest.

I got in the car and drove, just drove. And then, as if by magic, there was a Circle K in front of me. Maybe just one can of beer would take away the tightness, and what the hell, one beer couldn't hurt me. And no one would know.

Late October 1975:

Linder kept calling, but I'd let the phone ring. I had not answered it in five days. I kept the curtains pulled, wouldn't even sit by the pool for fear someone would see me with my tall blue glass. The kids came and went—all of us acting as if we could ignore what was happening. Eventually, the kids decided to stay with friends for a few days.

I hadn't shaved. I hadn't eaten. I had barely slept.

My head was crammed with facts and slogans about alcoholism.

> One day at a time. Just don't drink.
> It's a disease.
> One drink's too many, 10,000 aren't enough.

My blood was full of rotgut vodka. It wasn't quite working. I didn't feel anything physically, but the brain wouldn't stop:

> *How the hell did this happen?*
> *Why? Why me?*
> *Oughta be editing the news, not-*

I got up, stumbled into the kitchen with a half-full glass to get another drink.

I was scared someone would break into the house and take the booze away, and I'd have to try to drive down to the store without getting arrested in order to get more, but I didn't have enough cash to get much.

> *You're weak.*
> *You have no strength of character.*
> *You let the kids down.*
> *Hide the car keys. You may need the car.*
> *Is the back door locked?*
> *The look on Donny's face.*
> *Laura's eyes.*
> *You have no strength of character.*
> *This drink is diluted. Get it pure vodka*
> *before someone takes it away*
> *How? Did this happen to me? Why?*
> *Ohgawd Annie, Donny, Laura*
> *I never*
> *Meant for this to happen*

"Boyd? It's Scott. I've been drinking for 10 or 11 days straight. I need help."

"I can't, Scott. My boy's got plans for us today and besides, you're still drinking."

"Get me help, Boyd."

"Good luck, kid. I know how it feels. Call me when you're not drinking."

Oh God help me!

There was a knock on the door and it wouldn't go away. I snuck over to the front window, peeked around the curtain.

Luke! It was Luke!

I opened the door, shrank from the burst of midday Arizona sunlight.

"No fun, is it?"

"Thanks, Luke, for coming."

He nodded grimly. "Boyd got me. Where's your bedroom? I'm getting you a suitcase and getting you into a dry-out place here in Tucson."

"Do I really need that?"

He brushed past me grumbling, went down the hall toward my room.

"Stinks in here."

I watched as he threw pants and shirts into a beat-up bag he'd found. He kept talking about this disease but I couldn't mentally focus on what he said.

Try as I could, I couldn't quite stand up straight.

"C'mon."

I stumbled to the front door with him.

He went out first, turned and looked at me leaning against the doorframe.

And then huge, tough pipefitter Luke smiled the sweetest most loving smile in the world. He reached out with his right arm and just scooped me up by the waist and carried me to his car like a sack of potatoes.

West Center wanted me to dry out there for five days.

The second day I shook so bad they had to give me a lighter. Matches, said a nurse, were a suicide torch for someone shaking as bad as I was.

A few minutes later, as I sat on the toilet, I thought briefly about suicide.

It would be so simple. Just take the drawcord from the blinds and drape it over the shower rod and wrap it around my throat while standing on the edge of the toilet. Kick off and swing. I wondered if it would hurt.

On the third day, I walked out. I'd do it alone.

I'd stayed dry for three weeks. I thought I'd better find a job.

I had no idea what I could do. Who would hire a drunk, even if I wasn't as bad as other drunks? Maybe I'd just tell them I had a disease, that I'd had a relapse which was necessary for me to understand what one little drink might do to me.

It was 8:40 a.m. I sat at the dining room table, a big mahogany table I'd inherited, with a matching cabinet, from my grandmother's aunt.

Don was still sleeping. He'd miss two classes at least. I couldn't get him to wake up. He acted like I wasn't there.

Laura had gone to school without uttering a single word. She looked so cute, in a bright plaid outfit and shirt. But her eyes were so dark.

I couldn't stand reading the front page of the Arizona Daily Star. It needed editing, and I was a has-been who couldn't even pay the bills for a house for his own lovely children.

I turned to the classifieds. Was there an editing or writing job?

There wasn't.

I put my head flat against the mahoghany and cried.

You can't die.
You can't commit suicide; you have two kids.
You can't find a job.
You didn't want this, didn't deserve this.
Why? why why why?

At 3:10 that afternoon I made a surprising discovery. I was pulling into a liquor store on Speedway Boulevard and had no recollection of intending or planning to go to a liquor store. I'd been dry for 22 days.

There was no fight left in me. I bought two quarts of vodka, walked back to the car, unscrewed one bottle and pulled it up to my lips.

It was awful. Hot and burning in my throat.

But then came that warm familiar love in my gut. Ahhhh. To hell with finding a job today. I'll just drink a little today, let myself have a breather here. No one needs to know.

Five days later, even my terrier Rascal, who loved me obviously and dearly, wouldn't talk to me.

I didn't know where the kids were. It was 7 p.m.

I didn't know which day of the week it was.

I had almost no money for their lunches but I had to get enough to buy more vodka.

I couldn't remember anything that had happened in those five days.

And the FBI was chasing me. I was sure of it.

I refilled my glass. The bottle was about gone, and I saw no others around. What the hell? I'd have to stop drinking again, go through it again, but not now.

The car was dusty, as if it hadn't been used for a day or two. I got in, headed down Bear Canyon Road for more.

I didn't know why, but the FBI was putting agents out on the road to follow me. Every time I'd drive to the liquor store, there'd be another unmarked car behind me. Most of the agents looked like businessmen, but some were disguised as housewives.

Occasionally, I'd see a policeman behind me, but I knew that was probably just accidental. But the FBI cars weren't.

I wondered if they'd stop following me if I'd call Washington, D.C., and just turn myself in.

But for what?

I couldn't think of anything I'd done wrong.

Somehow, I made it back home. The kids still weren't there. I filled up, then sat down in the living room and tried to remember what I'd done that had gotten the government after me.

This time I dried out alone at home. The whirling images lasted two days. The shakes lasted four days. It felt like a month.

There was a new practical problem, though. Again I had become deathly afraid to make left-hand turns facing oncoming traffic. And that was just one of the constant, countless fears I felt.

A real estate friend dropped by after church. He said he knew what kind of shape I was in, physically and financially, and he wondered if he could help out by selling the house for me. I told him to go to hell. After all, I still had some savings secreted away.

I ran into an alcoholic who had been sober for three years. I started to explain my situation and how complicated it was.

"Make it simple, Scott."

"That sounds great, but it isn't simple."

"You can keep it simple—real simple. Like, just don't pick up the first drink."

"Yeah, yeah, I know."

That jerk, all he was capable of doing was making things simple, I thought. That was because he was a simpleton. I laughed at my joke.

I'd gone six days and felt great. I was eating again, swimming twice a day, even running with Rascal. Two blocks and I was done, but I felt better.

It was a Tuesday night and the board of directors for the start-up church had met. I was driving home, feeling good. The FM station cranked out "A Man and A Woman."

It felt so right, that song. Some day it would feel right with Ms. Right.

I swung off to the right, went around the block, screwed up my courage for a rare left turn back onto Bear Canyon Road and headed back toward town. I didn't want to go home yet. I felt too good.

Waiting at the light at Wilmot and Speedway, I saw a short blonde get out of a BMW, white skirt flashing in the evening breeze. She walked into a bar called The Living Room.

Gorgeous! She might be looking for me.

I hadn't realized how long I'd been there until the bartender grinned a "last call, sir" at me. I ordered another double. I still had four bucks in my wallet. I'd started with $20.

Funny, the wallet wouldn't fit back into the hip pocket I'd taken it from. I stood up, trying to push it in, and slumped against the barstool.

No one seemed to notice.

"So, buddy, where d'ya get a drink after you guys close?"

The bartender looked at me, then murmured that there was a bar on Grant Road that would serve after hours if you parked in back and tipped the guy.

I woke up about 10 and wandered into the kitchen to see if I had any vodka in the house. Ahhh—a whole fifth had been tucked away behind the white plates.

The kids weren't home. The house all mine. Empty.

Except for wonderful little Rascal. My buddy.

I called and he sidled over—wary, tongue hanging out, eyes mournful yet feisty.

That's what I loved about him—his feist. Was there such a word?

Or—wasn't this a weekday? Maybe they had been home when I got in, and had gotten themselves off to school without waking me?

I looked outside. The car was there and looked normal.

I decided not to make coffee, poured a KoolAid-over-vodka. Maybe I'd play golf for the day. The KoolAid tasted so good, how come I'd never had this before?

Then I noticed the scab on my right hand. It was about an inch long, looked like I'd gotten gashed there somehow, somewhere.

Oh well, I thought, just another little blackout. I probably just . . .

Ohmygawd, what if I cut myself on a rusty nail? I could have lockjaw and die!

I hurried into the bedroom and threw on a shirt.

Wait a minute, my drink's still in the kitchen. I hurried back out to make sure it was there. I knew I'd better keep it with me, so no one could get it.

I stopped to pet Rascal. His white, black and brown patches of hair were tangled, as if he'd been chasing through the desert underbrush.

Back in the bedroom, drink in hand, but I couldn't remember why I was getting dressed, where I was going.

Music! I needed music. I rushed out to the den to turn on the stereo. But I'd left my drink in the bedroom so to hell with the music. I went back to the bedroom, sat down on the floor, leaned against the bed and sipped. I wondered how long Nixon could put up with the press. They'll get him yet. No, that's right—he's out of office now. They did get him. Let's see, it's Ford now, with Rocky, right?

Gotta shave, I thought. But let's just wait until this drink gets to the system, so I won't be shaking when I shave. Don't want any cuts on my-

That's it—the scab on my right hand. Look at it! I was going to the hospital. Might have lockjaw. What if I have lockjaw and they put me in a hospital and make me stay there . . .

No, maybe I had better not go to a hospital to have this thing checked. Yet—I'd better take a drink with me in the car. The FBI'll tail me, no doubt, and I don't want to make left-hand turns, especially with government agents behind me, spying, waiting for me to make a mistake.

But if I don't go to the hospital, where will I go?

The liquor store. Then I'll decide.

It was two nights later when the kids went with friends for pizza and I drove down to the store for a little beer. Rascal wanted to go. Wonderful buddy Rascal. I hugged him, let him sit in my lap while I headed back down Bear Canyon Road.

On the way back, Rascal did his usual barking at the horses grazing in a pecan grove along Tanque Verde Road. I swung off into a driveway, stopped the car, opened a nice cold 16-ounce beer. Rascal was yipping excitedly, tongue hanging out, his eyes darting from the horses to me and back.

"Okay, fella, I love you—here you go." I opened the door and he bounded out and straight for the horses.

Such a joy, watching Rascal tease the horses. I sighed, leaned my head against the headrest and sipped my beer.

I'd had a solid 10 minutes of quiet—except for the roar of the nearby traffic—and felt rested.

"Rascal! C'mon, Rascal."

He stared at me from the field, maybe 50 yards to my left.

I knew what would get him. I started the car, turned around and opened the door. "C'mon, Rascal. Time to go home."

He just stared at me, feisty and playful, his eyes begging me to let him stay.

I turned off the engine, unsnapped another beer.

A few minutes later, I realized that Rascal had disappeared. He wasn't around the horses, wasn't anywhere in sight.

I got out. "Rascal! Rascal!"

No Rascal.

"Rascal, c'mon, fella. I'm leaving now."

No sign of him.

Dumb little bastard, I thought. Thinks he can get away with that!

I turned on the engine, closed the door, revved the engine, put my head out for one last call—"Rascal!" No sign of him.

I gunned the engine, ignored the traffic on Tanque Verde and swung out to my right. I'd just go home. That would show him.

The kids got home an hour later. Laura asked where Rascal was. I told her.

"Dad!"

"Well?"

"Dad, you can't just leave him there."

I called Donny. We got in the car and drove back down to the horse ranch. It was dark. Rascal was nowhere to be seen or heard. We called and whistled and called. No Rascal. As we drove away, I caught a glimpse of a mangled dead animal on the highway.

I could not bear to stop.

In all my drinking, I had never done anything this bad. In the morning, I would go to a hospital, do absolutely anything to get off this damned alcohol.

I had just killed my own Rascal!

Christmas came and went. I stayed in my oblivion as much as possible. In January I avoided everyone for a few days, but got too drunk to know where I was. Brownie drove me to a detox place for Mexicans in South Tucson. I stayed overnight, rode a bus back. Just two weeks earlier, I had told my children I'd be working.

I decided to become a freelance writer, and talked an editor into a piece on a longtime TV anchorman in Tucson, a man who was not respected by young hot-shot types. I spent long hours in the studio and in the man's home and wrote a sympathetic piece about him. Two weeks later, the magazine's editor phoned and suggested I might have been drunk when I wrote it.

That hurt. I had not been drunk, but my reputation obviously was that of a drunk and it was, I knew, an easy way to reject anything I wrote—just say Smith's a drunk; he didn't know what he was writing.

The classifieds always included ads for car salesmen and home fire-alarm salesmen. I interviewed for both, but couldn't get myself to accept any offers. So I did some part-time jobs cleaning up realtors' new listings.

The real estate guy came back and said I was something like four months behind on the mortgage—didn't I think I'd better sell the house? I didn't ask how he knew about the payments. I said I'd only sell if I made a big profit. He said I had let the property get run-down and I'd better fix it up or take a loss. I told him to go to hell.

Time blurred. Days, months, a fog flying through me.

Hunt Bennett came to town to see his parents, Homer and Elizabeth, in Green Valley. He phoned and said he'd meet me for breakfast at the airport before his plane. We drank bloody marys and he left. I drove home, had two more drinks, headed back into the city to look for a job.

An off-duty policeman pulled me over before noon and arrested me for drunk driving. I spent the afternoon, evening and night in the drunktank, the only white man there. I had called Brownie but help never came. A sheriff's deputy stayed near the door to make sure I didn't get attacked. I tried to sleep and couldn't. In the morning, a deputy said I'd been fortunate. I went to court and pleaded guilty.

Brownie told me he and Bob Linder had left me in jail because they thought it might help me.

I finally painted the gutters and sold the house. No profit, but at least I'd gotten some cash. I rented a three bedroom apartment so Don and Laura could have their own rooms.

I tried real estate school in the mornings but got drunk the second week. The blackboard and books were unintelligible to me. I quit.

There was a former beauty queen, now about 27, living in the apartment complex. I decided she would be my project in life. She said I drank too much. But she'd hang around me, usually in a bikini.

I decided to not drink and to try selling insurance. I even told my new boss, a pleasant guy, that I was an alcoholic but would never drink again. I lasted several weeks but then the company's headquarters said I didn't have enough sobriety to be a good bet. The boss said he would have to let me go.

I drank that night.

A recovering alcoholic told me that I got drunk because I drank. I thought that was the dumbest of all the dumb things I'd heard yet.

I was behind on the rent payments when Laura left for two weeks back East at Quogue with her mother and my family.

I drank for 10 days, dried out in the apartment for three days of shaking and pacing.

Then Don said he'd like to move in with a buddy's family nearby. I said he could try it, although it angered me.

> *My son, my sweet dear Donny, doesn't want to live with me.*
> *I don't deserve to be alive if he can't trust me.*

I left 10 minutes later for the liquor store.

I drank until I couldn't get out of bed.

I dried out on my own. It took three days of shaking and nightmares and not sleeping.

Then my mother called and said she had decided that Laura would stay back East permanently, that I was an alcoholic and could not raise a daughter.

Laura could live in Washington with Lynn, who was now in the title insurance business and doing well.

I was furious. I headed for the liquor store.

A swirling downdrift.
Flotsam
Circlespinning
Down.

I was alone, my daughter taken away and my son choosing to move out.

Dry again, I ran into a guy from a headhunting firm and tried that. I liked the work—mostly phone calls all day long—and I won the office contest for arranging the most first time interviews, although it was only my second week of work. The prize was a bottle of scotch. I told the boss I'd rather have cash. He said he'd change it later. I put the bottle in my trunk.

I worked another week and the boss, a young and cocky guy, still hadn't given me the money. I resented that. It could be dangerous for me. The more I thought about it, the madder I got. Finally on Friday night, I went out to the car and got the bottle. I was going to sell it to a neighbor. Instead I took it inside, got a bowl of ice and a glass, sat down in my favorite chair, and decided to show that stupid boss!

I'd drink at him.

By Monday I didn't know it was Monday.

By the end of the week, I got up enough vodka-driven courage to walk into the guy's office.

"Hey, Scott—what's going on huh?"

"Look, I just want to tell you one thing."

"Yeah? We're not used to someone not coming to work or calling-"

"I'm sorry. I started drinking again. It's not your fault at all. I'll have to just resign."

He stared at me for a moment, looked down at the carpet, then shrugged and said he'd mail me a paycheck.

I'd been trying some counseling from a warm, intelligent woman named Carolyn. She gave me pills which would prevent me from drinking—I'd get terribly sick if I drank at all.

I stayed on them for 10 days, then waited three days and tried a canned martini in the car before my weekly appointment with her.

I went into our session and she interrupted me to ask if I'd had a drink. I said yes and she took my vitals: pulse 120, blood pressure unbelievably low, something like 60 over 40.

I would die before I'd get to a hospital, I said. So she had me drive to a pharmacist, who gave me one little antidote pill. Then, still taking her instructions on faith but thinking I'd die, I drove home, took the pill, passed out and woke up the next day feeling as though I should have died.

I stayed dry for a couple of weeks. I got to the beauty queen.

We went to dinner and then danced. And I discovered that she loved to drink. As she ordered her third, I ordered "just one gin and tonic."

The fresh twinge of the lime in the nose . . . the tiny sparkles from the tonic in the nostrils . . . the heavy presence of the gin . . . I felt home again.

We danced in her living room, close and slow, undulating together. She asked me to undo her hair—it had been in a tight bun. We danced some more. She asked me to loosen the zipper on the back of her tight green dress so she could feel freer. We danced some more.

As we danced, her hand crept down into my pants. My hand went down, down inside her dress.

"C'mon—bed."

She purred into my ear: "This is so romantic! Let's do it now, here. Dancing."

"No, no, bed!" I pulled her with me, through the long hallway to her room.

She wanted romance. I knew "romance" would take too long. I was going to pass out soon.

At 5 I got up, walked to my place, poured myself a vodka on the rocks and went to bed.

The weeks went past in a drunken blur. The only money I had went for more booze. I could not stop.

Didn't want to drink, didn't want to stop.

Sometimes welcome oblivion. But mostly just drunk, day after day, night after night, sitting there in my chair, drinking and staring at the drawn curtains, my world reeling with nameless nightmares.

I lost that apartment and moved into a smaller one. And dried out.

My problem, I figured, was that when I drank I kept on drinking.

I'd try just drinking beer, and only during the Tonight Show.

The theme music at the front of the show became my favorite song. But I decided I didn't need to wait all day. So I was drinking round the clock again.

I kept the curtains pulled and the phone off the hook, seldom went outside except when the booze or cigarettes ran out.

No one would call by the time the Carson theme came on. I could sit back with a drink and laugh with Carson.

Free. No phone calls. No faces. No bill collections. No one one could see me, hear me.

The fears had been getting to me, though, and sometimes I'd have to fight them off even during Carson, fears that I was going to die, and hideously.

My body was going fast—the weight now at 130, the skin yellow, the eyes hollow.

2:05 a.m., a Tuesday night:

The spinning had stopped and I lurched off the bed, into the bathroom for the bottle. I'd outsmarted any possible visitors by keeping my bottle in the tub behind the shower curtain.

I poured until the blue plastic glass was almost full, walked out to the kitchen and got ice cubes. Stood with my back leaning into the kitchen counter, thankfully gulping down that pain-killer, fear-killer, conscience-killer.

When I drank like this, it made me feel even worse about myself, but it also gave me all the more reason to drink as much as I could get.

Oblivion. If I could just get on-going oblivion.

I couldn't find cigarettes anywhere. I reeled from room to room, rechecking every possible spot.

I knew I was too gone to drive.

Then I noticed the ashtrays. They were spilling over with two-inch butts. I picked one up, pressed the end of it back into a circular shape, and lit it.

Not bad. I could get through the night on these.

I opened the curtains and the sliding windows in the bedroom to let some fresh air in, then turned out all the lights so any night guards in the apartment complex couldn't see that I was home. They might be waiting to catch me. I didn't know what for, but it felt like they'd want to catch me.

I managed to get to a church council meeting one night in the home of a wonderfully normal, healthy guy named Otto. Instead of my usual argumentative drunk-self, I turned quiet. No one seemed to notice.

I had to be quiet: The room was turning sideways on me and I was holding onto my chair for dear life. The whole room would tilt up to the right and it felt as if we'd all slide right out of the house. I knew it was the booze and yet it seemed so real.

I dried out and after a few days got a job selling advertising space for a new magazine.

I did well, knocking on doors, cold-calling, always hoping none of my old students would see this wobbling, rail-thin me, or see what I was doing.

I opened two new accounts and talked one of them into an additional ad-agency arrangement with us.

I'd been dry for two weeks when I had a business lunch at the Plaza International, my old professorial hangout. My companion ordered a martini. I told the waitress to make it two of them.

Several afternoons later, I awakened to see the publisher of the magazine at the end of my bed, going through papers on my table.

"Hey!"

"I'm leaving now, Scott. Just had to get your paperwork on these accounts. Awful sorry about your situation."

He went out the door and I headed for the kitchen, where the bottle would be.

But no—the bottle wasn't there. What day was it anyhow? The bottle!

It was beside my bed, half empty. Thank God I hadn't lost it, or the publisher hadn't taken it. Ohmygawd, he must've seen it!

The rent was three months' past due and I had no job.

I phoned an antiques dealer. She came over and gave me $700 for my grandmother's aunt's dining room table and chairs and cabinet, plus H.R.'s old soft silver spoons with an "S" on them.

I paid off two months' rent and, knowing full well what I had just done, I bought three quarts of vodka.

A Monday morning in September 1976:

Dry. Three weeks, one day and 10 hours dry!

I wanted to get some sun. I had stopped by a friend's apartment and grabbed a copy of Editor & Publisher, the weekly trade journal for newspaper people. I would take it by the pool. No one would see me on a Monday, a workday.

I put on my swim trunks and caught a glimpse of myself in the mirror.

I could see every bone in the ribcage. The rounded edges of the shoulder blades looked angular, the skin too loose in the hollows just below them.

No wonder the little girls in the complex had called me Bird Legs one day! My thighs were about three inches in diameter, at the largest point. My arms were smaller.

The swim trunks had been for a waist 36.

I rooted around in some old boxes and found my college-days bermuda shorts, waist 30. I put them on and stood in front of the mirror. No, they wouldn't stay up when I dove. I found an old belt and used a corkscrew to push a new hole through the belt at 28 inches

I took a lounge chair in a hot, sunny corner, put my feet on another chair, and started leafing through E&P. I hadn't seen it in several years, but the format and type faces—even the headlines—didn't seem to have changed a bit.

I could still do it. I knew I could. If I would just stay dry.

I stopped in the classified ads and adjusted my thinking: I would not look for a big job, but a job that would get me back on my feet. I would have to tell any new employer what had happened, that I was recovering, that I met regularly with other alcoholics.

There it was:

The Allentown Morning Call, my alma mater, my first love in newspapers, needed a national editor. I knew what that meant: Someone to edit the wire-service stuff and to dummy pages, including page 1.

Hell, I'd done that when I was 22.

I went inside, got an iced tea, without vodka, and sat blinking in the sun for half an hour.

The warmth felt so good. I would have to start eating fattening foods, get some heft back on the bones.

Gawddammit though, if only I could drink beer.

In the afternoon, I picked up the phone and dialed Allentown, asking for George Nehrbas, my old mentor.

"Nehrbas."

His voice hadn't changed—still the same crisp thin blue-blooded George. I pictured his hair still so straight, slicked down the way Williams College guys did it in his generation.

"George?"

"Yes?"

"This is Scott—Scott Smith."

"Well, hello, Scott! Long time! How are you?"

"Great, George."

We chatted for several minutes about my leaving Washington and my two years teaching in Arizona.

"George, I saw your ad in E&P for a national editor, and believe it or not, if that's the same old wire-editor job, I'd love to come back, settle down in my favorite part of the country, and just do a good job for my favorite paper."

George called me back an hour later and said I was all but hired, but they would need to see me—would I fly into Allentown the next week, just to get through the formalities? I'd be talking to a great guy named Jerry Bellune, who was managing editor.

"Just one thing, George: I ought to tell you that I am a recovering alcoholic."

"No problem, Scott, as long you're doing all the right things about that ."

"I am, George. I'll be glad to fill you in on it when I get there."

Wow! The world is going to let me back in!

I phoned the few friends I had—Bob Linder, Lionel and Artie Brown, Bil Wilkins, and Bob and Luke. Scott was going back east to his old newspaper—wasn't it great?

They each sounded skeptical.

It had been a whirlwind two days—the interviewing had gone beautifully, I'd instantly liked Jerry Bellune, Allentown felt good, and I'd found an apartment overlooking a park.

I'd called Ann and Al from Allentown, told them what was happening, and flew into Cleveland the next day. As we walked along the airport passenger tunnel, my mother said she wanted to arrange for a friend in Medina to cut my hair—if I was coming back East, I wouldn't want my hair to look like that.

It had been a good but awkward visit, and I was glad now to settle back into a seat on American for the flight from Cleveland to Tucson.

It felt as though I'd been on stage for three straight days. I could finally settle back, be myself, make some plans and—geez, I'd have an income again.

I was back in the world again.

About 20 minutes out of Cleveland-Hopkins, the stewardesses came along with the cocktail tray. The man beside me ordered a canned martini very dry, the kind I'd used when commuting on the Beltway back in Washington. I felt thankful I was dry now.

"You sir?"

"Iced tea, please."

"I'm sorry, sir, we don't have any iced tea. We do have soda and juice—how about some juice or a tomato juice?"

The words surprised me as they rolled up through my throat: "Well, I'll have a beer, then."

The plane pulled up to the gate in Tucson at sunset. My first stop was the men's room, then the airport bar for just one more beer. It would only be my third. I was sure I could handle it.

And besides, packing up all my stuff and getting across the country would take a lot of energy and there was no way I could do it if I was drinking, so just for tonight I'd have three beers, no one would know it.

The world was letting me back in. I deserved to celebrate.

Eight days later, I pulled out of the parking lot at the apartment complex at 7:05 a.m., the Datsun heavy with clothes and stereo, books and records and typewriter and photos from the years in Tucson.

I swung left on Broadway and headed into the morning sun. Next stop Texas!

I was relieved to be on the road, getting the hell out of such a boring town. No wonder I'd had problems—Tucson was boring, the desert was boring, the people were boring. I'd be okay back East.

I reached down between my thighs and jiggled the can I held there. It was already empty. I swung into a liquor store, bought two cold six-packs and headed toward the Interstate, gratefully gulping down my fifth beer of the morning. It was 7:20 and I was on my way . . .

9

I swerved across the country, emerging from blackouts in Texas, Tennessee, and Ohio.

I knocked on the front door at my parents' house in Medina, Ohio, at 2:30 a.m. and couldn't waken them. It was a relief—they'd be so disappointed to see that I was so sick, and drinking again. I stayed in a Holiday Inn three miles from their house, got up and got beer and was back on the roads.

I felt that I could still drive safely. I cared about one thing: being able to drink without interruption.

That last night on the road, as I drank-drove across Pennsylvania, an elk darted out in front of my car. My right front fender was crunched; the elk limped away as if slightly hurt.

I kept on driving, finally pulling into a motel in the mountains near Interstate 80 about midnight.

The owners were homosexuals and they wanted to know if they could stop by my room for a little "good night." I told them to stick it up their ass, laughing loudly at my drunken humor. Later in my room, I was scared; they looked as though they could be violent and I'd mocked them.

I passed out, bottle beside me. I awakened four hours later.

You'd gotten sober again, kid. Now you've blown it again.
You can't stop. Blown it! Blown it! You're supposed to be back

on your feet now, you stupid s.o.b. You have
blown it. You
weak s.o.b., you might as well just die now—
why wait?

The motel seemed perfect for my own version of the movie "Psycho." I could use a knife—I'd get a serrated one— and die in a pool of blood in this godforsaken nowhere.

Or maybe use the curtain cords to hang myself by the shower rod.

The rod looked too weak even to support my bones. And the mirror said that's all I was:

Bones
Draped with pale orange
flesh. Weak.
No strength of character.
Weak.
Even let poor Rascal get killed.
Now again you've
blown it.
Blown it!, and you don't even have enough
guts to . . .

I dove back into my bottle.

At least the booze death would be within oblivion.

Or would it?

That afternoon, I checked into the Sheraton hotel in downtown Allentown.

"National editor" of the Morning Call. That was a laugh. I couldn't face telling George Y. Nehrbas that his old protege couldn't even stay sober long enough to report for work. And there would be Jerry Bellune, the managing editor, who also had believed in my sobriety. As I had.

For several days I almost never left my room, calling downstairs for room service every couple of hours—two drinks at a time. I was often delirious, wishing I could just die but wanting the next drink even more than that.

Each day I hoped I could stay in the oblivion. Each day I could not.

Finally, on a Monday, there was a knock on my door about 7 in the evening.

A man stood there, in his 50s with thinning gray hair and a bright look in his eyes. He said he was from the newspaper. They'd asked him to come over and see if he could help. He said he was an alcoholic, just like me. He'd been going to A.A. for six years and had not had a single drink. It worked.

He told me we were going to a hospital. I didn't fight. He drove me there, wished me luck.

The medical center's detox ward was gray, small, crowded.

After several gray, confused days, the executive editor, Ed Miller, and Jerry Bellune, the managing editor who'd hired me so enthusiastically, came to visit.

They offered me a vacation, suggested I might want to get away and straighten out, then come to work. Maybe the move and the pressure had just been too much for me. Their eyes were kind.

I thanked them and explained that I needed to throw myself into my job.

I checked out of the hospital, unloaded my stuff into my bright new apartment overlooking a park—I'd leased it sober, during my interviewing trip—and went to work. As national editor, to my surprise.

Each day I felt better, throwing myself into the work.

A couple of weeks later, Jerry Bellune wanted me to fly down to Washington with him to spend a couple of hours with the district's member of the House of Representatives. It would be neat, Jerry said, to see me return to my old stomping grounds.

I wondered how I would feel if I ran into some of my old colleagues—maybe McGrory wandering around the Senate gallery or . . .

We were to leave early in the morning. The night before, I got drunk. I couldn't understand why.

Jerry told me later that when I didn't meet him at the airport in the morning, he sent the police to make sure I was still alive; I can only remember telling someone at the door—presumably a police officer—that I was tired and wanted to be left alone so I could sleep.

When I did awaken that day and realized what I'd done—stood Jerry up, and started the booze again—I knew I could not handle the shame. I headed for the liquor store.

To hell with this routine about working, Smith.
Just drink
and it'll all go away. Just a little drink.

I drank for another five or six days, in and out of blackouts and liquor stores, a bottle always beside me, the oblivion never quite black enough to blot out the horror of what was happening to me again.

I made my second visit to the detox unit, and this time they took the gloves off. Doctors warned me coldly that my weight was about 130—'normal' was 170—and that I would die within months.

Nurses warned me that I was not getting any drug treatment that could prevent a fatal seizure during withdrawal.

I got the feeling that maybe it was acceptable for a newspaper editor to get drunk once—but definitely not twice.

Jerry Bellune warned me that this stuff could not continue, and that I would not be the national editor.

A guy who'd been sober nine years warned me that my "half measures" were killing me. He said I'd have to stop trying to stay sober my way.

I agreed to go to a counselor recommended by the publishers.

Wrong counselor. She was bright and gorgeous, and single.

She wanted to talk about my low self-image. I wanted to show her how great I was and convince her—without saying so—that she should fall in love with me. Maybe she'd be the one. That would fix me, I'd be able then to stay sober.

She casually volunteered one evening that she was in love with someone. I started drinking a couple of days later. This time I dried out on my own, but missed several days' work.

There were sober alcoholics all over Allentown. So, relenting to pressure from Jerry Bellune and my counselor, I started meeting with some of them in church basements and at the 'Y'.

They kept saying the same dumb things the ones in Tucson had said. Stuff like "Keep it simple—don't pick up the first one. One day or one hour at a time".

I knew it didn't apply to me, this simplicity they talked about. They were simpletons. I was a complicated, highly sensitive person, with special needs they could never understand.

I had my standard technique: Always agree with them. Get them off my back. Later, when alone, I could drink if I damn well wanted to.

November, 1976:

I stood at my kitchen sink one afternoon, door locked, phone off the hook, curtains drawn. I poured another bourbon into a short clear glass, skipped the ice.

That ice might splash and spill some of the bourbon.
And I do not want to lose any of this stuff.
Gotta go to work at 5:30 this afternoon.
Ought to pay the rent, but
Boy, that went down in a hurry.
More, Scott—before someone walks in here
and takes it away from you. More!
Geezus. It doesn't even taste good.
And it's not fun anymore.
I really am an alcoholic! Can't even enjoy the stuff.
Fuck it. Just keep going Scott, just keep slogging it down.
Oblivion. Just oblivion. I'll take oblivion.
It's better than facing those people or that goddam
hospital—to hell with those people—
and ohgawd what is wrong with me?—
and pour a little more, make it a big one.
No splashiepoo, just a lil drinkiepoo again.
Washontin. I was supposed to go to Washontin with—
what's his name?—Jerry.
No, no that was last time.
No, that was many times ago.
Who cares, anyway.
They'll know I'm drinking again if I don't show up.
But I can't go to work like this.
One more, jus a lil drinkiepoo.
Can't enjoy it, though.
Sometime I'll go sit in a park and enjoy the birds
and my booze and do it right.
Just pray I don't see a dog that looks like Rascal-
Ahgawwd give me oblivion!

I went back to the detox unit, not quite remembering how I'd gotten there, and not quite caring—curious, but resigned to—to . . .

Dying this way.

I stumbled out to the coffee room and plumped down into one of the tan plastic chairs, ignoring the other patients.

There was a sign in front of me. I squinted, trying to read it:

LET GO.

Huh?

LET GOD.

It was right. I knew it was right. There was no longer any way at all that I alone could handle this.

Now, if only God knew that I existed . . .

The medical people hadn't been able to help me. The other alcoholics hadn't been able to help me. My family had shut me off again.

And most importantly, I doubted that even I could help me.

If only, I thought, God knew I existed.

But I knew better.

In the summer, I managed to stay dry for almost three months. I got to know some people who were successful at it, and started to sense that somehow maybe I could make it.

One of the guys who was staying sober—he wore button-down collars and we seemed to identify with each other—invited me to go down to Philadelphia to watch the last day of a PGA golf tournament. I thought it would be a good Sunday in the sun for me. My weight was up to 135 and I was getting a little strength back. And the yellow was disappearing from the cheeks and chest.

The Saturday night before our trip, I stopped in a bar in Emmaus to see a guy who'd cash a $15 check for me. The beer smelled foul and I was so glad I wasn't drinking.

It happened on the way back to my apartment. There was no warning.

I pulled into a liquor store and asked for a pack of More regulars and oh yes, a fifth of Tanquerey, too.

I sat in the old chair and drank almost all of it—just enough to pass out.

Morning came and we drove to Philadelphia. The golf was boring and I went two hours before I casually walked away from my buddy, got two fairways away from him, and casually approached one of the refreshment tents. Just a little beer; it was so humid and . . .

I dried out Tuesday and Wednesday on my own. It was the briefest bender I'd had, and the withdrawal wasn't as severe.

Wednesday night (I think), I was awakened by a nightmare: Rascal was begging me to come and get him.

The guilt about everything—from my kids to Rascal to just the fact that I'd been drinking—was heavy again. But I was getting better at lying.

The golf-trip buddy asked. Jerry Bellune asked. Had I maybe had a problem?

No, no, I insisted, I'd actually been sick to my stomach. Of course I hadn't been drinking. I tried to sound offended. They both appeared to believe me.

One picture kept coming back in the night: Just an image of the house we'd owned in 1970 on Michael Court in Colesville: The low-slung brick rambling place with three fireplaces and pool and a state park to the right and rear.

Camelot.
For one brief shining moment . . .
And I walked away.

The image would always awaken me, always push me out of bed.

The medical evidence was making an impression on me.

Beginning back in Phoenix, the doctors had been doing all sorts of tests—body scans included.

The consensus from five thorough examinations over 22 months was clear: I had "acute chronic alcoholism," which the American Medical Association had declared a progressive, clinically identifiable, terminal disease.

My case would be terminal "sooner than you think", a doctor in Allentown told me.

I had liver damage and cirrhosis.

Imbalanced blood.

Chronic malnutrition.

Secondary hepatitis.

Emphysema. Steady decrease in lung function.

All these factors would put a huge load on my heart if I had to withdraw again. And that meant I might not survive the rigors of a convulsion.

The doctor also told me that I was amazingly lucky there was no discernible brain damage—"yet".

That same doctor was the one who told me I didn't need 'brain damage'—the problem already was my brain.

I would die.

They all said I would die. They were right.

I no longer feared death; at least I wouldn't have to drink then.

When dry, I'd hang around with recovering alcoholics.

Harry Philips was the toughest: stern, with straight white hair at age 45; he talked about life and death as the choices an alcoholic had to face. I didn't like him.

"You're the toughest kind in the world to get sober, Scott. You're too smart. It lets you concoct all these intellectual traps. There's nothing 'intellectual' about it, stupid. It's simple: you don't pick up the next drink."

"You'll die, all right."

Ed Schmidt was the bear. He was maybe 68 years, short, always with the stub of an unlit cigar jutting from a flat mouth that spoke only one language: sobriety, in a grunty sort of Pennsylvania Dutch voice. He had bright eyes, though, that carried love and tolerance. His crew cut resembled a white hair brush.

I had something deep in me about these guys—they spoke straight and didn't drink. I couldn't get it.

I walked down Eighth Street in Allentown toward the big bridge. Back in my days as a reporter, I'd helped the cops search for a guy who'd jumped off that bridge. I was the one who found him: a sickening flattened glob.

No. I could not.

It was a problem, this knowledge that I ought to just finish things: When I was dry, as I was this day, I was too scared to do it. When I was drunk, I just wanted the next drink.

I walked into an alleyway behind a large store. And there was my answer. The store had thrown out some large heavy cardboard cartons.

> *By this winter I will have lost my job, my apartment, my car. I*

won't have any thing or any one to worry about. I'll come over
here at night and pull a few of these big cartons down the
hillside and make a shack out of them, down under the bridge.
Other guys live there. I'll get enough money somehow to keep
drinking until I just die down there. Maybe the weather'll
do it, the snow and cold. Or a convulsion. Or maybe one of the
other guys'll do it to me. For me.

EIGHT DAYS IN AUGUST

This is what I remember:

Saturday morning:

What the hell was going on?

I was walking into a liquor store!

I'd been—could it be?

I'd already been drinking!

I was supposed to be playing in a little golf tournament in Lancaster later in the day, the guest of Judy from Medina and her family.

What the hell was I doing, walking into a liquor store?

I turned and opened the trunk. There was my suitcase for the weekend. No sign of booze anywhere.

But I was already boozed up.

I could not remember taking the first drink.

What the hell? If I'm already drinking, I know I can't stop. Besides, it feels good, and this time I'll just keep it to a minimum and no one'll be any the wiser. I'll just ease through the weekend and enjoy the golf.

I walked on into the liquor store, bought two quarts of cheap vodka and a six-pack of 7Up.

Sunday:

It was difficult to get out of bed on Sunday. I was in a Lancaster motel and when Judy arrived, she saw what kind of shape I was in. No matter how hard I tried, I could not hide the wobbly walk.

We drove to her father's home and chatted, then took a walking tour of the golf course. It had been raining and we couldn't play.

Got back to the motel in the afternoon. Judy waited in the room while I went to the car "to get something." I'd carried a fresh 7Up with me, poured it out on the parking lot and filled the can with vodka from the trunk.

Judy, a bright, warm, pleasant high school chum, lovely and now single, suggested we go sit in a field of tall grass and just "be there with each other".

We sat and I casually drank my 7Up, tossing it down as if it were soda.

I announced that I'd be right back—just had to go to the bathroom. I went into my room, can in hand, opened the bottom drawer of the dresser, pulled out a fresh bottle, filled the can, loudly went to the bathroom, and sauntered back to the field.

Hours later, I was sprawled on the bed, moaning, bottle beside me.

Judy was on the phone, asking someone if they couldn't just help. She'd hung up, said I should just rest until someone got there. I tried to say thank you, and I'm so sorry-

Monday:

Sometime in the afternoon, I realized I was back in my apartment in Allentown. The bottle was beside the bed.

Ohmygawd! I thought, I'd hit someone with the car.

> *The police have an all-points out and I'm*
> *wanted for*
> *manslaughter.*
> *Could it be?*
> *Why didn't I just kill me instead?*

I pulled on a shirt—I'd slept in my slacks and shoes—and went downstairs. Spinning with vertigo, holding the handrail for safety.

The car was parked where it should be. There were no new dents, no blood.

Tuesday:

It was noon and I was coming out of the blackout.

I was out of vodka.

Too shaky to shave, I put on clean clothes, edged down the stairs and into the sunshine. It hurt. My head pounded. I got into the Datsun.

I had to muster enough strength, enough moxie, to get more.

I drove slowly to the state liquor store in South Allentown. That would be safe. No one from the office would see me there.

There was a short line. Finally it was my turn. The clerk said, "Yes sir?"

I stared at him.

"Sir?"

I couldn't say anything. I felt frozen.

He peered into my eyes.

"Maybe some other time, sir."

I spun and walked out to the Datsun.

As I started the car, I thought that the clerk might know who I was.

Gotta get to another store
before he calls them, warns them:
don't give him anymore.

I slammed the car into gear, my mind suddenly clearing, focusing.

Cedar Crest Boulevard! There was a liquor store there.

I shot through the city streets at 40 to 60 miles an hour, oblivious to stop signs or the risk of getting caught.

My mouth was practicing the words: "A quart of vodka please—a quart of vodka please—a quart of vodka please."

I got there and straightened my body, sucking in the fresh air. I put on sunglasses—the frame was bent but they'd cover the eyes the other clerk had seen—and walked briskly into the store.

The clerk was on the phone. I stood waiting at the counter, acting impatient, as if I had somewhere to go.

He hung up.

The words rolled out smoothly: "A quart of vodka please." I handed him a $20. He got the vodka.

"Anything else?"

"Oh, let's make it two quarts. Two quarts of vodka, please."

He got another one, rang it up, gave me change, bagged the bottles.

I opened one in the parking lot, decided someone might see me, drove around behind the shopping center, pulled up beside a trash bin, and gulped.

Wednesday:

It was evening. I was slumped in the old red chair in the dark.

There was a knock at the door. I opened it and saw Joe Berg standing there.

Berg was a tall, muscular Montana cowboy with an education in cowboying, drinking and women. He'd gotten sober in Allentown and had befriended me months earlier.

"How ya doing?"

I shook my head, let him in.

I would not turn on the lights. I sat back down in my chair.

He sat down in the other chair. I lit a cigarette, took a pull on the blue plastic glass beside me, saying nothing.

"Thought maybe I could get my television back. I've got this woman staying at my place and she likes color television-"

"Take it."

He got up, unplugged the television, lifted it easily and went to the door.

"Scott, anytime you want . . ."

"Just go, Joe."

Thursday:

It was time to try enjoying my drinking! I'd had enough of my apartment, I thought. I hadn't opened the curtains nor turned on the telephone for—how many days was it now?

I got in the shower. I would clean up, enjoy the drinking.

The phone started ringing. I turned off the shower, ran into the living room. The line was blank. Nothing. They must've hung up.

Back in the shower. This time, though, I took my drink with me, so I could enjoy a long shower and not worry that someone would somehow get into the apartment and steal my glass.

Phone again. I turned off the shower, ran into the living room. Nothing. They'd hung up again-

No! The phone wasn't plugged in.

So how did it ring?

Got back in the shower, started the water, took a sip of the vodka.

The phone was ringing again.

Damn! Should I answer it?

I turned off the water.

The ringing stopped.

Huh?

Turned the water back on.

The phone started ringing again.

An hour later, I'd put on clean slacks, clean socks, and a shirt that had been worn only once or twice, and not when I was drinking. It would have to do. I had no more clean shirts.

It had taken several full glasses of vodka before my hands were steady enough to shave, but then it went well: no nicks, no blood.

I had shaved without ever looking into my eyes in the mirror. It was a major accomplishment.

It was time to enjoy my drinking!

I filled a jug with ice cubes, remembered that I had some olives and dumped them into the jug, then filled it with half a quart of vodka, got a nice glass, put it all in a fresh paper bag. I'd have a picnic in the park.

Food?

No, better not. Might take away the joy of martinis in the park. I had not eaten even a cracker since the preceding Friday.

I got lost trying to find the park, but eventually found it, drove far enough in that no one was likely to see me.

I'd brought a table cloth. I spread it out under a tall cedar, sat down and poured a martini into the nice clean glass.

Leaned back, waiting for the joy, for the big "ahh."

What if someone saw me?

Got up, picked up all my stuff, carried it to a tree farther back from the road. No one would see me here!

I'd spilled some of the booze, so I refilled the glass, lay back on my side, head resting in my left hand. The joy would come soon, the joy of just being alone and having a little martini in the park.

There was a bee buzzing somewhere near me. I stood up and screamed at it to go away.

Sat back down, and slowly sipped my drink. Strange, just to sip—no gulping when you're a Gentleman Just Having A Martini In The Park. Besides, I didn't need to gulp since I'd already had plenty.

Ohgawd! Where was this park anyway? I'd gotten lost finding it, and now had no idea where I was.

How would I ever get back home? Especially if I kept on drinking? My mind would get worse, not better. Maybe I'd never find my apartment, and that was where the rest of the booze was.

Panicking, I grabbed my stuff and hurried back to the car.

Friday:

(I do not remember anything of Friday.)

Saturday, August 27, 1977:

I felt clear-headed when I awakened. It was about 9. Went to the kitchen, checked the vodka supply. It was about gone. For some reason, that didn't panic me. I poured some into a tall glass, added ice cubes and water, swished it with my finger and took a slow pull on it. I had enough for half the day.

No way, Scott. This is not working. You couldn't buy enough.

Slumping into my red chair, lighting a cigarette, sighing, I recalled those sober people who were always saying: "Keep coming back."

Stuck. So damned stuck.

It would not work for me. That was clear. Their program was the most effective thing in the history of mankind in combatting alcoholism. But it was for people like them, not for me. It just could not work for me.

I was in the damndest spot I'd ever heard of.

Unable to drink without a disaster.
Unable to not-drink.

It had been like this for—how long? Ever since I'd picked up that can of beer six days after the hospital in Phoenix. What was that—22 months?—and I hadn't had the guts . . .

The guts to kill myself.

And didn't have the strength of character to stop drinking except when it got so bad that I couldn't continue.

That's right, I thought. It had run 11 days of drinking almost every time.

Let's see: this was Saturday. The eighth day.

I can't go another three days. I might as well-

I thought of the shakes and remembered the time at the detox unit when I'd come razorclose to a major convulsion.

And I remembered a guy, about 40, whose family was visiting him—his wife and kids—when he went into a convulsion and his heart gave out. I'd heard that last hideous scream . . .

I knew I just couldn't keep going. And I couldn't taper off. I knew that, too.

I plugged the phone in, got my address book, dialed a woman who'd been kind to me, a woman who wasn't an alcoholic but had found her only "home" hanging around alcoholics. She felt that she was an outcast. She'd been a minister's wife, had raised eight kids, felt empty, phony and trapped, and had just walked out.

I knew she'd be kind. And I didn't need any "tough love" at this moment.

"Hi. It's Scott."

"Are you okay? I've been worried. You haven't answered your phone for days-"

"Can you get me to a hospital?

"Again?"

"Yeah." I lit a cigarette, inhaled deeply, slowly. "I can't do it alone anymore. I'll just keep on drinking. I need . . ."

"Everyone said the hospitals wouldn't take you any more."

"They did?"

I broke into a sweat.

"They said you were just too hopeless, that there were other people who might get well and you would just be taking up space and . . ."

"Please! Oh God please!"

"I'll call some of your friends—maybe someone'll have an idea."

"Will you let me know?"

"Yes, but—I really doubt that any hospital's going to take you."

"I . . ."

"I'll try. Can you just stop long enough to wait until I call you back?"

I paused, took a slow sip of the vodka. "I don't think I can. And right now I'm rational, but who knows when . . ."

"Scott, do you feel like you want to get drunk again?"

" 'Get drunk'? I'm rational right now, but I'm drunk as all hell. Haven't had anything to eat all this week, not even a cracker."

"The usual, huh? When you get into it, you really do it."

"I can't stop without help. I know that."

"Well, I may just have to be the help. I'll come over and stay with you for however long it takes . . ."

"It wouldn't work." I need a sober alcoholic now."

"Let me call you back—just take it slow on the vodka, huh?"

"Thank you. And oh God please keep calling until someone . . ."

I poured the glass full and started pacing. I could hear the sweat dripping onto the hardwood floor.

She was at my door an hour later. A buddy named Jules, who always hung aroung Ed Schmidt, was with her.

Allentown Osteopathic Hospital had agreed to take me, she said. A doctor there said he understood.

She told me not to pack, just to go.

I nodded, put my shoes on, turned to my right and took one last slow pull on the vodka.

Jules helped me down the stairs and into the car.

The admissions lady took down my name, address, birthdate, Social Security number. I sat in a wooden chair thinking it was so slippery I'd slide right out of it onto the floor.

"And what are you here for?"

"Huh? I'm drunk!"

I laughed, thinking it was the funniest yet stupidest question I'd ever heard. All anyone would have to do was look at me and they would know:

He's drunk.
He's dying.
He's helpless.

Sometime Sunday night or Monday morning, there in the hospital, something happened.

Walking down the corridor from my room. Rapid breathing. Shaking worse than usual. Unshaved, unsmiling, knowing this detoxing could be the fatal one.

Something
way inside the core of me,
just below my chest, above my stomach

moved

shifted
I felt somehow different.
I got back in bed and was able to sleep.

9 a.m. Monday:

Jerry Bellune came through the door into my room and I knew what was about to happen.

"We've put up with—no, that's not even it, Scott."

"We just can't . . .

"We . . .

"Have to terminate you."

I felt relief for me, sorry for Jerry.

Scott, a county welfare department counselor, came right after Jerry left.

"Isn't this getting a little old, Smith?"

"Just tell me what I have to do." I meant it, but also knew too well there wasn't anything anyone could do now.

"I do have a thought . . .you're out of work now."

"How'd you . . ."

"Mr. Bellune and I talked."

I stared out the window. These poor guys, all decent guys, were wasting time that could be otherwise productive trying to figure out what to do with S. Smith, who was dying of acute chronic alcoholism. Didn't they know there was nothing, absolutely nothing, they could do? They should be enjoying their lives, not worrying about someone like me, who'd gone beyond hope.

"I think you ought to consider going to . . ."

He named a rehabilitation center in the Pennsylvania mountains. I'd heard of it often, and always as the worst place possible, a place where they-

"Are the stories about that place true—that they make people do all that crazy juvenile stuff, and they get real tough physically and emotionally?"

"I don't know. They may be true, or they may just be folklore. I do know that the place is our only, last resort for you."

I didn't think about it.

"I'll go."

His head shot up. "You will?"

"If that's the one shot I've got, I'll take it."

"You got to understand, Smith—it's mostly inmates from the federal system up there—guys who're in for murder and whatever who need to be cleaned up for prison. Judges sentence 'em up there for the first 30 days of their sentences."

"Then how can I go?"

"They take noncriminal, 'paying' patients, too."

"I can't pay . . ."

"I know. But I think Lehigh County can do it for you."

"I'll go if you can arrange it."

Right after he'd left, I got a moment alone to smoke a cigarette in the corner chair. No nurses, no noises. Just me.

I felt flat, matter-of-fact. I'd just agreed to go to a place where . . .

But I had no emotions about it now. I'd just do whatever anyone suggested.

Ed Schmidt came charging through the door, his eyes dancing.

Behind Ed came a cadre of people I'd seen—alcoholics who, with Ed, got together at lunchtime on Mondays and Fridays in a room at the 'Y'.

"We're gonna sit here, Scott, in your room. You get back in bed."

I got back in bed. The sonofabitch never even asked me how I was feeling! Tough old bastard. What the hell was the point of bringing all these people up here anyway?

Then I realized: he's trying to help me! That mean old sonofabitch brought all these people up here just to try to help me!

I got out of the hospital on a Wednesday and immediately met with Ed and some of the others who'd visited my hospital room.

I had two dollars and forty cents in my pocket. My checking account held maybe one dollar and there was no more money.

Ed passed a plate, a collection to help down-and-out alkies.

I put the $2.40 in the plate.

Might as well. There's no money where I'm going. I'm going to die.

Later, I walked back into the apartment I would have to give up. It was time to start packing—with nowhere to go.

I stood there, remembering the hope with which I'd rented the apartment the previous autumn—I'd thought back then that I would make it.

Then I raised my arms, palms up, in the most heartfelt prayer I'd ever uttered:

"God: If you even know that I exist, please help me—I'm out of money. Please help me with the checkbook."

Within an hour a woman knocked at the door. I didn't recognize her. She explained quickly:

"You lent me $20 a month or two ago. At a bar, I think. I don't have any idea how I knew where you lived but I did, and I have no idea why I drove this street today or remembered it, but—well, here's your twenty."

What a coincidence, I thought.

After she left, I went to the store and bought a carton of cigarettes.

Later in the afternoon, Jerry Bellune called.

"Scott, I have no idea why I'm doing this. But I'm going to act as if we owe you a few days' vacation pay."

Huh? Another coincidence?

If you'll meet me on the company parking lot—if you're going to see some of your alcoholic friends tonight—well, I figured you wouldn't want to be seen in the newsroom."

"You're right, Jerry."

"Meet me in the parking lot at 7:45 and I'll give it to you in cash. It's a hundred and eighty-seven-something."

I had given away my last $2.40. I had prayed from the heart. Within hours, out of nowhere, for no rational reason, two people had put more than $200 in my hands.

The next morning, I tried praying the same way, but this time asking that if He knew I existed, maybe He would help me not to drink that day.

JUST DON'T

10

I had to wait 19 days to get admitted to the "rehab" up in the mountains. It felt miraculous that I got through the workless days and sleepless nights and finally got there.

It was worse than I'd anticipated. I'd heard about confrontational therapy. It hadn't meant anything to me.

The people at this place knew me without having met me, could "read my mail," in their vernacular.

Part of the therapy was to get tough. They called me "the smart guy," sneered that I'd been a college professor.

I liked to read. They wouldn't let me read.

No pens or pencils or papers.

No chance to be alone or think.

They worked my tail off, 6 a.m. to midnight. I polished the big refrigerator and scrubbed clean floors. I sat through group therapy sessions with teen-age criminals—and was treated just as they were.

About the 20th day, while mowing the lawn, I looked up at the mountain sky and felt a flicker of hope.

Every other minute there was hell. Yes I could leave.

One of my roommates, age 17, was in for manslaughter or murder. He'd often awaken in the black of the night, screaming his memories of what he had done to an innocent old lady.

I was treated the same way he was—which I thought was unfair.

I was to stay 30 days. On the 27th, disgusted, I walked out.

I lugged my suitcase down the mountain road. One of the counselors pulled up in a car, and asked if I'd like a ride to the nearest town. He seemed "new" to me—suddenly relaxed, friendly. I got in.

"Tough up there," I told him.

"Yeah, well, we wanted to show you something—that your old ways didn't work. You've got to try new ways of living and thinking, or you won't stay sober. You'll die, Scott."

"I know."

"You've got to reprogram yourself."

"I know."

And I did know; what he was saying was right.

Yet something bothered me. I soon knew what.

"Scott, I find you very attractive-"

"Go to hell, asshole."

I got out of the car, checked into a cheap motel. I phoned Jim, a friend in Allentown who'd said he would pick me up when I got out.

Jim arrived 12 hours later. Somehow I was still sober. It felt miraculous to me—but then again, I didn't want to have to go through another "rehab."

I'd been praying not to drink, the same prayer I'd said each morning for 46 days now.

I'd chosen a guy to help me stay sober—a wonderfully nice guy with five years of sobriety and a good education. He lived in a good Allentown neighborhood and even wore button-down shirts.

But Harry Phillips, in his characteristically gruff manner, took me aside one night and pushed me into a wall, his hand gripping the front of my shirt, his eyes jabbing at me:

"You can't have a nice guy helping you!"

"I can't? Why?"

"You need someone who'll cut through your intellectual bullshit. Maybe Ed Schmidt would be the right guy!" His eyes were on fire.

"Ed Schmidt?"

It was ridiculous. Ed was a friend, yes—but he was nothing at all like me. We had nothing in common. Nothing but . . .

"Listen to me, stupid. You're too goddam bright for your own good. You've got all these complicated intellectual ways to outsmart people—and yourself.

"Your life is at stake, Scott. This isn't some little con job in the office so you can get ahead or please people, kid. This is your own life and you're going to die unless someone gets through all those layers of bullshit." He stared at me from about nine inches away. His blue eyes were blazing.

Speechless, I looked down at the floor.

"Do it!," Harry said.

When Harry got like this, I was afraid he'd punch me if he didn't have my full attention.

"But. Look, uh, Harry, I uh . . ."

"You said you want to stay sober."

"Yeah?"

"Have you ever been able to, depending upon your own intellectual brainpower?"

"Well this time is . . ."

"No different than the last time, stupid."

I hated him, trusted him, loved him, all in that moment.

"Well, Scott?"

"Okay."

The muscles in his face eased back a bit.

"You need Ed, Scott. You need someone to pull you out of that goddam brain of yours. You're like me—too goddam smart to stay sober."

"Huh?"

"The guys who helped me, back in Virginia, geezus the stuff they did to me." He laughed. "Anyway—you need Ed. I just hope he'll do it . . ."

"You mean he might not?"

I had assumed that Harry knew that Ed would do it.

"Just pray that he's in a good mood when you ask him."

That was really ridiculous. Not only did Harry want me to ask Ed to help me, but now he wanted me to pray that Ed would say yes.

The next morning, after I said my "thank You and please help me not to drink today," I added a P.S.: "If, Lord, Ed Schmidt's right for me—well, I'll leave it up to You, Lord. I personally don't think so, but if You think so . . ."

I'd lost Ed's phone number and didn't ask anyone for it, nor even look in the phone book. Instead, I just watched for him, figuring that if he didn't turn up, it meant God agreed with me that this was just too preposterous.

Several nights later, Ed was at a meeting I was attending. His cronies were standing around with him. They were discussing the Phillies' chances.

I edged up to the group, waiting for a moment when Ed might be alone.

I can't believe I'm going to do this.

My heart was thudding as if I was about to ask Cleopatra for a date.

It was ridiculous. Ed Schmidt, a runty little Pennsylvania Dutchman in his late 60s with a third-grade education, a retired cabdriver who always wore the stub of an unlit cigar in the corner of his mouth, a guy who grunted instead of speaking, advising *me*, with my education and experience and sensitivities? Ridiculous!

He saw me hanging near him but kept on chatting. Finally he got free.

"Wha'd you want?"

"Hi, Ed. How are you?"

"You okay? You look kinda ratty."

"I'm uh . . ."

"You watch the Phillies? Or's that too 'simple' for you?"

His eyes were dancing at me.

"I, uh, wondered if you'd uh, uh . . ."

"I know, Scott. Yeah, I'll do it."

"Huh?"

He said nothing.

I had to say something. "So . . ."

"Don't drink tonight, call me tomorrow."

"I haven't had a drink in 57 days."

"I said 'tonight'."

"That's all? Just don't drink tonight?"

"For you, that's a goddam miracle."

I phoned him at 8 the next morning. He said he thought I ought to go with him to a little meeting in a church basement in Catasauqua at noon. I said okay.

We met there, chatted as if nothing had happened, almost like we were old buddies. Somehow, suddenly, I felt like we *were* old buddies.

I was staying with my friend Jim and his girlfriend, Pat. They'd given me a bedroom and lots of good food and made me a sort-of older brother.

They urged hot-fudge sundaes on me every night. Sometimes I ate two. As a result, I was rapidly getting back to my normal 170 pounds. But I couldn't get to sleep at night because of all the sugar in my blood.

Jim was staying sober and we both depended upon Harry Phillips for a lot of advice.

My Datsun, the car I'd thought would fix me back in Tuscon, was repossessed. I'd parked it at Harry's overnight. It was gone in the morning.

That banged-up Datsun was my only way to get around town. I had never, since age 16, gone without a car.

Jim drove me to Philadelphia and the "repo yard" where my car had been taken. I got my personal stuff out of it and on the way back to Allentown told Jim that it hurt. Back in Tucson, I'd hung out with a guy who'd wanted me to help him write a funny book about his experiences repo-ing cars.

I had no car, no job. I saw a lot of my fellow alcoholics, often several times a day. I read a lot from a big book about alcoholic recovery and how it works. And I got hooked on strong coffee.

The days added up, days with Harry or Ed or Jim . . . or another guy named Harry, an insurance man who had two years of sobriety but always seemed to want my advice on things. I found that funny, but it probably was good for what little self-esteem I had left.

I went to Ed for a long talk when I had been dry about 75 days. I explained that I thought I really ought to go back to Washington now, to rescue Lynn from life without Scott. I talked for two straight hours, and Ed barely said a word. But his eyes said he loved me and understood me.

At the end of my two hours of nonstop explaining, I asked Ed: "What do you think? Should I do it?"

The stub of the cigar wiggled slightly, his eyes moist with love or humor—I was never quite sure which.

"Jus' don't fuggin drink."

"Huh?"

"That's my advice. Jus' don't fuggin drink."

I drove back mulling over Ed's advice.

By the time I got to Jim's house I'd decided that Ed probably did not think I should go back to Washington.

Lynn, in fact, was doing well. So were the children. My motives, I realized, were selfish—I missed them terribly, wanted to start making amends to them.

Later, I asked Ed about it. He shrugged and said he had said everything he had to say in that one short sentence he'd repeated.

"Jus' don't fuggin drink, Scott."

Shopping centers had become the new American small town. I developed an affinity for the Whitehall Mall just north of Allentown and within a bus ride from Harry's.

At first I'd just sit there, watching the would-be shoppers.

But then I felt somehow led one day into a bookstore and to the history section. And there in paperback I saw the granite wisdom of Tom Jefferson's face, and intuitively felt I should read the book: "Thomas Jefferson/An Intimate History" by Fawn M. Brodie.

I was intrigued within minutes, and spent many hours sitting in the mall, day after day, reading about a man who amounted to something.

My next talk with Ed was about my income taxes. I told him I was scared the IRS would come after me for late or back tax taxes. I'd had no real income, true, but . . . Was I just being paranoid?

Ed listened and finally grinned and gave me one sentence of advice about my taxes: "Jus' don't fuggin drink."

The room Jim and Pat gave me was down the hall from theirs. They watched television in my room. They were incessantly necking, French-kissing, fondling. It got to me.

One night I told Ed how horny I was getting.

He suggested that I could take care of that problem myself.

I laughed out loud.

"No one has the right to deny you biological release.

"But if what you want is a lot of affection—get a puppy."

"You kidding me, Ed?"

"Nope." The way he said the word had a sort of thump in the throat to it.

"Nope."

"A puppy?"

"You need affection, Scott. Puppies need affection and they're real good at giving it. Get a puppy."

I can't believe it! I need a woman. And this silly old fart wants me to get a goddam puppy! "Tough Love" is one thing, but this is ridiculous! I want a woman!

Ed seemed nonplussed about the whole crisis:

"I know a guy who runs a little pet store. If you want, I'll call him.

"No thanks, Ed."

"And as far as your biological functions are concerned, I'm not going to to tell you to deny yourself—just don't go falling in love now."

Two afternoons later, I got a puppy—a bright, feisty little terrier just three months old.

I named him Rascal II.

I talked with Harry Phillips about my not having a girlfriend, having a puppy instead.

Harry nodded, eyes glistening in humor.

"Ed's got you pegged.

"Left to your devices. Scott, you'd just try a whole string of half-measures, and you'd die. This is life or death, Scott. Getting a girl and 'falling in love' would be dangerous, emotionally.

"I know that death doesn't scare you—but think of your kids! They wouldn't want you to die a hopeless, helpless weak-ass drunk vomiting to death in some scumbag hotel. Would they?"

One Monday night I ran into a guy named Joe who'd gone without a drink for five years—a span I still couldn't comprehend.

Joe was a financial type. He had managed a brokerage firm. I told him about Ed's advice on taxes.

After he finished laughing, Joe said that I had not had enough income to worry about taxes anyhow.

He was right, of course. How could I have worried so, when I didn't have any income anyway?

The next Monday night, I told Joe I thought I'd better start making some money again.

"Why?" He was smiling. "How old are you, Scott?"

"Thirty-seven."

"Look, Scott, why don't you just take six months or a year off—don't work at all—and enjoy getting sober? Be easy on yourself! Life's short. This is a very special time in your life. Just six months 'off' won't hurt you."

The next time I saw Joe, we were standing beside each other in the men's room at St. Catherine's Church on a Tuesday night. He stared at the wall but spoke directly to me: "Go get yourself a copy of the book 'How to Be Your Own Best Friend'. It's helped me a lot—and you need it more than I do."

It was the same almost every night.

In bed about 11:30 or midnight.

Tight band across the chest.
Ohgawd I hate this!
Roll over—maybe that'll relieve it.

Still awake at 12:30.
Still awake at 1.

Why?
Why do I want to drink?
Damn!
Roll over the other way and count backward from 435 this time.

Awake at 2 and 3.
It was usually 3:30 or 4 when I'd get to sleep.
I told Harry Phillips I was worried about it.
"Why? No one ever died from undersleep."

Mean tough s.o.b. goddam sonofa goddam mean bastard-

"I suppose that's true, Harry. Thanks."

One afternoon I explained to Harry that I had to get a job or even a volunteer job somewhere; I was going nuts just doing nothing.

"Scott, don't just do something. Sit there."

Tough, mean sonofabitch. Mean Harry. God-dam . . .

"Thank you, Harry."

I decided in late October that I wouldn't seek work. I'd live on the $41 a week I got from welfare and devote several months to not drinking, one day at a time. Harry and Joe each had five years, and both recommended that I not work.

It felt irresponsible yet liberating.

Besides, how was I going to work when I was only getting two or three hours of sleep at night?

Someone bought me a typewriter.

I don't know who.

It was just there at the front door one day. A big green used typewriter.

That afternoon, I borrowed a car and drove out to the store where it had been purchased. The manager would not tell me anything.

"Anonymous."

I put it on the table in my room at Jim's and thought how I could write letters with it. That was good. Letter-writing would help fill up my days.

Still, I couldn't figure out why someone had done it. I was an editor, not a writer. Maybe it was just someone who didn't understand me.

When I told Harry Phillips about it, he suggested that I not try to find out who'd done it.

Aha!, I thought—Harry did it.

"I know your mind, Scott. You probably think I did it, because I'm telling you not to look into it. That's on the surface, Scott. Look a little deeper. Whoever did it wanted to be anonymous. You should allow them that."

I didn't understand.

Thanksgiving Day, 1977:

We'd stuffed the turkey the night before. In the morning, Jim and I set the table—they were having Jim's mother and some other friends over for the afternoon's feast.

I borrowed a car and drove over to Harry's. There was something I wanted to ask him about. I'd noticed that Jim, who was doing well in his new found sobriety, was taking several 8-hour cold tablets every day.

Harry frowned, then asked details. He said it didn't sound dangerous, yet those capsules did contain something that could alter the metabolism a little, so "let's just keep an eye on it, and if it continues, I will mention it to Jim."

"There's something else, Harry."

"What?"

"I still can't sleep at night. It's been three months!"

"Tough shit, kid."

Jim's mother arrived, then the others, and about 3:30 we all sat down for the traditional turkey dinner.

"Honey," Jim said to Pat, "I don't want you to lift one finger for the rest of the day. Scott and I will do everything."

He turned to the others. "I never had a brother. Now I've got Scott."

His mother added: "And you two really are like brothers!"

Jim asked if I'd like to say a prayer; I suggested the Doxology.

As we ate, my heart welled over.

Was it 1968? Dwight and Helen came. Was that when Don and Laura and Lynn and I were all

so happy? And Dwight and I ate so much
we walked two miles through Chevy Chase afterward,
And my mother's Thanksgivings!
What are my parents doing today?
Do they know I'm okay?

The tears felt hot on my cheeks. I jumped up, fled up the stairs, threw myself on my bed and sobbed.

I wanted to drink.

Of course you want to drink.
That's what alcoholics do—they drink.
Just before they die.

In early December I went to Ed Schmidt about my career. What did he think I should do? Maybe I should go to work right after the first of the year.

It was doubtful that the Morning Call would hire me back. But possibly the afternoon paper, the Chronicle, would. Also, sales jobs were advertised. I could work on commission. I might be good at it. Or I could apply for . . .

"The answers are usually right under your nose, Scott."

"Huh?"

"That's my experience," said the bear. "When you're really searching for an answer about something basic to you, the answer will be right under your nose."

It was too simple, but I nodded and thanked him.

That night I had coffee and pie with a member of Alcoholics Anonymous at a diner and we got into a discussion of why the A.A. program is the most successful in history in treating the disease.

He said it was partly because of the anonymous part.

"What do you mean?"

"People can come in our doors and they never have to identify themselves—we don't even care, frankly, who or what they are. Bank president, judge, ditch-digger—it doesn't matter; we're all just alcoholics trying to help each other.

"But just the hint of any publicity and a lot of us wouldn't ever come in the doors—we'd stay out there, killing ourselves because of our silly pride. And anonymity is more than just a way to protect peoples' identities. It's the spiritual foundation of our program."

It sounded ridiculous. I could understand that it allowed new members to not worry about being seen at an A.A. meeting. But how could this guy call it a spiritual thing? It sounded more like a recruiting tool.

He went on: "We're willing to try, at least, to put our principles before personalities. Sometimes that's tough. Somebody wants to make a speech or make a name for himself—or some woman."

"What do you mean? Don't they want to stay anonymous?"

"Not all of 'em. Hell, some of us get so excited we want the whole world to know that we've found an answer to an incurable disease. But we must be willing to stay anonymous about A.A.

"At the level of press, radio, TV, books, stuff like that, it's important that we not let our egos override our message."

"Let me explain. We have to maintain our anonymity on two levels:

"First in public: We just don't say that we're members of A.A. If we want to say publicly that we're recovering alcoholics, that's a personal option. But A.A. itself is no one personality. It's a body of simple principles that work for us. So no one personality can speak for us or represent us.

"On the second level, within the program itself, and outside too, we have to stay above personalities and stick to what's important: the steps and traditions of the program.

"But the point is that the program works, not that this person or that person got sober or stayed sober, or got drunk—that's what I mean, it's principles, not personalities."

We ordered more coffee.

"Now, you're a writer, Scott . . ."

I stopped him. "No—I'm an editor."

He laughed. "That's right, I forgot. You're an out-of-work editor . . ."

I was learning a strange truth for me:

Attitude follows action.

If I "acted as if" about something and continued to act that way, my attitude about that thing would gradually change.

So I acted as if I did not want to drink. I acted as if I would be okay for another day. I acted as if I was enjoying not working. I acted as if I was healthy.

And I kept noting the "coincidences"—my prayers were being fulfilled, somehow, and I was somehow programming my own reality.

In the first week of January, I sat at the desk in my room on a snowy afternoon and thought about all the jobs *not* open to me.

What was it Ed had said?

Ed had become a giant to me. I'd never been around someone with an uncanny ability to cut through things like Ed could. Not even Harry Phillips, who kept telling me not to worry, some day I'd probably be publisher of a goddam newspaper somewhere in paradise.

What was it?
Something about -
about -
"right under your nose."

"Right under my nose." That was it.

I grinned and turned my eyes toward the tip of my nose.

I closed the left eye and looked with the right. I could see the nose tip. I looked just past it. Just the table and the typewriter.

Crazy old Ed.

I closed the right eye and squinted down at the tip of my nose with the left.

Looked past the nosetip.

The TYPEWRITER!!!!!!!

There was a woman who was a few months behind me in sobriety. Short hair, fine features. And every cell in me said one thing about her: She's very sexy.

She asked one day what I was doing to keep myself busy.

I said I was on the 90th page of my second novel.

Instant sweat popped out on my forehead.

She asked if she could read the first novel.

"I've got to tell you the truth. I didn't write a first novel. I just wanted to . . ."

"Just wanted to what?"

"Wanna go see a movie someday?"

The fact is, I'd been writing almost every afternoon, mostly long pieces of 'fiction' about newspaper people in Washington. The stuff wasn't any good and I knew it. But I had to keep doing it. But it helped me take inventory of myself—which helped me stay sober.

The winter weather brought pictures of Tucson into my mind almost daily. Saguaro cacti and golf and the Catalina mountains and hot sun.

I typed a letter to the headhunting company I'd worked for in Tucson. The letter was straightforward. I was an alcoholic and finally getting sober. I had enjoyed my brief try at headhunting and wanted to get back to Tucson.

I had decided I would not want to work for anyone who didn't know I was alcoholic. If an employer knew that I was alcoholic and trying to stay sober, pride alone might prevent me from trying to sneak a drink on them. Furthermore, I didn't want to work for someone who didn't have some compassion for what I was trying to do.

Jim and I were having sandwiches at the diner. He was talking about business prospects in his sales job.

I interrupted him:

"Jim, I'm having a really wild sensation right now!"

" . . .And these guys are buying-"

"Jim!"

He looked up.

"There's, I don't know, *there's something going on*, Jim. I have knowledge."

"Knowledge?"

"I know something is happening in my life, it's very important in my life, and it's happening a long ways away from here."

"Uhh . . ."

"It's the truth, Jim. I know it is. In fact, I want you to remember that I told you this now."

He went back into his business problems and we finished lunch, then drove home.

There was deep snow everywhere. We found a place to park and were talking about more snow-shoveling as we walked up the front steps of Jim and Pat's home, where I was staying.

The phone inside the house was ringing.

Jim raced to the door, jammed the key into the lock and ran inside.

I knocked my boots on the side of the porch railing, laughing. Jim was always like that—acting as if business was the most urgent thing in his life.

"It's for you." My skin suddenly tingled.

"This'll be it," I told him. "It will be the thing I told you was going on."

The voice on the phone was male.

"Scott, I'm Bob Thorne, in Tucson . . ."

He had bought the Management Recruiters office where I had previously worked. And he had received my letter.

"You had a real good start here before your, ah, problem. If you have the plane fare to get here, I've got a job for you."

I had to pack and leave within a week. I took some clothes, the typewriter and my golf clubs.

My savings account, built with small deposits out of my welfare checks, had $185 in it. The lowest oneway plane fare to Tucson was $183.

How'd this happen?
Damndest thing, these coincidences.
They just keep happening.
And they always seem to coincide with my prayers.

I flew into Cleveland and spent an evening with Ann and Al.

There was no way to tell them what had happened. And when I tried, Ann stopped me: "I don't want to hear it." As much as I wanted understanding and love, I didn't blame her. The story of her little boy was not a pretty one.

The next day, I took a late flight from Cleveland to Dallas, then a midnight flight west to Tucson. A silver-bright moon shone down on the desert. I felt somehow blessed. I didn't know why. But it was as real as the moon.

Tucson
Springtime 1978:

I stayed with Lionel and Artie Brown and the current seven dogs she gave life to in Bear Canyon. He lent me his old Datsun pickup truck and I went to work in Bob Thorne's office. I liked it. The work was fascinating, much like that of a reporter—finding people and getting them to talk.

I called Bob Linder. He said the church was growing rapidly. When I said I was just a few blocks away, he seemed wary but asked me to come over.

Bob Linder the minister and Bob Linder the man had both been through hell with and over me. I didn't blame him if he was leary of letting me back into the leadership of the church I'd helped to start as a drunk.

He greeted me cautiously on the driveway. We shook hands and went out to his back patio, sat down with iced tea and chatted briefly about my year and a half in Allentown.

He interrupted one of my Allentown stories and, leaning forward with a rare earnestness, told me:

"In all my years in the ministry and in life, Scott, I've never seen such evidence of the Grace of God as you are."

Maybe it should have offended me, but I threw back my head and howled in delight. It was true.

"Your face—I've never seen you look healthy before, I guess. You look healthy and natural and relaxed."

"One day at a time, Bob."

"I don't care how you're doing it, keep doing whatever it is. It's got to be the Grace of God!"

After two weeks I rented a scruffy little apartment just north of Speedway Boulevard. The best things about it were the little pool, the fact that it was "mine" and it was just a block from a Wienerschnitzel, where I could get cheap dinners.

I had been sober for seven miraculous months. To stay that way, I prayed a lot, walked a lot, and got to know other sober alcoholics who hung around a "bingo hall" on Pima Street.

But my two greatest sources of strength didn't hang around there at all.

I heard Bill Worthington telling some people about his early days of sobriety. He was wearing a white shirt—it looked like the $50 type from Brooks—and cowboy belt and chino pants and enormous shoes. He was in his 60s, tall and distinguished, yet a touch gangly and boyish.

Bill'd gotten sober when I was 10 years old, and he'd stayed sober ever since. He'd gone to Rice University, spent a year with Texaco in Texas, then nine years with IBM ("sell all day, install all night"). Then he'd gone to work with American Hard Rubber in New York, a success in sales but feeling like hell inside.

He'd gone to his doctor, who'd suggested the problem was booze and had called in a man who had been able to quit drinking.

"I was still functioning, still had a job in New York with American Hard Rubber, and was two years maybe from being put away in an institution or dying."

"Just plain luck. And God.

"After nine months of dryness, I was sent to Saudi Arabia for ten months with Emerson Engineers. I didn't drink."

Bill had gone on to a career consulting on computer systems, and finally retired, although he still owned and oversaw a ranch back East. It specialized in something called

Limousine Cattle, which sounded to me like a rather exotic strain of beef cattle.

At age 60-something, he'd entered the University of Arizona to get his doctorate in computer sciences. At 68, he would be awarded his PhD.

I was hearing a man tell about success-after-alcoholism.

On a Sunday night, after I had spent my day hurting inside—hurting in loneliness memories, I walked up to him and started a conversation. We seemed to hit it off. I asked him if he would be willing to help me stay sober. He said yes, that he was in fact helping a couple of men in Tucson and a guy who'd moved to Florida. I should call him the next day and we'd get together.

I ran into Dodie Gust in a similar fashion. I overheard her talking about staying sober.

Everything about Dodie said intelligence, humor, depth. She'd been sober for eight years, was now about 50, single, happy.

I asked her what she did for a living.

"Oh, I have this crazy newspaper here in town, and I do all sorts of other things. I write, I paint, I . . ."

She'd said all I wanted to hear. My intuition said she'd be a friend for life.

Coincidences . . . I'd needed friends and support, alone and sober in the desert. In a relatively brief time, I had found a man who'd been sober 28 years and a woman who'd been sober eight years and they both had the sort of intelligence and background that I could respect.

Tucson was looking better. I was even starting to make some money. I had not had a drink in eight months.

I returned to the Tanque Verde Lutheran Church, and enjoyed the new building, but declined any suggestion that I get involved in church activities.

God had come to me through other alcoholics. The church had never "gotten me sober." It was crucial that I do exactly what my minister friend, Bob Linder had said: Keep doing what I'd been doing.

Bob Thorne had brought in a bright, chirpy, bearded guy named John McGuinness, from the home offices of Management Recruiters in Cleveland, as a managing partner in our office.

Both took a liking to me—and vice versa. They saw that I had enough cash for groceries or rent. And McGuinness then lent me his blue Scirocco to drive. He also had a BMW and was buying a Jeep. His wife Kathy, who was working for us too, had another car. They both had the rare ability to lend me something without making me feel less-than.

John and Bob sat down with me at the Plush Horse bar downstairs one evening after work. They were having beer and ordering "unlimited Cokes for Scott", which they found funny. We talked business for maybe 45 minutes and then I noticed that Bob was staring at me

"You've really got strength, kid, sitting here while we drink."

John interjected: "We admire it so much."

Where and how do I begin to tell them?

"Well," I began, aware they were both watching and listening intently. "It's not me at all."

"I know, I know," said Bob, winking at John. "It's God."

"Well, yes, damnit, it is." I felt a surge of frustration.

John stepped in. "Well, whatever you're doing, it's working—right?"

"Bob, it's like an old thing I learned about writing."

"Yeah?"

"You can't write about Alaska," I said, "if you haven't been to Alaska. What I'm trying to say is, I know this from my own experience. There is no way that I had the strength to quit drinking, and stay quit."

John leaned forward. "Wait a minute." He was frowning, but his eyes were gleaming. "It's okay for you to give all the credit to someone else, or God or whatever—but it's a fact that you had the strength not to order a drink tonight. It's not God sitting here—you are the one who didn't order the drink."

"You don't understand!"

"Yes I do."

"No! I didn't have what you call 'strength'. I do not have it, alone, now. I was given it—given it like a free gift. And all I did was ask for it. That's all."

John threw his hands up as if I was the one who didn't understand.

Bob turned in his chair, trying to catch the waitress's eye, saying back over his shoulder: "Well, anyway, I hope you get more of that when it comes to making placements!"

We laughed. And I knew right then I would have this same conversation, this difficulty in explaining, for as long as I stayed sober. As long as I was talking with people who had not been through it—or who hadn't been 'to Alaska'—they would not be able to understand.

The office was fun, mostly because of a recruiter named Ray Herring.

Herring was a genius hiding behind the guise of a hillbilly, with a sort of nonchalance that would charm a queen. He had been career Air Force, "retired" after his 20 years, was now in his 40s and having fun making money.

He showed me ways to get names of potential candidates for the jobs I was trying to fill. It was fun, sometimes hilarious.

One Friday night after work, and his first couple of beers, he decided to celebrate by "placin' a little job order with one of those highfalutin' headhunters in the big city." He phoned a firm in Los Angeles, claimed that he was in the furniture-covering business, owned a huge ranch in New Mexico and wanted the recruiter to find him a manager for the ranch—someone who knew ranching and had experiencing raising naugas . . .

He said later the recruiter didn't even get the joke.

Ray taught me how to "ask for the order," how to laugh about people who didn't keep their word, how to deal with my own failures.

He said recruiting was the second-best thing in the world.

Every time he made another statement like that, he announced that he was "serious as a heart attack."

One night I walked from the "bingo hall" on Pima Street to my apartment, marveling at the palms swaying against the brilliant desert sky. "Thank You, Lord, for putting Ray Herring in my life!" I was shouting it.

Ray's the Ed Schmidt of my business life, I thought. Funny that I learn the most from the guys who keep things simple.

Mid-July 1978:

I was sitting at my desk poring over resumes of candidates for a vacancy with a local construction company. I glanced up and saw McGuinness joking with a slender brunette.

I'm going to marry that woman.

I stared, wondering if she was the woman from Cleveland he'd been telling everyone about. Denise de Ville, 21 years old and coming to work for us.

Yes yes. She's perfect. Just look at her!

Two weeks later, I phoned Kathy McGuiness at home and asked if she and John thought it would be out-of-line if I asked Denise to have dinner with me.

"We think it'd be great!," Kathy said. "In fact—we wondered if that would happen."

Denise and I had dinner dates every night for 21 nights.

She was of Italian and French blood, had grown up in the Cleveland area, almost finished work for her degree at a community college there, and had joined M.R. sensing that "something'll happen" in Tucson.

We were 16 years apart. I thought she was just like the women I would have dated when I was her age if I hadn't been married at 18.

We spent evenings after dinner sitting in parks talking about houses and children and family life. I spilled my story to her night after night. She listened, usually just nodding.

And we necked, passionately every chance we got.

Finally, late on a Friday night in mid-August, she suggested that there wasn't enough room on the couch . . .

The following morning, we sat sipping coffee on the carpet in the living room of her tiny one-bedroom apartment. I felt strangely excited and steered the conversation toward our relationship. She agreed that it was special, that we shared the same needs and desires: a family, kids, a nice home.

"So: do you want to get married?"

"Are you asking me to marry you?" We had been dating for just 22 days, she said.

"Yup." I grinned.

Why didn't I feel more drama? Why didn't she?

Her eyes closed for a long moment.

"Well . . . I guess so."

"You do?"

She smiled, nodding.

Two hours later, we sat in the open back seat of a Jeep, headed for lunch with John and Kathy McGuinness. I'd told them: I'd move into Denise's place because it was so much nicer for her, and we'd be married Sept. 28th.

I was 37 and about to celebrate one year of sobriety. Denise was 21 and about to get married and have kids.

She was getting her desire.

I was getting mine, although I couldn't articulate what it was. Not even to myself.

I asked Bob Linder to marry us. He insisted on the "formality" required by the Lutheran church of "premarital counseling." It felt absurd, but I went along with it.

"Do you plan to have children?"

"Right away," I said.

"Don't you think maybe you ought to have some fun first?"

"But-"

"And have you thought about just having fun together—really getting to know each other—before you even get married?"

"Look, Bob: We both know what we want and we want to get married and have children, and that's just the way we both feel."

He sighed, as if he felt helpless.

With perhaps 65 friends on hand, we were married at the Tanque Verde Lutheran Church on Thursday night, Sept. 28, 1978. We spent the night at the Arizona Inn, a gracious old-style hotel near the university campus, and flew the next morning to San Francisco. I'd wanted the honeymoon in Monterey and that sounded just fine to Denise since she'd never been there.

I had no temptation to drink, nor to run. Everything felt just fine.

On Monday, I got tearful when we had to leave the ocean. We flew back to Tucson and were back at work the next morning.

On October 28th, we were making love and a wave of knowledge swept through me. I had no question that it was right.

"Do you feel something extra?" I asked.

"Yes."

"I think we're creating a baby right now."

"Yes." She was smiling, a Madonna serenity.

"Denise! There's someone else here!"

"I know."

I turned and looked over my left shoulder, toward the bathroom. I saw no one.

"Someone, some spirit. It might be—is . . ."

She nodded, her eyes glistening.

"There's someone standing right there and we can't see him!"

"I know, I know."

We talked about it later and agreed that both experiences were real: We were conceiving a child, and that there had been a spirit standing there with us, loving us.

In late November, we confirmed that Denise was one-month pregnant.

We'd married Sept. 28. We'd conceived October 28. We decided that 28 was our lucky number.

McGuinness and I got into a confrontation in January. I didn't like his style of handling some problems in the office. He thought me arrogant and fired me.

I smiled and felt relieved. I told him I wouldn't drink over it, gathered my stuff and my wife, and left.

Within two days McGuinness and I were friendly again. We understood and respected each other. And neither of us would back down.

At home, I knelt in front of the window, looking up the rocky face of the Catalinas.

"Please help me. We're having a baby. You already know that. Please, just take care of us. I put myself in Your hands."

Alan Schoenberg, president of Management Recruiters International in Cleveland, phoned me several days later and suggested that since I'd had a year at Stanford and loved the Bay Area, I should call MR's general manager in San Francisco, Bob Read.

Denise smiled knowingly. Schoenberg must've arranged things, she said.

Several days later I flew to San Francisco. The office was on the 35th floor of the Union Bank building. As I stepped out of the cab I felt the pace of the financial district, the canyons of the city, the excitement of A New Life. This was it, I thought.

I interviewed all day and was hired to recruit in "process engineering and management" under the M.R. manager, Eric Wheel, who reported to Read.

A week later, Denise and I stuffed almost all of our belongings into her old brown Saab, and took two days to drive to San Francisco.

And we were both aware that we'd prayed a lot.

We stayed in a motel while we hunted for an apartment. The third day, we rented a two-bedroom place above a laundromat on Irving Street in the Sunset district.

We had no furniture. And I'd spent our only cash to get the apartment.

We tried the furniture-leasing places in the phone book, even picked out furniture, but they all said my credit was not strong enough.

We decided that we'd just live on the floor and maybe buy a bed out of my first paycheck—except that we'd basically committed those funds to the rent.

Denise was three months pregnant. I couldn't let her live that way, yet saw no way out of it.

We were getting into the elevator, back at our motel after breakfast. In desperation, I thought of the principles that had helped me get sober.

Let go.
Let God.

I closed my eyes and just said in my mind: "Please! I can't handle this. You can. I'll let You do it. Please!"

Back in our room, I glanced at the Yellow Pages, still lying open. I'd phoned every one of the furniture-leasing places. We had no cash. We were stuck. God would have to get pretty inventive.

"Scott? Did you call this one?"

She was right. There was one small listing I had missed.

I called and asked for the credit manager.

"Yeah?"

"You're the credit manager?"

"Yeah."

"I, uh—well, I just moved here from Tucson. My name's Scott Smith and . . .

"Yeah?"

"My wife's pregnant. I have a good job with Management Recruiters at 50 California Street and, I should, uh, should make at least $30,000 in my first year with them."

"Yeah?" It sounded like he was simultaneously running an adding machine, probably not even listening to me.

Let go

I took a deep breath. I'd never done this.

"Well. Here's the thing: I'm an alcoholic. My credit's terrible. But I've been sober more than a year—almost a year and a half."

"Scott Smith huh? Tell me something, kid: Do you hang around with a bunch of alcoholics who aren't drinking anymore?"

"Sure do!"

His voice became warm: "C'mon down here, Scott."
"Huh?"
"My dad was an alcoholic. Some guys like you got him sober and he stayed sober for the last seven years of his life. You got all the furniture you need, pal. Just c'mon down and pick it out."
What a coincidence.

April 1979:
Hollow. A hole in my heart. Tension across my chest.
No matter how well the job went or how good our sex life was, I felt hollow inside. That same old hollow I'd felt in Washington when I'd been drinking.

Why why why why?

In the drinking days, I'd tended to talk out of the side of my mouth whenever close to someone else, so they wouldn't get a heavy dose of the alcohol breath.
Now, however, I not only did *not* have alcohol in me; I'd discovered the joys of Scope mouthwash.
My breath was clean, fresh. And the Scope felt so good on the occasions when I intentionally swallowed it. So warm down deep.

Denise went into labor July 27. It lasted 44 hours.
In a delivery room at Children's Hospital, San Francsico, about 9 p.m. on Saturday July 28, I saw the grayish crown of a child's head emerging. Shocks coursed through my body. I couldn't say anything. The doctor took the baby to a blanket, washed her and handed her to me.
Denise was worn out and elated. I was quiet, just rocking the newborn and feeling Love coming to me, through me. There were no words for it, just 20 minutes of holding my daughter and knowing that just two years earlier I'd been damned near dead.
We named her Jessie Bennett Smith.
I took note of a coincidence:
My father had died at age 28. Denise and I had been married on the 28th of the month (September). The child had been conceived, with a third presence in the room, on the 28th. The child had been born on the 28th. And my sobriety dated to Aug. 28, 1977.

The birth got me wondering. Why was I given this renewed, and new, life? It seemed egotistical to wonder about it, yet I did.

Was there some 'mission' for me? Was I given new life so that I could—what?

It only made sense that each day was a gift, and that there was some purpose to it.

Several days later, there was an abnormally strong earthquake in San Francisco. It was 5.8 on the Richter scale.

The Union Bank building did as it was designed-to-do: it swayed. We were 35 floors up, and desks in the office were starting to slide with the ominous swaying.

This was it! I asked God to help me, said I didn't want to die now, but mentally said good-bye to family and dear little Jessie, who'd just gone home from the hospital a couple of days earlier.

I announced the next week that I wanted to move down to the Peninsula—Silicon Valley—and help open MR's new office in Menlo Park. Eric and Bob said that was perfect; they would want me to manage that office.

Perfect, I thought. Now I would feel better inside.

We rented a three-bedroom house just off El Monte Boulevard in a quiet residential part of Mountain View. It seemed just right.

But something was amiss. No matter how nice the family and house, no matter how well the job went, I still felt hollow.

Why why why why?

11

Sunday, April 20, 1980:

I'd met with some recovering alcoholics in a meeting hall near the community center in Menlo Park, then had swung up through some back streets in the quiet neighborhoods, a "back way" to Route 280, which I would take south toward our home in Mountain View.

The time was about 9 p.m. The car, the weather, the traffic were normal.

Suddenly I felt a chill race up my spine, then back down.

The chills continued. (They lasted for about 15 minutes, I later noted.)

Then, suddenly, I had a strange thought: that my grandfather H.R., who had died in 1970, was in the car with me.

The first thing that struck me about it was the feeling that it was okay, was real, was not at all to be doubted. I looked around inside the car, half expecting to see his spirit sitting there grinning at me. No. I reached out with my right hand, waved it through the space in the back seat of the Pinto, then through the passenger space to my right. Nothing.

The chills were still coursing back and forth in my spine.

"Hello H.R."

I heard a voice replying instantly: "*Now* will you stop worrying about time?"

The inflection and tone were more like he'd sounded in the early 1960s than in the months before his death. I didn't care whether the sound was real in a material sense. It was absolutely real to me.

And I was dumbstruck by the remark. I had always worried about time, and I never told anyone about it. Not about my deep worry. And probably hadn't ever even indicated it to H.R.

On the surface, my mother and others knew that I was perhaps abnormally conscious of hours and days passing. I'd often remark that "48 hours ago we were—" or "just 38 more hours and we'll—". But I'd never told anyone that I had a deep fear that time was robbing us. This was tragic to me. And I had a dread of time because it would bring death, and perhaps oblivion.

H.R. had died nine years and eight months before this February evening. If he was talking to me now, was visiting me, it meant that he had, as he'd expected, lived on. And it meant that I needn't fear death.

His voice again: "Your job will change soon."

I had no idea why that would be true, or why he would say it.

I sensed that his spirit was behind me, and had a sensation of his hand crossing his face, as in the sign of the Trinity.

And he was gone.

The chills stopped several minutes later.

I felt joyous, warmed. And at peace with myself and everything around me.

Yet there was ambivalence: Intuitively I knew the experience was real; intellectually I knew others would question it. My mother, for example, probably would not believe it was real.

When I got home, I sat down at the kitchen table and scribbled notes about the experience. I wanted a record of exactly what I'd "heard," and I sensed it might be the start of something.

I put the notes inside a book, and then I told Denise about the experience.

She seemed unimpressed, saying she didn't doubt it at all. "Lots of times I get the feeling that my grandfather is around me," she said, "but I don't ever tell people about it."

I tried to press the conversation. I wanted to talk about spirits, about death and life after it, about God. Denise said there was a program on TV she wanted to see, and she needed to get some sleep.

It hurt. But it was also the way our marriage seemed to be going. She said I was too serious; I said that she was avoiding discussion of anything important.

I knew I was doing one thing right: Every month I'd send off another $37 to a bank in Arizona—paying off the loan on the Datsun that had been repossessed in '77. Making amends. Part of spiritual progress. I hated it, yet found the process—whether with that bank or an old emotional 'debt'— cleansing.

I was also, quietly and privately, trying to make amends to my first family—Lynn, and Don and Laura.

Denise was wonderful about it, said she understood—even though we were always strapped for money.

But the hollow kept returning.

May 12, 1980:

The emotional pain was a dull,long aching. Something was amiss in the marriage and in the work I did.

Yet everything in my life seemed so good . . .

I tried to talk about it, but it just didn't work. I hoped the whole thing would just go away, whatever it was.

Then came physical pain. It had been stabbing at me for five days now: The cyst on my bottom was the size of a plum and no matter how hard I tried I couldn't break it.

It hurt to sit. It hurt to stand. It hurt to walk. It hurt to lie on my back, on my side, on my stomach.

I wouldn't go to a doctor. It would cost $80 to have it incised. It would still hurt, and besides, doctors had told me that these things were simply "external ulcers," and I did not want to hear about that.

Denise felt, to me, like she was more married to house and daughter than to me. Every time I'd tried to talk about it, I'd gotten nowhere.

It wasn't her "fault," I knew—nor mine. It was just the way things were.

Somewhere deep in me I knew that I felt stuck, with no one who could understand.

About 7 p.m. I drove to the Walgreens drug store on El Camino to see if I could get some drawing salve.

I was limping through the store, and there it was.

It made absolute sense!

A huge pyramid of 16-ounce bottles of Scope mouthwash—18 percent alcohol—on sale.

I grabbed a bottle, found some "Boil-Ease" and went to the cash register.

The register tape jammed and the clerk had to summon the manager to try to fix it.

I knew it was my chance to pray, to avoid what I was about to do. But if I prayed I wouldn't get a chance to drink it, to get out of the pain.

I can pray.
I wouldn't drink it if I'd pray.
Screw it! I want this!
I DESERVE SOME SORT OF CHEMICAL RELIEF.

At 9:45 that night Denise was in the kitchen and I was sitting in my robe on the couch. In my left hand, a glass. Three ice cubes. And the liquid was bright blue-green!

Scope on the rocks.

Oh My God!
What the hell am I doing?
This is insanity.

I dialed a guy who had 20 years of sobriety.

When he answered, I groaned. "Scott here. I uh—you'd better come over.

"Is this Scott?"

"Look, I-"

"What's wrong, Scott?'

"I am sitting here in pain and I am drinking—you'll never believe it—Scope mouthwash."

"You're drinking it?"

"Drinking it. On my third glass, I think. I'm getting high and . . ."

"It's got alcohol in it!"

"That's the point."

"You're drinking Scope mouthwash?"

"Yup. It's on the rocks, 18 percent alcohol."

"I'll be there in 20 minutes. Don't go anywhere."

"Thanks."

I took another swig of Scope.

Absolute
Insanity.

I jumped in the car, raced up to a 7-Eleven store in bathrobe and slippers and bought another bottle of Scope.

Made it home in time.

He was at the door in less than 20 minutes. We went straight to the kitchen, where he ceremoniously poured the

Scope down the drain, just as he might've done a bottle of vodka.

He turned and looked in my eyes.

"Okay: Where's the other one?"

I looked at the floor.

"C'mon, c'mon!—the other bottle!"

I had to laugh. It was ludicrous. He even knew I'd have a second one!

"In the garage."

"Get it."

It went down the drain, and we agreed that he would ride with me to a doctor's office in San Francisco the next morning.

Two days later I sat down and wrote out an inventory of every feeling I'd been going through—every guilt, every desire. And I added the actions I didn't like, the stuff I didn't want anyone to know about. It was a relief to write it all down, even read it aloud to the nighttime sky, but I realized that I would need to talk it through with someone.

And that meant telling someone that my life was not what it appeared—it was, in fact, a long dull ache, a nightmare within sobriety.

But I knew that if I wanted to be sober I had to do it.

About 15 months previously, I had done an "inventory" of my life and problems. Now I had to go through the same process.

It was the old truth about "half measures." Even in the little things they wouldn't do anymore. I had to get rigorously honest about everything, and leave the results to God. And the marriage was going to be No. 1 on my list of issues to ask Him to handle.

I prayed that God would remove my insanity, and told Him that I couldn't remove it myself. Some form of drinking could happen again, and next time it might be so much worse I didn't want to think about it: A long binge, slow awful death.

The recovering alcoholic who had helped me with the Scope agreed to hear my inventory, and the following Monday night I unloaded on him.

My "inventory" seemed catastrophic until I somehow had the objective distance to hear me, to hear, "apart from myself," the things I was telling him. They were little more than annoying details in a seemingly ordinary life—mostly about the marriage and my frustrations. They just didn't feel as "big" to me now.

But I was an alcoholic and I'd been holding them in. And obviously I had filled with pain to a point of spiritual caving-in: That moment at the cash register when I'd thought 'screw it' . . .

June 8, 1980:

There it was again. A little book I read every morning had that June 8 message again:

"Your life has been given to you mainly for the purpose of training your soul." I knew intuitively it was right. But I could not understand or explain it.

Within two weeks, I'd told every sober alcoholic I knew exactly what had happened to me.

It became funny, and a few people started calling me Scope Smith. It was a useful reminder.

Not one of them criticized me or seemed judgemental. They understood.

Telling them instilled something in me—a feeling that I'd be okay if I'd be open and honest and pray a lot.

Those guys in Pennsylvania had been right all along: Half measures would not work.

I felt that the world was coming into focus. I'd never seen it quite this way, before.

As I looked back, I could see that no one else had ever been "the problem"—I had been the problem.

Lynn had finally remarried—it appeared to be a good marriage—and had started a title insurance firm. I felt genuinely pleased for her, and tried to make amends.

Don had landed a good job with a good company and was making steady progress as a manager with it. I tried to make amends to him. Lynn had hired our daughter Laura, who'd always been sharp with numbers. And now Laura seemed to be headed straight ahead with a solid career, and a good relationship with a young man who was apparently "serious" about her.

Making amends became a test of my patience. There was just no way that a quick "I'm sorry" would ever make restitution for the emotional havoc I had caused in their lives. I would have to make the amends slowly, over time, ever mindful that if I stayed sober I could help them when the call came. The first steps, I knew, would involve simple things like phone calls and birthday presents and the simplicity of just "being there," loving them.

June 1980:

It was 8:10 a.m. and unless I hurried, I wouldn't be the first person in the office, and I took pride being a manager who was usually the first to arrive.

I took a last swig of the coffee, grabbed my file folders, started out the door.

It happened just as I crossed the threshhold:

A little boy's face. Brown eyes, brown hair, right before my eyes. He was staring at me.

"Denise!"

She came to the foyer, hair still wet from the shower, coffee cup in hand.

"This is very strange! I'm . . .it's gone."

"What?" She had a questioning yet knowing look in her eyes.

"We're going to have a little boy."

"I know."

"I just saw him! Not in person, but a face inside my forehead."

She showed no shock at all.

"I saw him, Denise! Right in front of me. He's got brown hair and I think—this is strange—I think he was sort of looking at his new daddy."

Denise just nodded, smiling.

As I drove toward Menlo Park, I started singing a song I had never sung to myself: "Prepare Ye the Way of the Lord," from Godspell.

I did not allow myself to wonder if the marriage was holding up well enough to bear another child.

(In August, two months later, Denise confirmed that she was pregnant. The child had been conceived in June. I found it difficult to believe what had happened that morning in June. I'd never heard of such a thing. Denise said she never doubted that the experience was real. When I asked why, she said she didn't know why.)

Worried about my salary, I opened a conversation with a friend, Ewing Philbin, about a 50/50 partnership in a recruiting business.

July 1, 1980:

I'd bought the book—very quietly—one week earlier, on the suggestion of a recovering alcoholic who said it helped change his attitudes. "The Power of Positive Thinking," by Norman Vincent Peale.

I'd heard so many of my more intellectual friends scoff at it that I was surprised this man had recommended it—he'd gone to Yale and read gray spiritual treatises. I had always assumed that it was "in" to look down the nose at Peale.

Yet I had strange feeling that somehow I was "supposed" to read it, and that my friend had been somehow "guided" or "led" to recommend it to me.

I sat down on our patio and opened it. Several hours passed before I could stop reading or thinking about what Peale said.

Denise said I was boring her. How about taking Jessie to the park?

On July 3, I spoke with my mother by phone and told her what I was reading, although with some trepidation—I figured she'd be likely to scoff at Peale's "simplistic, rose-colored thinking."

She was silent for a moment, and then said with a rare softness:

"Your grandfather H.R. loved Peale so much . . . That's interesting."

I hadn't told her about H.R.'s apparent "visit" in my car April 20.

July 4, 1980:

I got up at 5:15, made coffee, took a shower and drove to the public course at Fairway Glen in north San Jose.

The fog was heavy and there were only five or six cars in the parking lot. Inside, several older men were drinking coffee, probably waiting for the fog to lift or the dawnlight to turn to bright morning. I paid my greens fee and started playing alone.

I played quickly and well, feeling peaceful and healthy. I didn't have to wait on anyone, I could study my shots, even use a second ball on the more interesting shots.

I hit a strong, straight approach shot to the sixth green, dim in the fog—about 220 yards—and was walking up the fairway. I could see that my ball was on the green and noted to myself that I should use that 2 iron more often.

I felt a chill.

H.R.'s at the green waiting for me.

Chills coursed through me. The same feeling as that night in April, I thought.

I walked along, trying to memorize the moment. The fog was lifting. The air was heavy. The time was about 7:35. The green was wet. Something way down deep inside me felt bemused.

As I put my bag down and took out my putter—I would have a 15-foot putt for par—I got a happy, wonderful "hello Scott!"

"Hi—I knew you were here."

"Do you want to ask me anything?"

"What should I do?"

"You're on the right path now."

It was H.R.'s voice, and very real. But I wondered if I was hallucinating.

"Scott, you doubt too much."

"So that *was* you in April?"

"Ask anything you want, but hurry."

"Should I leave Management Recruiters and start a company with Ewing?"

"You'll be a better man for it."

He was gone.

I took no time at all with the putt. And I sank it, to my surprise. I had that same warmth and peacefulness I'd felt April 20.

The chills dissipated about the time I teed off on No. 7, wishing he were still there. I had so many more questions! Especially about wherever he was.

I felt no doubt at all that it was real, that he had been there, that his advice meant I should break away from M.R. and start a recruiting firm with Ewing Philbin.

Later in the day, I read more of Peale, then phoned Ewing.

As July 1980 ended, I closed out my work with Management Recruiters. Bob Read was marvelous about it, telling me that if my partnership with Ewing Philbin wasn't what I hoped it would be, "don't have too much pride to call me—we'd want you back."

Ewing and I went to work as Smith & Philbin.

We did all right for a start-up, but by late December I was slowly running out of money and felt I had to make a change. Denise was pregnant and we were going broke. I remembered H.R.'s "advice"—I'd be a better man for the experience. It cut with a razor's irony: I had needed this experience.

I did go back to Bob Read, and by the spring of 1981 Bob had broken away from the M.R. corporate structure, bought the Menlo Park office as a franchise and hired me as manager. It took off like a rocket.

As time went along, several guys in the Palo Alto and Mountain View area asked me to help them stay sober.

One, Jerry, was a winner, one of the rare ones. A kid named Greg lasted two weeks and disappeared. A bright, sweet man named Steve lasted several months, then started drinking again, and drifted away.

Another Steve got drunk. I took Jerry with me and we pushed on into Steve's rat-hole apartment late one night, scooped him up and drove him to Valley Medical Center in San Jose. He was later transferred to a halfway house and eventually I ran into him; he had two years of sobriety.

I was discovering a paradox: Whenever I tried to help another alcoholic, I was the one who got the most benefit. If I put help out there, I got help back, whether the "subject" drank or stayed dry.

January 1981:

My son Don flew in to visit for a few days. We golfed, walked, watched whales, talked—a young man and his father finally starting to know each other.

Over hot dogs at a picnic table near the Pacific Grove golf course, I tried to tell him that "my recovery proves to me, and to anyone, that God loves me unconditionally, and that life is positive and I'd better have positive attitudes, because they work, Don, they really work."

That's okay for you to believe, Dad. You have to, uh, believe in something, I know.

"But there is no God, and you should know, with your education, that the universe was created at random chance by the accidental collision of cosmic chemicals."

I changed the subject. Time would handle this—and God would, I thought.

March 17, 1981:

Denise was in pain but efficient. The doctor was cool. I stood at the foot of the bed as the small gray crown of the head began to appear.

I was amazed at my own calmness, as if I'd known in advance exactly what would happen: Our son would be delivered smoothly at Stanford Hospital and everything would go beautifully.

And there he was. Huntley Raymond Smith, red, screaming and healthy.

Denise had graciously gone along with my idea for his name: It combined my grandfather H.R. (he was named Herman Raymond but he hated the Herman part) and my favorite cousin/good friend, Huntley Bennett. And it combined both sides of my own heritage—the Smith family from the East Coast, and my maternal side, the Bennett and Huntley families from northern Ohio.

I was healthy. I wanted to make sure, though. I had two young children.

A very thorough internist did the physical exam over several hours. I told him I wished my reporters back in Washington had asked as many questions.

Finally he shook his head with a grin: "I'd expected to see damage, then find out how bad the damage was, and treat you if necessary.

"There's no damage?"

"It's amazing."

We talked about recovery from "acute chronic alcoholism", and I told him about the coincidences I'd been experiencing since the summer of '77—the things that seemed to happen in direct response to whatever I'd prayed. He nodded with a smile.

"Can I ask you a question before I leave?"

"Of course."

"That little spot in my eye that I asked you about, the one I've had ever since I saw it on an airplane trip about 1970—was it caused by drinking?"

"Oh I doubt it—it's just a very routine thing that people get." I later decided that my subconscious apparently had seized upon the "spot" to warn me of my problem.

As the new M.R. office got rolling, Bob Read said he wanted to take out key-manager insurance on me—$1 million worth.

A longtime Aetna guy came to see us. I told him everything about my medical history. He asked a series of detailed questions about my efforts to maintain sobriety. Then Aetna had me take two blood tests.

Several weeks later, the Aetna man came back and explained to us that Aetna could not give us the lowest-low premium on a million dollars of insurance on Scott Smith—because Scott smoked.

I thought I'd die laughing.

The evening television news brought news that the Washington Star had died. There on the network I saw Mary McGrory and Jerry O'Leary and the old newsroom and the building.

I can't handle this.

I turned the T.V. off, changed my mind, switched it back on but to a different network. Two minutes later, it did its own "Washington Star dies" story.

I'm sober.
That's all that matters.
The Star 'died' in my life long ago.

I had a wife, daughter and son now, all given to me in my sobriety. We were living in a good house in a wondrous area of the world, and I was making a livable wage with the career issue seemingly decided. I was healthy and there was this string of coincidences trailing along behind my prayers . . .

But why did I still feel so hollow inside?

Why why why why?
oh damnit why?

12

August 5, 1981:

As I awakened, I felt unusually eager to get going. It was a Wednesday and my job managing the new M.R. office in Menlo Park was going well. I enjoyed both headhunting and managing. I didn't miss newspapering and felt thankful to have a job that I enjoyed.

I reviewed the day ahead: I was going to have lunch with Ginny Dean. I'd known Ginny maybe 10 months, but only in safe situations that carried no acknowledgement of any other feelings. I did know she was about 26, single, brilliant, intuitive. And a recovering alcoholic.

I'd run into her in Palo Alto the preceding week. We'd gravitated toward each other, then stood talking—first about trivia, and eventually about the lack of romance in her life. I'd stayed cool, trying not to show any particular interest.

When she had told me she lived in Menlo Park and wasn't working, I'd said my office was around the corner, near Draegers' supermarket. She had said we ought to get together sometime for lunch. I'd given her my business card, told her to feel free to call me. She called two days later and suggested lunch.

The Wednesday morning went quickly. I left the office about 11:55, drove the three blocks and found her place: A tiny one-bedroom apartment, bookish, cluttered and pleasant, seemingly too 'normal' for a woman of class, money and godawful problems.

She was ready and, I thought, talking too much and too fast—about nothing. We left quickly.

I drove to an unpainted little restaurant in the redwoods where we'd feel at ease, a place known for its great hamburgers and greasy-wonderful fries.

It took time for my senses to focus on what Ginny was saying, rather than on her hair, golden to the small of her back, and my sense of truth in those eyes.

". . . Mom lives with this man she met while she was still with Dad." She toyed with her cigarette. How come I was glad she smoked?

"Gawd! I shouldn't say 'lives with'—they're married! Gawd I talk like . . ."

Something reminded me of something.

"Dad works in San Francisco, very handsome, not very open, real straight." Her eyes bore into me. "He still thinks I'll be something. I was going into the law, but . . .

"All through my childhood, I just couldn't live up to my potential, and certainly not up to . . ."

I broke in: "Yeah. One of my problems has always been this damned 'potential' they say I've got. My mother's a leryer and she always . . ."

"Your mom's a leryer?" Her eyes were smiling now.

"Well, a lawyer. I don't know why I need to joke about it. She was a judge before she was a lawyer."

I didn't have to wait. Her laughter sounded genuine.

"Anyway, Ginny, did you go to law school?"

"No. I worked as a paralegal for a while, but I was drinking and it wasn't going to work for me. I was a mess, that's what."

I was staring at the hollow in her throat. The high forehead, straight nose, deep eyes—and now this marvelous hollow in the throat. The single guys have it made, I thought.

"How long have you been in the personnel business," she asked.

"Headhunting, not personnel. Since I had about seven months of not drinking—since March 1978. What we do is called headhunting because companies pay us to find certain types of people for them, usually in management or in some discipline like, say, chemistry or software.

"I started down in Tucson—there's a real miracle in that part—and was transferred to San Francisco maybe 10 months later. I'm an ocean person, and I loved the Pacific and had to get back here."

She was honestly interested.

"I'd been at Stanford on a fellowship for a year, 1970, on a leave of absence from the Washington Star. I'd been under a contract, literally, that uh, forced me to go back after my fellowship. They knew what they were doing, making me sign that. Otherwise I might have quit and stayed out here then.

"Anyway . . . I made it a sort of life commitment, a life-goal, to get back out here and really live here someday."

"How big was your job there, anyway?"

"Where?

"At the Star."

"The Star, when I got there, was the biggest, best paper in Washington. The Post was coming on strong, but the Star was the paper with integrity.

"For several years, I sort of ran the day-to-day stuff on the national staff—White House, politics, Congress, the Vietnam war, assassinations, the space shots. Quite a job. Competed day to day with the Post, the New York Times, the Wall Street Journal, the networks, the wire services. I loved it, yet-

"Anyway, at the end I was metropolitan editor, sort of a super city editor job."

She was flowing into my eyes. I couldn't quite tell if she was listening or just absorbing me, or both.

I was feeling *equal*. I'd never felt quite this way.

"Ever see that Ed Asner thing on TV? That was like my job as metropolitan editor." She wasn't impressed.

"But the jig was up by '73—they'd spotted my behavior; they knew."

She nodded.

We ordered cheeseburgers and fries. I was forty-seven thousand million miles from the office, and my wife, and . . .

The hollow in her throat was about a third of an inch deep, just the size of the tip of my tongue. What the hell was I doing, thinking like that? Ginny and I had a spiritual and intellectual relationship. And I was married, with a devoted wife and two little children!

I'd like to waggle my tongue in there 'til she giggles, then slowly slide it upward.

"So, Scott." I could feel that she wanted to get my background scrolled across her memory so we could get on with something else. Oh geezuz, had she read my mind?

"You seem to understand about a family that expected too much," she said.

I nodded. "Maybe you'll know what I mean here: My family didn't give much physical love—hugs, touching, stuff like that. They gave me strokes for achieving.

"So that's why I started achieving and kept on achieving and doing well, but never quite . . . Much later, I really understood the title of John Dean's book, 'Blind Ambition' ".

She was grinning, nodding: "And that explains so much emphasis on your job. To get love."

Her smile had a turn to it now. "And not just real spiritual family love—you've lacked physical love." The eyes were knowing, warm. "So you were this big success-type in Washington, D.C., so early in life. And all that's supposed to have changed now."

I sensed what was coming, and hid behind my cheeseburger.

"But I mean, my gawd, you just work all the time, don't you?"

"You mean now?"

"Yes. You—it seems to me that you just work all the time and—when do you have time for your wife? Is her name Carol?"

"No, It's Denise."

"Denise. Okay. So when do you have time for her?"

This was getting too awkward. And now she was asking about the basic problem I wasn't going to discuss with any female.

"I . . ."

"Does Denise give you the physi . . ."

"I . . .

She stopped chewing, looking at me with wide, deep eyes that said it was okay.

"Well, I play golf, too. I love it. I get out there on the Palo Alto Municipal and for five hours I don't even think about business problems or my life at home. Do you play golf?"

"Oh gawd no. Daddy'd like it if I did, I suppose. But you're trying to change the subject, and I want to know . . ."

"Know what, Ginny?"

"You know damned well what."

"Great cheeseburger, isn't it?. And the fries . . ." I hoped my eyes conveyed some sparkle, some humor about a topic that terrified me. I knew it was okay, knew she was with me, not cross-examining me.

"No." She wore a wry half-grin, a knowing, it's-okay-Scott look. "I'm not letting you do that." I felt warm, secure. I shrugged and she leaned forward, the hollow disappearing behind the strong, squarish chin.

I ate for a moment, hoping my mind would break through the confusing feelings—here was a woman who was almost my mirror, but I had a wife, and children, and . . .

"Look, Ginny. I know I give people this image that I've got it all together, but . . ."

"I knew you didn't."

"You did?"

"Sure." She nodded. "Go on—tell me! Who do—no this isn't my business—yes it is—so who do you talk with, I mean really talk with?"

"No one, I guess. My friend Bill, but he doesn't want to hear anything about any problems with . . ." I fell silent.

Her voice went soft.

"Just say it, Scott."

"Say what?"

"Stop detouring, you jerk!"

We both grinned.

"Just say whatever you need, deep down, to say—maybe not so much need to say to me, per se, but need to tell anyone, just tell them out loud. You can't just stuff this!"

"Okay, okay!" I bit into the cheeseburger, wondered whether I'd be able to see her again soon.

She knew it. She
put her hand in mine, and yes
she knew it

"There's this song running through my . . ."

"You're evading, Scott Smith! You're—I've already told you more about me than I . . ."

"Don't you want to know what song?

"No. No, I don't. I want you to answer."

"Denise is a wonderful woman and . . ."

"This is your second marriage, right?"

Sometimes this felt like the sickest thing I could ever tell anyone about me. Ginny's expression didn't even change!

"During the time that I was so very sick, after my first marriage had broken up, I—I drank more than a bottle of Tanquerey gin one day to have the nerve to—gawd this is embarrassing to me—I, well, I married a woman back then who was sort of my drinking partner and nurse. It wasn't really a marriage—I mean, I don't think of it today as having been a marriage at all—and it broke up very quickly."

Ginny shook her head impatiently. "So what about Denise? I don't care about the stuff when you were drinking—at least not that way. What about Denise—you okay with her?"

> *I can't. It feels too ungrateful. Oh God. Denise is at home in our nice house with Jessie and Huntley, wonderful wonderful little Jessie and Huntley, and Denise's probably ironing my shirts and I'm with this woman at lunch and I can say almost anything to her—the kind of things that really matter to me, that Denise doesn't want to discuss—and I was about to talk about how Denise and I don't really communicate, how alone I feel almost all the time. No, no—it just isn't fair to Denise, to tell this beautiful bright woman all the things that I should be saying to Denise—except that that's exactly the problem. Geezus, what's happened to me?*

I felt a tightening inside my chest, the same feeling I used to drink to get rid of. But these days I knew I didn't need to drink over it. Was this what caused it—holding my feelings in?

"Look, Ginny: It just feels too damned selfish to . . ."

"To live your life honestly?"

"To say how I feel when . . ."

"It feels too selfish to just be yourself, doesn't it? Feels too selfish if you start to get really straight with someone?"

Oh damn her! I marveled at how precisely she'd shot through the complicated parts and hit the truth. She could do that. "Just go ahead and say what you feel, Scott. You're sitting there judging yourself like you've got some alcoholic jury in your head—just like me. That's it, you're just like me. Except—well, I may not be as healthy or long-time sober as you are, but by God I always go ahead and say what I . . . of course, sometimes it gets me in a lot of trouble.

"Maybe that's what you're afraid of—that I would repeat it. No, no Scott—this is just between us. Now, are we going to be real, or you going to let this slide past, la de da, like you've got everything together and you're the all-American wonderful guy who came up from the absolute bottom and now loves his wife—who he always will say is absolutely perfectly wonderful—and loves his family and—the great martyr, that's what you're doing. You're doing the . . ."

"You're right. You're right."

I let my shoulders down, sat back, looked at this woman who, suddenly,

> *So suddenly, she was making it feel like the truth was okay, not a nightmare. Not a nightmare? No, that feels so wrong to call it a nightmare. My God, I've got this great house and I have a good job now and I prayed, oh Lord how I prayed!, to have this wife and this daughter and son now and—it feels like I'm kicking God in the balls to say the truth like this, but—*

"Just talk to me, Scott."

The waitress came with the check. I made a production out of extracting the wallet from the hip pocket, pulling out a ten, calculating a tip. I wondered if Ginny noticed that I didn't have any credit cards.

"I want to see you, Ginny." The male firmness in my voice surprised me. "This has been—well, just wonderful."

"You bastard! You're on the spot and you—oh, I shouldn't blame you. You've done a helluva lot and I really respect you for it. Really, Scott." Her eyes bore into mine. "Really. Do you know that?"

"Know what?"

"That I really respect you?"

"Well, no, I don't know—or well, I guess I sense that you like—that we have a lot in common, beyond alcohol."

"So you can feel open with me. I am not here to hurt you."

She said it softly, yet as if reading from a Tablet. She had me. I knew it, she knew it.

I got up, pushed my chair back, saw, really saw, into those deep, knowing eyes. And again that hollow in her throat. Was it pulsing?

"When?"

"Whenever's good for you—you're the one with the job and the marriage and the golf and all that."

Now I felt dirty again—almost dirty, almost dishonest—to have a wife at home. Oh damn.

"C'mon. We can't just stand here in the middle of a restaurant trying to decide this."

We both laughed, and moved with unspoken relief toward the door.

The door, the door. It gave me a chance, finally, to touch her. I held the door open with my right hand, looked outside and ever so smoothly reached for her elbow with my left.

I touched some woman's left breast. Smack on. There were three ladies leaving their Woodside luncheon in their just right Levis, going back to their just right Woodside homes and they'd somehow gotten in front of Ginny. But the woman whose breast—firm, no bra—I had just poked, she didn't seem to notice. That's weird, I thought. It felt more like a tennis ball than a breast.

Ginny caught up with me at the car.

I got in and started the car and pulled out into the road. Neither of us said a word. Were we sad that lunch was over?

Back up Woodside Road and then a right onto Whiskey Hill Road. There were horses on the golden summertime hillside to our left, lazy and comfortable and natural. She broke the silence.

"That was a good cheeseburger. How'd you find that place? I mean, my Gawd, it doesn't have bathrooms, and that's where you decide to take me for my big lunchdate I'd told Maggie would be my . . ."

I glanced quickly at her. Her voice stopped and she glanced back, a silly smile.

Hadn't known there were women like this,
women I could share my emotions with.

There was another long pause. I broke it as we crossed an overpass above Route 280.

"I want to see you."

"In time." Her voice had gone soft again.

September 1981:

I went in-search-of . . .

I didn't know what it was I was in search of, yet it felt natural and somehow similar to how I'd felt most of my life.

My life had been "searching" and I couldn't explain it to me or anyone else.

I was just driving around, stopping in bookstores, window-shopping. Tower Records at El Camino and San Antonio at the southern edge of Palo Alto brought one answer.

I'd casually wandered into a little room they'd set aside for posters. And there it was: Earthrise.

I didn't care if it was just a $4.95 poster, part of the pop culture, home to the druggies. That NASA photo of the Earth, seen from orbit 65 miles above the moon, spoke to the inner me. And I felt grateful not only that I felt it, but that even the stoned hippies apparently felt the same great truth.

Something's changing on this Earth.

I bought the poster and a frame and took them home.

The next day, I hung it on the wall across from my office desk. It was behind visitors: it could remind me that no matter how sticky or stupid business got, there were greater truths in my life. I was an organism and a spirit, walking and moving and growing on that wondrous blue and white sphere hanging so miraculously in space.

I knew that no matter where I worked in the future, I'd want my Earthrise near me, reminding me.

Or was it prodding me?

If so, to what?

I didn't know. And knew I didn't know.

Ginny and I had dinner one night in Palo Alto, and a week later went to a Stanford football game together.

I didn't tell Denise who I was going with. "Just another recovering alcoholic." I was deeply confused over just what Ginny and I were—lovers? brothers? friends? All of them?

December 1981:

There was nothing I could do for Ginny.

I'd parked the Fiat in the covered lot, entered the mall through Macy's, checked the sale items in the men's department, gone out the mall side, turned right, wandered to the end, checked the mens wear at Emporium, then at Nordstrom's. I'd looked at desk items at a leather goods store, at posters in a pop gallery, at soaps in a store that smelled like perfume.

Just nothing.

I sat down on a bench and smoked another cigarette.

Nothing.

Ginny has gotten drunk.
My heart has gone somewhere.

On the surface, my life was fine. The family and the job went up and down but just fine, thank you; just fine.

I couldn't feel the job now. I couldn't feel Denise now. I could get enthused about dear bright Jessie and Huntley, and I could still get enthused about God and spiritual matters. But the stuff of every day was a dim, dull blur.

Ginny has gotten drunk. Ohgawd!

The anger in me had nowhere to go. I wasn't mad at anybody, including Ginny.

So this is how an alcoholic's spouse or family feels.

My anger was at the very disease for which I felt gratitude. If I wasn't an alcoholic, I wouldn't have gotten to my knees, where I belonged.

But if Ginny wasn't an alcoholic . . .
Damn damn damn!
She's a true best friend. And now she's drunk!

I realized that this was the fourth night in eight days that I had come to this shopping center—and just wandered. I had bought nothing except some coffee. I'd spent the other nights with recovering alcoholics. I had no interest in sitting around the house with the television.

In fact, I thought, I've been doing this for months. For what? I knew that I did not know what I wanted, or needed.

Ginny had been on and off for several weeks now. I'd done everything I could—listened, talked, taken her for help, ignored her, gotten angry, prayed and prayed. Nothing worked.

Nothing.

Crying. That's what I'm doing. I'm crying inside.

I stood up, sighing. I'd go home, enjoy the children and do my job.

March 1982:

It was a strange phrase, "out of body" experiences.

I was intrigued. I'd heard of them, and now encountered a magazine piece about them. The nub of it seemed so incredibly significant that I couldn't see why society shunned investigation or discussion of "OOB" reports.

If a human being, lying in bed fully awake and conscious, could "float" up out of the body, could see or hear or sense things and people in other places . . . It was proof of the existence of the soul. That would be proof that we do live past "death."

What was wrong with this society that out-of-body experiences weren't a focus of major federal research, weren't front-page headlines?

I had not had the experience. But now there were indications that "it" could be induced.

I was fascinated, but did nothing about it.

July 1982:

Some of Ginny's friends and some of mine were shooting hostile glances at me when I'd run into them. Apparently they felt that I had led Ginny back into the bottle.

It was unfair, but there wasn't anything I could do about it. Slowly, over the months, I started to see that their reactions gave me a chance to try turning the other cheek. And as soon as I did that, my resentments went away.

Something told me it was a good lesson for business life, too.

I was sitting up in bed, lights on, smoking a cigarette. The house was quiet.

Suddenly I saw something:

Three figures playing somewhere, a place I'd never seen.

The first was H.R. He was much younger than I'd ever seen him, maybe 45, and wearing a cast on his leg. His hair was darker!—I'd never seen him like this! The second one was wearing a hat and a coat and had his back to me. They were laughing and playing catch with a football.

There was a third figure, dimly to my right, about 5-10, wearing a raincoat. A man. He looked familiar, even from the back.

I had a sense that I was seeing this in Real Time—in some other dimension. And I sensed that the second figure was my father, Don Smith, who died in 1942.

They were so happy!

Was that third figure somehow me?

The image lasted about a minute. I felt calm yet fascinated. Intellectually, I assumed it was a scene from memory.

Later I called Ann with a question. No, I had never seen H.R. playing football, nor at age 45.

I had no idea why I suddenly wanted to buy a house near the ocean. We had to get out of a lease arrangement in San Carlos and meet the requirements for a loan. It would take some sort of a miracle to satisfy all the five parties involved. On a Sunday afternoon, I got in bed to take a nap, and prayed about it.

When I awakened, I made some coffee, sat on the deck and looked out at the distant bay. Suddenly I thought of a complicated financial arrangement which would satisfy all five parties. It worked.

The deal was simply too sophisticated financially for me to have thought it up alone. I knew that.

Coincidences. No matter what they were or how they happened, I could only experience them if I stayed sober.

A week later, I was sitting upright in bed about 10 p.m., smoking a cigarette. Denise was asleep at my side. The light was on.

I closed my eyes and felt my shoulders relax.

Suddenly I was floating. I saw a bright red two-story barn. I was floating at the level of the peak of the gable roof. I could see every detail.

Out of body!!

I was instantly back in bed. My mind raced with possibilities and improbabilities. Would I ever know whether I'd been "out there"?

Two months later, we moved into a modern four-bedroom house near the ocean. Denise and I celebrated; we'd been married four years on the day we signed the papers to close the deal.

I thought the new house would change the marriage.

Denise got sick and had to stay in bed for days. There were two kids and I was running an office of headhunters, managing the house, staying sober. It was too much.

On a Thursday night, I pulled the car to the side of the road, lowered my head, closed my eyes: "Please!—Please help me to slow down!"

The next Sunday morning at 9:15, I was standing on the deck, not moving my body but yelling at the dog.

I heard a loud crack, like a rifle shot.

I was suddenly falling.

Before my body hit the deck, I knew the truth:

> *The prayer! My ankle just broke! I'll have to slow down.*

I was laughing immediately.

Then the pain took over. Denise, who had recovered from her illness, drove me to a hospital to get my ankle put in a cast.

The X rays showed a thin crack—just enough, the doctor said, to require a cast for three or four weeks. He said, literally, that I would have to slow down. I said I understood.

I kept running into a guy who would talk for 15 or 20 minutes straight about absolutely nothing—the price of the draperies his wife was considering for her mother's house in the Midwest, for example.

One night I stopped my car at the library and said a simple prayer aloud and from the heart.

"Dear God, please help me gain tolerance."

Two nights later, I was at the hospital to see some of my recovering alcoholic friends. A short, bald man with an Okie drawl yelled out to me.

"Scott!—Hey Scott! Will you work with me? Please."

"I don't know. I don't know you."

"I'm gay!"

"I'm not." I responded.

"I know," he yelled. "That's what I need—someone who's not."

My prayer, I thought. I'd asked for tolerance, and in the last several years I hadn't felt very tolerant of homosexuals.

"Okay."

We agreed to have coffee the next Saturday.

Dick Holland and his mate, Corky, had just moved to northern California from Omaha. Dick, in his late 40s, had been sober about six months.

They'd been living in the smallest house trailer I'd ever seen. It amazed me that Dick had been able to stay sober at all under those conditions. Especially when I saw that Dick's friends had left a quart of bourbon on the driver's seat.

We went to a pancake place near their trailer park and drank coffee.

Dick explained how he and Corky had fallen into their good fortune—yes, he said, good fortune.

They'd been in trouble, he said, financially, professionally and "sort of spiritually" back in Omaha. They'd run a storefront that sold vitamins and novelties in one of the city's less desirable areas.

Dick, who had a college education and a quick mind, had gotten so sick with his drinking—a case of beer a day plus whatever else he slid into—that he had finally asked for help.

After several months, they'd run into someone who was selling franchises for a house-cleaning service. Dick and Corky took their $25,000 in savings and bought franchise rights to an area in San Mateo County, just south of San Francisco.

I interrupted. "Dick, I just don't know how you can stay sober, living in that tiny little space with people drinking all around you and bottles everywhere. And you're under the pressure of getting a business started."

"Isn't God beautiful?" His smiling round face was full of joy. "We live right by the sea—me, an Okie, just a dingy, gets to live here by the Pacific Ocean, and we have our business. I've never had it so good.

"I went to a diocesan seminary in Little Rock, for four years and—can you imagine this?—I was in charge of the wine cellar? I helped start a pizza thing that's now one of the big national chains. Just a dingy like me!"

He rattled on. I nodded to the waitress that yes we'd take more coffee, and then I leaned back and tried to get a handle on this happy, grateful "Okie boy" I'd agreed to help.

This guy's got it.
He's positive about everything.
He'll stay sober.
He'll probably be a millionaire, too.

I'd prayed for tolerance and Dick had shown up. Somehow I sensed he was a blessing. And, I noted, I didn't give a damn that he was homosexual.

Coincidences.

BEGINNING OF THE BEGINNINGS

13

Tuesday, March 1, 1983:

We lived near sea level, a quarter-mile from the surf line. My office in Menlo Park also was near sea level, along the flatlands bordering San Francisco Bay. To get to work and back home, I had to cross a mountain ridge via Route 92.

That's where it happened. On Route 92.

The morning commute up the mountain had become symbolic to me: I felt as if I had to "pull" myself over an emotional mountain these mornings of 1983 before I could be an effective, upbeat manager of a group of headhunters whose work was naturally discouraging.

On this Tuesday morning I was sadder, more deeply upset than usual.

My right brain was flickering a message:

The marriage isn't right.
Is that why I feel so hollow?

The rational left side of my brain also had a message: The job was not right for me anymore. I wasn't enjoying the sales work, and as a manager I didn't get to do the detective work on the phone anymore. The business was losing its appeal for me.

I shuddered, slammed the little Fiat up into third gear and started up the mountain. I did not feel it coming. It was just there in an instant.

I was screaming loudly:

"Oh dear God, please help me!"

Before I left the office that Tuesday evening, I wrote on my weekly planning calendar: "some of my hardest days ever."

As I again crossed the summit on the way home, I prayed aloud but quietly:

"Please help me! I'm willing now to look at journalism again. I am willing."

Thursday March 3:

The drive up the mountain this morning was even worse.

My mother had called with word that Uncle Carter had died Tuesday—about 11 a.m. Eastern time (just when I had screamed that "help me!" prayer).

Dear, sweet Carter Bennett, the uncle who'd help me have some faith in life when I was a child, had left us, sitting up in his bed at the Pythian Sisters Home in Medina, Ohio, within eyesight of my parents' home. It was the same bed in which I'd last seen him—a pathetic figure, withering, in and out of his mind. The eyes were still there but gone was the Santa Claus twinkle that I had grown up with.

Mom had died. Uncle Homer had died. Now Uncle Carter. A generation was gone.

I was 42 years old and life was sweeping past me so quickly.

My calendar for this day showed "lunch with S.," a recovering alcoholic who was now back on his longtime drug-of-choice: cocaine. I canceled it. I was too drained to think I could help someone else—I needed help myself.

About 11, I phoned Denise, whispering so no one would overhear, even though I had closed the door of my office. I asked her to call the library in Redwood City, the town just north of Menlo Park, and see if it carried Editor & Publisher.

She called back, said the women at the library "thought they did."

I left the office at noon without telling Margaret, my right arm and administrative assistant, where I was going or when I'd return.

I'd go to the library in Redwood City and look at the job ads in Editor & Publisher, and it was no one's business except mine. It didn't occur to me that I was edgy, defiant about it. Just a whim, I thought. I'd just look.

I swung right onto a street I knew went toward Redwood City.

It was crazy, I decided. My mind listed the reasons: You don't know where the library is. You don't even know where this street goes. There is no reason why a library in Redwood City would have a trade paper for newspaper people. Redwood City's a labor town, and small.

I decided I'd give up on that whim and just go find a McDonald's and have a Big Mac. I drove along looking for a McDonald's.

And there it was, the Redwood City Public Library.

There was a parking lot, but I could only find one open spot on it, a space marked "Police Cars Only."

A policeman was just pulling into it. He looked at me, then put his car in reverse and motioned me to take the parking space. I waved a 'thank you' and pulled into the spot, my cream-colored Fiat, top down, in a "police cars only" parking space, invited there by a policeman . . .

A chill shot up my spine.

Something's going on.

The lady at the front desk looked bored. I thought she probably didn't get a lot of bookusers in Redwood City.

"Do you happen to carry Editor and Publisher Magazine?" I knew she'd say no.

"Oh yes!" She smiled proudly. "But no one ever seems to look at it. There's a whole stack of it in that room over there." She motioned toward an empty reading room. "I'm so glad someone wants to read it."

"Thank you."

The chills were still coursing my spine.

I found the magazines, took them to a reading table, and started thumbing through them, looking for familiar faces, glancing at the job ads.

I had the room to myself. I wasn't hungry for a Big Mac anymore. I'd just take my time. After all, I'd said in my prayer Tuesday evening that I was willing to consider journalism again.

Issue after issue, I saw nothing of any great interest. Maybe the next one—

"Excuse me."

I looked up.

A pleasantly rumpled guy in his early 30s. Glasses, inquisitive eyes.

"Yes?"

"Sorry to bother you. You're, uh, still interested in journalism, huh?"

"Oh, sort of." I smiled self-consciously and continued thumbing through a magazine.

"Didn't you used to be in newspapers?"

"Yeah." Why was I so reluctant to talk to this guy?

"Where?"

"Washington."

His eyes narrowed slightly. "Washington—at the Star?"

Did he know who I was, I wondered.

"Yes, the Star. In my last job there, I was the metropolitan editor."

We introduced ourselves, shook hands. He was a reporter for the San Jose Mercury News.

"So, what happened? Why did you get out of journalism?"

I sensed that he might know the answer.

I have absolutely nothing to hide.

"I'm an alcoholic. It got really bad. I almost died, couldn't work. And when I started to get sober, the guys who were helping me suggested that I stay out of journalism for at least five years."

"Five years? Why five years?"

"They figured a newsroom and the chaos there might trigger my drinking. So, I've done it."

"How long has it been?"

Now I felt stuck; there was no way I could try to tell him about drinking Scope mouthwash in 1980. So I'd just forget about the Scope.

"I started getting sober in August, 1977."

"Wow."

I thumbed through the next E&P in the stack. He just sat there.

"So, what are you doing now?"

"I manage a headhunting outfit in Menlo Park."

"Yeah? You working with electronics people?"

"Yup."

He had a funny look on his face, and then it came out: "Oh boy do I know some people who'd like to talk to you!"

"What do you mean?"

"Well, I just interviewed with these guys, and—I doubt if I'll get the job. They want someone with . . ."

This is it.

"Scott, they're looking for someone just like you—someone who's been maybe a city editor or metro editor of a daily, and also knows about the Silicon Valley and has contacts here."

"Who are 'they'?"
"Some guys from—you'll laugh—Kansas City."
I wasn't laughing.
"They want to start up a business weekly here. A business journal they call it."

This is it.
I'll run that paper
and it will succeed.
IT'S ALL BEEN ARRANGED FOR ME.

"Keep talking. I'm interested."
"Well, I just happen to have the business card from the guy who interviewed me. Don Keough is his name. Here."
He handed me the card.
"Keough started one of these papers for them in Kansas City. Now they want to find a guy—like you—to start one out here. They're real entrepreneurs, these men. Developers, real successful in Kansas City."
I thanked him and left in a hurry.
That night I told Denise I was going to go back into journalism. She asked where. "In the Silicon Valley, running a newspaper," I said. She thought that my tale of the day's events was intriguing.
I said I felt I'd had "precognition" about the paper's success.
The next morning I phoned Donald L. Keough in Kansas City, Mo.

Events moved quickly. The next Tuesday night, at Keough's suggestion, I met with the paper's startup publisher, Jim Smith. We had dinner in the coffee shop at the new Red Lion Inn in San Jose. It went well; I liked him. We said it was funny: two Smiths.
On Saturday the 12th I met with Keough in a hotel lobby in San Francisco. He said within minutes that I was the right man, but the decision would be up to Mike Russell, his boss back in Kansas City.

Wednesday March 16, 1983:
I stood in the lobby of the Red Lion hotel In San Jose. A tall thin man approached me with his hand out and a smile. "You're Scott!"
"Mr. Russell?"
"It's 'Mike'."

"Good to meet you."

"Let's go find some food."

I was keyed up but not nervous. Russell was my kind. And about my age.

Jim Smith, who had been parking a car, caught up with us at the maitre d's desk in the buffet luncheon room.

A waitress took us to a table—bench space for two people, a chair for one person.

"You want the booth or the chair?" Russell asked.

"Hell, I don't care. I'll just kneel, if you want. I've been on my knees half the morning anyway."

His brow arched for an instant and we sat down.

For the next 90 minutes, Mike Russell and Scott Smith went at it, moving through every topic we could, fast and straight. We did not mince words.

He was the first guy who ever did to me what I had routinely done when I interviewed someone to work for me: He asked me what made me tick.

After I'd talked about my alcoholic bottom, the recovery and the Grace which was my sole source of strength or power, I asked him what made *him* tick.

I learned a lot about him. I liked and respected him—just as my "reference checking" on him by phone had said I would.

Now obviously wealthy and one of the hottest young leaders in the Midwest, he had grown up on the other side of the tracks, a poor kid whose father had told him he'd never really make it.

His father had been a drinker, he said, without elaborating.

The family had gone through an un-heard-of procedure—divorce—and Mike had been told he'd never be a success. He'd proved them wrong.

He also said he was on a spiritual path and that he too saw much more to "failure" than met the eye. He'd been through enough to convince me he knew what I was talking about.

The important thing, he said, was learning to "give it back."

At that the moment I felt certain my "precognition" about the newspaper's success had been right.

The whole conversation went that way—two guys volleying and enjoying. Over the entree, I saw his shoulders drop and he said, "you win". I knew that was significant but did not know why.

The check arrived and we walked out.

Mike and I went to the men's room.

Standing there, each carefully staring at the wall ahead, Mike said: "We'll have fun."

It was his confirmation that I had the job. It was all he said, all I needed.

Early the following Monday, Keough phoned me to offer the job. I said I couldn't accept until I had seen their newspaper and the Russell-Worley offices in Kansas City.

I called a friend who called a high-level source in Kansas City. The word was that Russell was smart, successful, paid his bills on time and had developed a reputation as a business and political leader "though something of a maverick." He and his partner William Worley were clean and solid.

Wednesday, March 23:

I flew in and out of Kansas City in a day.

The men around the Russell/Worley complex at 3535 Broadway seemed bright, savvy, tough, yet easy-going.

Newspapering was new for them—and only a sideline of Mike's, not one of their "real" businesses. Real estate development, one-hour photo drive-up stores, ministorage warehouses, small energy companies—these were their meat and potatoes.

Don Keough, who'd done a start-up business weekly in St. Louis, had felt that Kansas City was a natural and had approached Mike Russell in 1982 about starting a business journal in Kansas City. Russell liked the idea.

Russell tried to convince his partner, but to no avail, so he took a stack of the St. Louis papers to Worley to read for a weekend. By the end of June, they'd secured four start-up budgets from Keough.

They gave him the go-ahead then, with no idea that they were creating what would become in four years the largest chain of local business weeklies in the world.

Russell felt that Kansas City had a negative opinion of itself and that a business journal might help change that.

It was the fashion in the cocktail circuit to talk about how down the city was—even though, in Russell's eyes, "all the comers were doing deals and making it."

The Kansas City Business Journal hit the street in October 1982. Russell and Worley had expected to see a profit much later, but the paper took off and was obviously going to give them a handsome return on the $750,000 they'd invested in it.

Typically, Russell looked into the future. If a business journal would fly in Kansas City, would help business pull itself up by the bootstraps, then why not a chain of them? And why not start it in the Silicon Valley?

As I toured the new offices in the renovated old brick building at 3535 Broadway, Kansas City, Keough told me that the two partners believed in letting an experienced editor hire good reporters and "do it right." The offices and furnishings fit that concept.

The Kansas City Business Journal seemed tiny and precious to me—a gem starting to grow in a news world populated by clumsy giants.

I felt at home there. Keough and I sat in his office, and Russell bounced in, smiling.

"Hello your editorship." He meant me!

"Hi Mike."

"Just work everything out and get started."

He was gone.

"Don—does he always assume like that?"

"You mean assume that you've accepted the job? Yes, always." Keough was chuckling. "That's Mike."

It was a busy time in Mike Russell's life. The partnership was trying to effect a turn-around in a gas-exploration deal with some high-flying Canadians, Keough said. To me, that translated into: They're letting Keough do his thing with the newspapers.

We didn't talk salary until Keough and I were about two miles from the airport. He said Mike would match what I'd been making, plus a little.

I accepted.

I was told two years later that before our Red Lion lunch, Mike had intended to tell me that he would not hire me. The stated reason was going to be money, but there was some question about putting the product in the hands of an admitted alcoholic. According to this version, my reference to kneeling and the Grace that had saved my life had helped change his mind.

The mail brought the formal offer/confirmation from Keough on Monday, March 28. I lingered over lunch with my friend Jerry Kelly, then set my jaw and walked back into Management Recruiters to resign.

So much had happened—just six years earlier, I'd been almost dead.

Despite the problems I'd felt within me in the recruiting business, I still had an enormous awareness now of what

Management Recruiters had done for me. It had been a cornerstone in my recovery. And now, for the second time, I was quitting the company.

My head was full of visions of Bob Thorne and Ray Herring and John McGuinness, of Alan Schoenberg, Eric Wheel, and the people who'd worked on my own staff there in Menlo Park, people who seemed to bank on me.

We had some good people and I'd gotten fond of them—especially Mike Paratore and Don Meagher and Marilyn Berry. It would be a shock, I knew.

Bob Read was kind about it, as if he'd always thought I would go back to newspapering. He was genuinely happy for me. I was relieved, and saw in him a lesson about business: Help people go where they belong naturally.

The next week, the staff threw a party for me, gave me a marble ashtray engraved "A Great Manager," and I left.

Part of my life had just ended.

I took a four-day weekend in Pacific Grove, played golf and took Denise to restaurants, then reported for work: The Business Journal, 1435 Koll Circle, San Jose—our startup space, cramped, almost windowless, wonderfully abuzz with the excitement of creating a newspaper.

The Business Journal would publish its first edition May 3, 1983. Keough would be the startup editor, I'd be managing editor. After two or three months, he'd move elsewhere to start another paper and I'd take over.

The startup was a store of energy: Two dozen people of vastly different backgrounds. On the sales side of the room (it was divided by low bookcases) we had Arnie Buckendorf selling classifieds and Madelon Holland as sales manager—poles apart in lifestyles, yet both with the same infectious enthusiasm.

On the editorial side we had two editors, six reporters.

Peter Finch would cover real estate, which we knew would be a critical beat. Finch was green, straight out of Stanford. It was a risk, giving such a good beat to such a green reporter. An older, more experienced reporter, Susan Waugh, would cover local banking. An Irish kid from New York, Mike Brennan, would cover high technology. They were wildly different, yet fresh and enthusiastic.

The paper would be a tabloid devoted to local business news, published every Monday. Regular features in addition to lots of news reporting would include a personality profile, two pages of editorial comment, a summary of one company's proxy statement (including executive salaries), a digest of insider trading, and a list of the "top 25" companies or people in a given field each week.

In addition, the paper would carry several pages of recorded business transactions, including new business listings. I was floored by how many names and numbers and details would go into each edition.

I wrote the paper's first profile. It was on Hoot Gibson, one of the founders of SRI, the big think tank in Menlo Park. And I wrote the first issue's lead story, on an investigation I'd heard about back at M.R.

It was wonderful, writing again.

Where have I been? I should've been writing.
—Getting sober, stupid.
All those wasted years-
—They'll pay off.

I had to forgive myself for my alcoholism over all again. But I was working too hard to think much about it.

The paper was popular within days of its debut. It deserved to be. It was good reading. If you were in business in the Silicon Valley, we were providing you with a local Wall Street Journal.

Unlike my jobs in Washington and Allentown, this job required me to express myself in public—to comment on issues.

Having to write editorials showed me how much I'd bottled up during the Washington years. And I quickly saw that I could have an impact—could effect, for example, the city of San Jose's development of its downtown.

For our fifth issue, I stayed up until 1 a.m. on a Sunday writing an "Editor's Notebook" column expressing my disgust at so-called media events, staged only to pander to press or television.

Denise had been watching television and said it didn't bother her that I was absorbed now in writing. She didn't ask what I'd written. I decided not to let it bother me.

A couple of weeks later, I wrote another "notebook" column, this one about my "out-of-date" love of the American flag.

People started telling me that I ought to write more columns, so I tried one about a guy's emotions in business. It was based on a man I knew, and the column felt awfully 'emotive'.

There was even more encouragement. People liked it.

My personality, my thoughts were becoming part of the package.

I wished that Denise was more interested.

One of the paper's principal supporters in San Jose was Phil Boyce, founder and chief executive officer of Pacific Valley Bank. He was making phone calls, opening doors for us—and giving me news tips. There was something about Phil that I intuitively trusted. And Russell had promised him an option on stock in the San Jose paper.

I did a profile on one of the local developers, Lew Wolff, and we hit it off as friends. He steered me to his lawyer, David Mitchell, managing partner of Hopkins Mitchell Carley, the biggest firm in the city. I liked him. And felt amazed to find a man with degrees from Stanford, Harvard and USC in San Jose!

Within weeks, I was starting to feel deeply involved with a group of highly charged go-getters who were building companies and a city.

Don Allen, who was community-affairs vice president in Boyce's Pacific Valley Bank, asked me to join the Downtown Rotary, which was the Establishment's meeting ground. The club had developed a reputation as an out-of-the-ordinary Rotary because it had once thrown the town's leading citizens out when they didn't attend often enough.

I wouldn't have believed that I would ever join a service club. I did, though, and I was glad. They were good people, and the meetings were a high spot for me, although I was offended immediately that there were no female members.

I was finding gems in a city I'd once mocked.

The paper was getting read and quoted widely.

And all the while I had Mike Russell and Bill Worley behind me.

We were all dedicated to the notion that our little weeklies could help regenerate local entrepreneurial enthusiasm. We might differ on politics, but we all knew the benefits of free enterprise.

As we reported local politics as it affected business, I was feeling genuine excitement about the rebirth of San Jose, and I started generating editorials and news stories that reflected it.

In a way, San Jose's downtown was a start-up too. When I'd first seen San Jose, in 1970, it had looked like a West

Coast burnout: an expanse of empty buildings, the streets nearly deserted except for hillbillies, Mexican laborers and vagrants.

Under a young mayor, Tom McEnery, who'd inherited business and land interests, the downtown area was being reborn. Developers showed me plans for what the city could become in another five years—hotels and office buildings, a huge convention center, new retail stores. I was hooked.

It all felt so right—a guy who'd been pulled out of desolation and almost certain death, a start-up newspaper, a city that was trying to regenerate itself.

The flag should fly with no apologies

With hands deep in hip pockets, eyes down on my dirty Adidas, I asked the clerk at the Thrifty whether his store sold the flag.

"Flag?" Apparently I was interrupting his progress in hanging 79-cent Bic lighters on the cash-register display.

"Uhh, yeah. American flags."

There was no hesitation: "No, We don't sell 'em."

"I thought since you're sort of a general store, that—well, where do you suppose I could find one?"

"Try the hardware."

A very pleasant man at the hardware store seemed to feel almost as awkward as I did about the topic. The store, he said, hadn't carried American flags for several years. He suggested the old grocery with the upstairs store full of old-fashioned gear like coal pots and rolls of calico. Maybe it would have a flag.

EDITOR'S NOTEBOOK

Scott B. Smith

The lady there hadn't had an upstairs customer yet that morning, so she huffed up the steps with me before asking if she could help (which made me feel all the guiltier, because I could see that this place was into fashionable old-fashioned stuff, not American flags.

"No," she said, "flags are a specialty item. Maybe you could find a flag store in San Francisco. . . ."

I got back in the car and headed home.

No one had treated me with any unusual disdain. I hadn't been razzed or quizzed or squinted at, hadn't even gotten the "you-some-kind-of-Bircher?" look.

Nor did I get my flag, although I was later to learn that Lucky stores sell them, in fact would put them on sale a couple of weeks hence.

That was the Sunday morning before Memorial Day Monday. Driving home, I made what I thought was a wonderfully half-disciplined decision: I would not get angry, and thereby would avoid all the negative thinking that could tarnish a sunny day off.

And what the hell? I'd gone all these years, all these holidays, joining my neighbors in not hanging a flag. What's one more time?

Down in one of my psyche's many dark corners, there was relief: I wouldn't have to worry about what my neighbors thought. No flag, no attention. No flag, no questions, no gossip or secret jeering of "the house with the flag out front."

And that's too bad.

Dammit, I'm going to stop apologizing for being an American. Or even feeling that maybe I should apologize.

But it *is* a touchy subject, isn't it?

For a 43-year-old who grew up on George M. Cohan songs sung boisterously on July Fourth (and on Christmas night, too, for that matter), there's something gone awry when an average citizen has even a tinge of feeling the *fashion* that it's gauche to hang a flag on a holiday.

Remember those protesters during the 'Nam war, the ones who took matches to Old Glory? (I was one of the many editors who put their picture on the front pages then, and it was news.) Those flower children had more power than we realized.

It doesn't matter, in this context, whether Vietman was a moral war, whether Jack Kennedy got us over there, whether Barry Goldwater was a nut.

One sliver of what happened to us as a country was a general disdain among what I call the *Gucci intellectuals* for anything smacking of liking one's country. And it wasn't just on the East Coast cocktail circuit. Flags came down across the land. It was slow, insidious.

It was media-led and predictable. No matter how many millions of us there are, we're a nation of individuals, with personal insecurities, normal neuroses. Most of us most of the time prefer being somewhat popular to being hung in subtle ridicule for hanging a flag.

The lingering effect of our national grand mal over Vietman—the very real, honest self-doubts about our role in the world—has been to make some of us, maybe many or most of us, uncomfortable about being what we are.

It shows up in the business community in subtle ways.

It's not just the discount chain that doesn't sell flags. It's also the Fortune-100 companies that think nine times before running ads bragging about their defense products (and often cancel the ads).

There are engineers and secretaries in this valley who take it on the chin for working at a company which makes, say, radar receivers. They can get called that worst of all words, *mongers*, accused of building bombs and favoring the extinction of all children.

There's a scientific-applications programmer in Mountain View, for instance, who owns his home (probably worth $165,000), has two kids, drinks beer, loves backpacking. He happens to work for a company which makes electronic systems which go into airplanes, some of which are military.

He's Joe Normal until a stranger asks where he works.

"Apple Computer" is his standard reply.

He's no dummy; he doesn't want to get cornered at a party.

Nor is he a right-winger. In fact, he's probably a left-of-center Democrat.

Well, to hell with it. In two weeks there'll be another national Monday of leisure. July Fourth. It's supposed to honor our independence. We're going to hang a flag from the front porch, maybe grill hamburgers out back. If the sky's clear and the kids don't have colds, we'll go enjoy a blanket and some of the evening's fireworks.

We're biting that little bullet and hanging the flag. It doesn't make us new left, old right, anti-intellectural, conservative, liberal or any other label. Except grateful.

I told a buddy who was running public relations for Rolm, an electronics company, that it was the old cliche: "right time, right place." He nodded, grinning.

More and more, I was starting to understand something through helping others:

Jerry, a gentle man, graying and about 50, had asked me to help him stay sober, but I was the one who was getting the gain. We'd talk business—he was in public relations and I was an editor—but there was always the underlying understanding that our friendship was built upon the love of one recovering alcoholic for another.

It was a miracle for me to feel that love. I couldn't express it. I could only hope Jerry knew.

We had hired my assistant from Management Recruiters, Karen Evanoff, now 24, to be our office manager.

She understood me. There was a bond that even our individual problems would not break.

Her mother Jean, hadn't had a drink in a couple of years.

During the paper's early months, Jean and Karen went through a nightmare: Jean had surgery for cancer. I was scared for them both, kept praying for them—specifically that Jean would survive, and would not drink, and that Karen would hold up emotionally.

It was sustaining for me to know that office and news problems—even the marriage problem I didn't want to have to face—were relatively small when you got right down to it. Karen and Jean were up against cancer and alcoholism.

Jean's cancer did not reappear and she did not drink. And Karen held up beautifully.

Just as we'd prayed.

Coincidences again.

For the paper's sixth week, I interviewed an astounding woman, Agnieszka Winkler. She'd been a Polish immigrant, now had two degrees. She'd gone to work part time at a commercial graphics agency in Palo Alto, and eventually had borrowed enough from friends to buy the company.

It was now an ad agency in Santa Clara, doing $12 million or more a year in advertising, most for technology companies, including one of the valley's hottest, Diasonics.

Some day, she said, she'd want to get out of business and do something important. The quote ended up in the Profile I wrote, and I knew I wouldn't forget her saying it. And I knew we'd be friends for a long time to come.

After a couple of months, it was decided, mostly by Keough, that I should take a reportorial trip to Hong Kong and Bangkok for 10 days. I wondered if someone was testing my sobriety before giving me full reins over the startup paper. After all, they'd invested more than a million dollars in it.

I flew to Vancouver Saturday, July 23. I took a Cathay Pacific flight the next afternoon up around the Gulf of Alaska and then down along the Aleutians, across Japan lengthwise and down into Hong Kong.

Everything was First Class, from the airline to the Rolls that picked me at the airport—everything.

All this
for a broken-down alkie?

After five days of an exhaustive schedule, meeting and interviewing dozens of key business and political leaders in Hong Kong, I was scheduled to go to the China border on Friday.

At 2 a.m., back from three frantic hours of shopping in the back streets of Kowloon, I got down on my knees in my room in the Peninsula Hotel.

I was still was an alcoholic; I was tired; there was good gin, scotch and ale in the mini-refrigerator in my room, and there was booze all around me socially. I asked God to keep me close to my recovery.

I met my guide for the next day's trip in the hotel lobby at 7 a.m. He was very, very British, proper and quite at home in the genteel setting of the huge lobby with its stately white columns and gold trim and violins.

He said he didn't normally give tours; his job was more in the writing end of promotional work for the Colony. In fact, he said, he would not have done this, except that someone got sick overnight and he was the only person available.

I ordered a second pot of coffee for myself.

"Drink a bit o' coffee, heh?"

"Maybe too much—but it sure beats what I used to drink."

"M'too."

I remembered my prayer just five hours earlier—that God would keep me close to the source of my recovery.

I broke the silence.

"I don't drink booze anymore."

He leaned forward: "It's been two years for me."

"Nineteen seventy-seven for me, except that I drank some goddam mouthwash in 1980."

"Mouthwash, m'gad Scott! That's frigghin' hilarious, it is!"

We ordered more coffee.

He knew the same program and principles I knew—stuff that had saved each of our lives. For two precious hours that morning, we "strangers" sat in the back of a van, roaring up through the mountains and to the China border, discussing our experience, strength and hope.

Hey, God -
These Coincidences . . .
Do they just keep happening?

I had four days in Thailand, stopped overnight in Hong Kong and flew home. The following week I was named editor. Keough was going on to Milwaukee to start the company's third paper there.

I'd gone out on a reportorial limb, arguing that Hong Kong would not be swallowed by China, that Peking could not afford to close the $8 billion funnel of Western business. Also, the Hong Kong coverage gave me a chance to talk about the results of "pure" free enterprise, where taxation wasn't penalizing successful entrepreneurs the way it was in the United States.

A public relations consultant lined me up to appear on three talk shows— the ABC, CBS and PBS stations in San Francisco.

Helped by the talk shows and with rapidly rising ad revenues, the Business Journal was making it, and fast.

We also were putting in 15-hour days routinely. And on the Wednesday nights before deadline, I was often staying overnight at a hotel near the office—check in about 11:30 p.m., check out at 6 a.m. Denise said she understood.

At times there was beer around the office—late on a Wednesday night, for example—and I was stunned to hear myself offering to buy. I thought it was a natural, good thing for the staff. Nevertheless, I'd let everyone know that their editor was a recovering alcoholic.

In mid-September we held an editors' meeting in one of the Russell-Worley properties in Kansas City. Russell said something about using my column in the Kansas City paper. I reacted nonchalantly.

I made two decisions I was to stick by during the next months and years:

I'd steer clear of boozing evenings "with the guys," and I would support Don Keough even when my own experience caused me to disagree with him. The guy was good, maybe a genius, and I had enough of a job just getting the San Jose paper on its feet. I was working 70 to 80 hours a week, including the 55-minute commute from our ocean town to San Jose.

The great thing about a start-up company, I decided, was that I could devote me to it, and not worry as much about problems at home.

Driving home, 11:15 p.m. on a Wednesday night, 1983:

I was pushing hard on Route 280, the Chrysler stereo carrying me with a Sinatra song that touched the heart of what was happening in me.

Spiritually, I was going somewhere. I had no idea where; I just knew I was on a path that was going to open out into a new world. As if I were pedaling the bicycle and God was steering it.

All across this country tonight,
there are alcoholics like me, staying sober
one day at a time.
Physical disease, spiritual answers.

No one ever played the Sinatra thing on the radio. It was on a tape I'd bought.

"Here's to the winners.
"Here's to the battle, whatever it's for—
"To ask the best of ourselves,
"And give much more.
"Here's to the heroes,
"Those who move mountains,
"Here's to the miracles
"They make us see.
"Here's to all brothers,
"Here's to all people,
"Here's to the winners
"All of us can be."

Aha! It was **not** just the alcoholics! It was the Russells and the Worleys, the Boyces and the Kellys and the Hollands and the Wolffs and the Reagans and the Winklers and the cab-drivers and—

We all, every one of us,
have our battles.
and our progress.

And I was seeing that the business leaders I knew all had a common characteristic: The good ones gave a lot back to their communities. It made moral sense, and business sense. Everyone won.

On October 3, I had dinner with a woman I'd met before the Hong Kong trip. Donna Wilson managed a center for entrepreneurial studies at San Jose State University. She was warm, bright, gorgeous, funny, spiritually connected, and single. I was a married man with a startup newspaper in my lap.

I felt an enormous warmth. We were tied together in a way I did not understand.

November 1983:

As I hurried back into the office from lunch, our receptionist said that Mike Russell had called from Kansas City and I was to call him immediately.

My mind searched its own files: What had I done wrong?

The switchboard in Kansas City recognized my voice—which seemed abnormal—and put me straight through to Mike.

His voice was distant. He was on a speaker phone.

"The board members of our company are around the table here, Scott . . . We just wanted to congratulate you. We've just named you publisher, as well as editor."

"Holy shit!!!" It was all I said.

I'd never wanted or expected the publisher role. But there was no way I could turn it down; the money was too good.

As the company expanded into the Milwaukee and Portland, Oregon, markets, our operation in San Jose grew. The column I was now writing weekly was building a following. I was amazed to find that the more open and candid, even 'spiritual,' my writing was, the more positive comment I got.

Mike Russell understood what I was trying to do with the column, and supported it. Pretty soon, it was showing up in the Kansas City Business Journal, and later it was to appear in other newspapers which he and Bill Worley started or bought.

Mike had hired a radio sales guru, Jim Taszarek, to manage our sales company-wide. He was a fast-talking wit who knew how to generate sales. And we had a lot in common and became after-work pals.

Taz fired our sales manager and brought in a young salesman out of Milwaukee, Don Waier—who pushed our revenues up quickly and helped get our operation into the black. I was relieved. There was no doubt now that we would make it financially.

I was part of a group of competent people who were making a mark. It put me on my knees in a daily "thank You—and please help me not to drink today." I was running on sheer adrenalin, and loved it. The job was creative and productive, for everyone. If I was exhausted, it seemed a small price to pay.

Occasionally I wondered if my steadily growing responsibilities and public position helped keep me sober. Was pride helping me not take that first drink?

The answer, I decided, was "no." My sobriety depended upon my spiritual condition each day, and that, in turn, was reinforced by staying close to others who were recovering from my disease.

And then our classified manager, Arnie, wanted to talk with me, said he had a personal problem. I'd been watching him, waiting for this. Oh what a gift it was to get another chance to give away what I'd been given.

Coincidences.

I kept feeling changes within me that I had never expected.

One of them was an overwhelming need or desire to reach out to those who were still caught up in the alcoholic trap that had almost killed me.

I saw them on the streets; I in my business suits carrying a heavy briefcase, they in their ragtag outfits. I'd say hello and grin, if they'd look at me—most felt too much shame to look strangers in the eye. I knew how that felt.

I saw them in hospitals, where I'd finally get a better chance to tell them what had happened in my life.

I saw them, too, in business suits, getting on planes and sitting in bars and waiting in lobbies—men or women who, to my one quick glance, were the "me" of just eight years earlier. I'd walk on by, wishing there was some way to tell them . . .

I'd never expected to feel compulsive compassion. But I did, and it felt good.

Phil Boyce had built a $440 million institution, Pacific Valley Bank, from scratch in 10 years. We sat talking about his philosophy of business, and it sounded strikingly like that of two other entrepreneurs I'd grown to admire, Mike Russell and Lew Wolff:

"Do what's right. Give back to the community."

I knew that's what I and my newspaper had to do.

14

Friday, October 14, 1983:

I had that "something's-going-on" feeling.

I drove to Monterey to interview Bob Talbott. As editor of the paper, I wanted to do a thorough story on Talbot Ties, which I'd heard was an almost ideal company.

I had no idea what the effects would be on me personally, nor what the weekend would draw up from deep inside me, nor that I would get inexplicable guidance.

Talbott, now in his late 70s, and I sat in his office for much of the interview, then toured his plant and went to an outdoor restaurant for a Friday-afternoon lunch in the sunshine. We hit it off almost instantly; the rapport was strong, firm.

I wrote a long piece afterward. It began with a description of Robert Talbott at age 45—highly successful on the East Coast yet feeling something amiss, something hollow.

Robert and Audrey Talbott had left their big home and lifestyle back east in 1950, when he was 45. They followed their heart to the Carmel headlands of the Pacific, and started a company devoted to practicing the art of good manufacturing, and to doing business the Right Way.

They'd chosen the tie business, and over the years Talbott had become a symbol of fine traditional clothing.

It wasn't his ties nor the quality control nor the office/plant built from old Oregon timber that got to me. It was Talbott's clear eyes, and his equally clear example. He'd been himself at his best. It showed. I wanted to be the same.

After our four-hour interview/conversation, I was tired. I needed a break, I decided—a break from the pressures of work and the tensions at home. It was time, I knew, to do another inventory of myself. I dreaded it and yet I knew that it would relieve pain, not cause it.

I got a room at the Hyatt Del Monte, phoned Denise, then showered and drove to my favorite place in Pacific Grove for dinner—a place by the surf, where I'd always been able to slow down and do some quiet thinking.

After dinner I stopped at a convenience store for a six-pack of 7Up, a yellow legal pad, some cigarettes, and then drove back to the sprawling hotel. The room seemed large and oh, so empty, even though I had thought I would enjoy the alone-ness.

I changed shirts, brushed my teeth, threw on a sports coat and took a slow walk around the hotel's grounds. The music from the main building was lively—a flute floating above an upbeat band. It was seductive and I was tired.

I felt it was okay to walk into the lounge. I knew exactly what I was doing, and the music was worth it. I ordered a Coke and just stood with my back to the bar, listening, watching.

After three songs, the band took a break and I wandered about the big lobby. Couples sat talking near the open fireplace. Couples sat at the lobby bar. They looked warm and happy, even carefree.

I was anything but carefree, even though it seemed I had everything going for me: Editor of a good paper. A wife, two beautiful children. A big house with a back deck from which I could see my Pacific. A new car, good friends, a good age—43.

I was miserable and would not discuss it, although Ginny, Jerry, and a few others knew it.

I wandered back into the bar, saw an empty table for two and sat down, along the left-hand side of the small dancefloor.

The flutist was excellent, the music danceable. A woman at the bar kept glancing at me. I kept glancing back: Maybe 5-9, trim, short dark hair, slightly bobbed nose, green eyes, intelligence in her face.

I turned away and watched the dancers.

A tall brunette leaned into her partner, her groin jamming her white skirt into him, her left hand toying with the nape of his neck, her eyes wistful yet hot.

The waitress, tall and blonde and friendly, came to me.

"I should leave," I grinned.

"You just got here." Her smile was open, warm, inviting. Bright teeth, clear eyes. Oh gawd, Smith, get out now.

"I'll try a tall orange juice."

She nodded, writing on the little tablet on her tray. "That sounds healthy."

"Well . . ."

Her eyes, oh her eyes. And the soft hollow in her throat. I looked away. The woman at the bar was smiling at me.

I drank the orange juice, silently praying for more than physical health. It would be a long night and I knew it.

By 8:15 the next morning, I'd scribbled two dozen pages of notes to myself.

Where I'd been.

What I'd done wrong.

The pain my alcoholism had inflicted on Lynn, Don, Laura.

The breakup of that marriage.

Billie and what she'd meant to me.

How I'd mentally felt about women.

Denise and the hollow, empty feeling now.

My feelings for Ginny and the sense that it could never work.

I never really loved.
It isn't anybody's 'fault'.

I cried, and cried, thought I could not stop. Images swelled up inside me.

Jessie's knowing eyes.

Huntley's trust.

Donny's strength.

Laura's pain.

My mother's courage.

I howled in spontaneous pain.

Huntley, dear sweet Huntley—the little boy now 2, just the age when my own daddy went away. Would Huntley's daddy leave him now?

I slid off the bed, the sobbing uncontrollable. I wondered if my body would just quit on me.

Room service knocked, with my second pot of the morning. Just seeing someone else helped me pull myself together, but not for long.

This, I knew, was my bottom in sobriety.

I missed H.R. so desperately now. I so terribly needed a knowing, loving, wise male, a father who could guide me.

I cried aloud: "H.R., oh H.R., please be here, help me!"

The notes grew, page after page, interspersed with sobs that seemed to erupt from somewhere deep in the gut.

I'd always needed, craved intensity and openness with a woman. I'd wanted to share my emotions with one woman. Sex had become a physical outlet for whatever I hadn't been able to express, either because I was afraid to say what I'd felt, or because the woman was afraid I'd say what I felt.

This will keep happening until you change it.
You will change or you will drink again.

The thought reminded me of where my strength came from, and I slid to the floor again, this time to my knees.

"Dear God, please be right here right now and help me . . ."

The prayer lasted several minutes and I climbed back onto the bed, lit a cigarette, and started writing more notes.

If I didn't live honestly, openly and comfortably, then my sobriety was at stake. My future. And my children's well-being. And others'. The joy and freedom I'd always wanted hinged upon sobriety and being honest with myself. Absolutely honest. And then acting in concert with my emotional truth.

I will get this right no matter how much pain it takes.

I saw that my emotional and spiritual needs had been so consuming that they prevented me from being a good father. It had been true in the past but was never more true than now, with Jessie and Huntley.

I felt that somehow Denise might never understand, nor help me. It was not—ever could be or would be—her fault, any more than my drinking had been Lynn's fault.

I had an eerie sensation that I was on a stage, surrounded by others, yet very, very alone, and that I had to learn my lessons through interaction with others.

Did that make the others victims of my weaknesses? Why would God set things up this way?

They have their own lessons to learn.

My pen flew across the page:

"If there was one person I'd want with me if I had a week to live, it would be: ______

"The fact is, I don't know. H.R. isn't here."

This was a big chunk of it: My need for a father, especially right now.

You have a Father.

God's protection and grace were not enough, I thought. I need to be able to talk. That's it, I decided: I need to say all these things aloud to God as I go. Sort of like a prayer. Or was it a confession?

"Father, I have consistently risked losing my own family—two of them now—in my need, my search for emotional closeness—for unconditional love.

"It hasn't been fair to others. Please forgive me.

"Father, I've consistently stacked so much responsibility on my shoulders that I started feeling hemmed-in, from 18 on, and then I started needing to 'escape'."

I wondered how much of my behavior had been rebellion. Rebellion against what?

These rules you've believed in—
They don't work for you!
You have to change.
Ann and Elsie and everyone
just did it the way they were supposed to—
they did their best,
but it did not work for you.
Don't ask why.
Just change.

The pen continued to race.

"I have never laughed very much, which connotes a lack of 'free' feelings in me."

The 'rules' I'd just thought about—they explained that one.

Then a clear conclusion:

If I was absolutely honest, with myself and with everyone else, I would have to break up this marriage.

My sobriety is at stake here.
Truth.
If I stay in a painful situation,

> *The insidious disease within myself will get me.*
> *Yes: My sobriety is at stake.*

"I have been living dishonestly, yet trying to do my best and get along.

"I am not happy.

"I haven't been comfortable on a routine basis with Denise for—?—three years?

"I want sobriety and spiritual growth.

"If my house were my home, I wouldn't wander around shopping centers night after night."

I poured more coffee, stretched my aching legs.

"It seems," I noted in suddenly slanted cursive, "as if everything I'm writing is justification for splitting up."

It felt like I was just a goddam cad!

Self-doubt welled up in me again. I went to the bathroom, and caught a glimpse of my own face. Looking into my eyes, I felt that my low self-esteem caused that doubt, always—but that the tears had been the evidence that this stuff I'd been writing was real.

Back in bed, another cigarette going, I pushed on:

"What's keeping me?

"Guilt and fear.

"Guilt regarding 'abandoning' my kids—will they be badly hurt by it?

"Fear of a mistake.

"Fear of my mother's reaction.

"Fear that what I did in 1969-70 was a mistake and now, although sober, I'll make the same mistake—because ***I have refused to trust my own truth.***"

Images of our home swept past me: The big stone fireplace, the enormous bedroom, the distant oceanview from the deck.

Or was it "our home?" It was Denise's, to be sure, and it was the kids', but was it really a home to me?

"Opposite points:

"The kids will be okay; God loves them and they're His rather than mine.

"It's possible I might be a better father if I felt right inside.

"I can't be a good father if I'm unhappy—especially if I might lose this precious sobriety.

"Then they'd have a drunk father or a dead father.

"Denise might be better off if I leave."

My mind wrestled with that one. Yes, I loved her in a way that made me want her to be happy. Would she be happy if I wasn't happy? And was I her kind of guy?

"Fear of my mother's reactions obviously is a childhood remnant of wanting her approval.

"She might approve now of whatever I do if it makes her son happy.

"This is my life, not hers. Her reaction is not the issue here."

Then came words uttered out of months or years of stiffled knowledge:

This marriage—was it
a recapturing, a rebuilding,
of what I lost in my alcoholism?
Yes yes yes yes yes.
I was rebuilding. Yes yes.
I must forgive myself. I must.
My sobriety's at stake here. My life's at stake.

The words rang right.

I emerged from the hotel at 11:40, threw my gear and the notepad into the car trunk, sucked in the fresh air, and headed north up Route 1.

Just north of Monterey, the highway is wide, sweeping, as it winds up the coast. I held my speed to 55 and tried to not think, tried to simply appreciate the beauty of my beloved Monterey peninsula behind me.

There was a sudden, familiar chill down the nape of my neck.

There's a book
I'm supposed to read-

I knew the intuition was right. It startled me. I'd never felt led to a book.

The highway narrowed to two lanes just past Castroville and I felt that I should make a left turn. I did, and as I approached Moss Landing, a tiny harbor town, I swung left onto the old road.

A bookstore was on my left. An old mini-sized school bus stood on blocks in the unkept field outside the store. A new sign on the aging bus said "paperbacks 25 cents." I felt pulled, the chills still running down my back.

Inside the old bus, I was surrounded by musty air and cartons of used paperbacks.

The chills continued.

Logic said I was out of my gourd. This was idiotic, wandering into a musty old school bus, thinking somehow I was being led to a book.

My gut said it was real.

I saw nothing on marriage, divorce, alcoholism—the problems on which I'd just spent so much of my heart. I turned and started to leave.

Something bright metallic orange caught my eye. It was a paperback, cover down. The back was a metallic orange-gold color.

Yes.

I picked the book up. The chills continued. I turned the book over.

On the cover there was a line drawing of a man and woman standing close to each other—just their faces and shoulders showed. His left hand rested high on her shoulder. She looked as though she was moving into his arms.

The title and author jumped out at me: "The Second Coming," by Walker Percy.

Strange: The jacket of the book said it was about a man who, like Talbott, had seemed to have everything going for him, but felt hollow, lacked a reason. I shrugged. I had bigger things to ponder: How would I tell Denise that I had to break up our marriage?

I found the owner of the store inside, paid the 25 cents and drove away, the book tucked into my briefcase.

Sunday night, I sat up late in the den, writing my column. It was about the value of work in our lives.

Monday I left the office at 2 and drove homeward up 101, praying to stay calm no matter what. I swung left onto 92 and crossed the mountain—and remembered that it was, after all, the same road where my prayers had brought such dramatic results less than a year earlier, when I'd needed to get back into journalism.

"Lord, just help me, Just be with me. Help and bless and protect us all—especially the children. Please, Lord!"

I led Denise into the dining room, sat down and looked into her eyes.

"I've got to leave now, Denise."

15

I drove slowly south down Pacific Coast Highway. I'd packed two suitcases, told her that I'd phone her to tell her where I'd be, that I'd be back on the weekend to see the children.

Her face was a mask; that I had no idea whether she knew how resolute I felt—or how she felt. My pain was heavy, yet not as bad as I'd anticipated. I was shaky but okay.

Was there relief?

Something sparked in the corner of the mind: Would Denise feel relief? Was this what she'd wanted subconsciously?

There was nothing I could do about the past. Where I had been wrong, all I could do now was try to make amends for the past, and not repeat the mistakes in the present, or in the future.

I had to get right with me.

Besides, I knew that deep down, I had never been as callous as it might have appeared from a distance.

I had seen too much emotional pain in my life. Not just my own, but also my grandmother's—her first husband had died—and then her second husband. And my mother's—her first husband too had died.

The pattern of the past was clear: When pain was present, I had always tried to walk away from it, thinking time would wash it away.

I couldn't just walk away anymore. I had to walk through it.

I could see coincidences everywhere, every day. What an irony, that my worst weakness, my alcoholism, had allowed me to see the patterns now.

And within the patterns I saw yet a deeper "coincidence": In my sobriety, I was re-experiencing almost all the choices and tests I'd experienced in my drinking days. Sometimes it felt as though I had taken a series of life's exams and flunked most of them—now I was getting to take the exams again.

For three months I holed up in motel rooms in Capitola, pouring everything into the San Jose Business Journal, but always knowing that my first job was to not-drink one day at a time.

We had wanted to make the marriage work.

Denise agreed to counseling but soon gave up.

There were moments when I thought I would drink, usually moments of nameless guilt and images of Denise, Lynn, Ginny—and still of Billie, 13 years later.

Thanksgiving was the bottom. I'd spent the day with the children, and the emotions came crashing down on me in waves. I ended up on the living room floor crying, finally dragging myself away to recover over coffee with other alcoholics also struggling to face emotions they'd previously covered over with booze. Holidays are hell for alkies like me, I said.

Often after the long days, I'd seek out live music, wherever I could find it—coffee houses where University of California/Santa Cruz students performed, quiet saloons where I felt comfortable alone with my grapefruit and 7Up and some soulful guitarist.

I kept thinking about a longtime friend from Palo Alto: A brilliant, witty lawyer who'd gone back to drinking just when it appeared to me that he'd repaired the damage from early problems.

And I'd sit there with a silent prayer for him. It would remind me how easily I could hit that awful moment when I would have no effective mental way to stop the first drink—unless I was keeping my spiritual house in order.

The danger to my sobriety was no longer being around alcohol. It was now clear that sobriety hinged upon feeling right with myself and with God.

I finally read that book I'd bought in the old bus—"The Second Coming" by Walker Percy, a marvelous big novel about a man who sought God and love and had the courage to follow his heart. The woman who gave him his life back was a girl who'd escaped from an asylum. She asked real questions and made the rest of the world look like it, not she, should be given shock treatments.

This confirmed something that was happening inside me. I was beginning a spiritual search, and I was convinced that a woman would have to be part of it—a woman who'd help me be Myself at My Best, my longtime prayer.

This book I'd been led to was giving me an explanation of some of my feelings—and giving me hope.

Denise was torn up, too. She suggested that I spend Christmas at home. We spent Christmas Eve in church with the children. It didn't help.

Funny. I was depending on God to give me strength, to help me stay sober each day during all this trauma. But in church, something was missing. The ritual was wonderful—the music, the Cross, the stained glass and chalices. Yet, church didn't seem to have the answers I'd always assumed it would have.

I had been rescued at the last moment, by a single thread, from death. If I wanted to stay sober, I'd found, I had to ask for help from that source of power and grace—God as I understood Him (or Her or It—that was just semantics). And the God I was getting to know in my life was all-loving, positive.

If He judges us, then surely I would have died and gone to the hell or oblivion befitting a drunk.

Instead, I'd been loved and forgiven.

So God as I understood Him did not judge me; He simply loved me.

That's not what I had heard in the churches, nor from the pious types. Some always spoke of evil, Satan, hell and damnation. I didn't believe it. As far as I could see, man's hell—at least, the hell I had felt thus far—had been *my* doing, not God's.

What about Hitler? Or the deaths of little children?

How would the God I was finding, knowing—how would this God allow such things to happen? The churches didn't have an answer that made intellectual or emotional sense to me.

I heard a guy named Chuck from Los Angeles say something that rang exactly true for me. He hadn't had a drink in about 30 years, and he'd been as far down as I had been, then had come back up. Now he owned a home overlooking the Pacific, and was successful in business. His son was a movie star.

I'd met Chuck a couple of times, and I liked his face. Although he was old and getting weak, he seemed to have the gleam in his eye that H.R. had had. There was something very right about him.

Chuck said he didn't believe in "good" and "evil" worlds.

"I believe in one world," he said. "I believe this is an experience. But it is not reality."

That rang true. It was the way I'd felt as a child, as a drunk and as a sober manager and writer stumbling through divorce.

Chuck quoted and worshipped "The Carpenter," and it was the same sense of Jesus that had been developing in my heart: A gentle all-loving spirit.

I borrowed $1,800 and rented a two-bedroom condominium. I was surprised at how quickly it felt "mine."

And I finally started telling people in San Jose what had happened.

If they judged me a cad, I would just have to live with it—at least, I felt, I could live with me.

The condo stood on a hillside above a wide, white beach. The house was yellow and white, two story, bright and modern yet conventional looking.

The interior felt right for me: modern, lots of wood, a fireplace, windows with panes and, most of all, an expansive view of the ocean.

I didn't mind that I had very little furniture; I was comfortable on a blanket in front of the fire in the evenings, usually listening to Sinatra.

I noticed first that I was listening mostly to Sinatra tapes while commuting, then buying Sinatra records for evenings alone at home. He was feeding me, giving me nurturing I needed. Something in his voice matched my own sense of sadness and, at the same time, simultaneous wisdom and hope.

The Business Journal was growing, and I was working into a comfortable routine: Up at 6:15, coffee and a few minutes just looking at the Pacific, leave for work at 7:10, get back home about 9:30 in the evening.

I was both the editor and now also the publisher. My column was gaining a following. And I was on several boards of directors.

The paper was pushing past $2 million in revenues, and our projections were bright.

Things were changing. Our Kansas City base was growing. It was now the headquarters for a string of papers.

There were systems and procedures and accountants who told us how to do what we had done previously by the seats of our pants. There was talk of selling stock to the public.

When I got home at night I'd be exhausted. I'd listen to the surf, build a fire and enjoy it and music for half an hour, then go to bed early.

On Tuesday nights I'd drive from the office to the house where the children and Denise lived—we'd put it on the market, but there were no quick takers.

On most weekends, I'd pick up Jessie and Huntley on Saturday morning and have them until Sunday evening. It was a 120-mile round trip, but it felt wonderful to be free and still to keep commitments to my children.

I knew that Jessie and Huntley were getting more of their father this way—more of his attention and love—than they'd been getting when we all lived together. That knowledge didn't stem the waves of sadness, but I could see no alternative.

Jessie was magnificent. She would override her sadness with fun, laughter. (But where had Jessie gotten the touch of tragedy that was evident long before all this had happened? She'd had that look in her eyes, ever since she was about 18 months old. Maybe someday I'd understand.)

Huntley didn't quite understand what was happening, so he was a spontaneous, beautiful light.

They had their own room in the condominium with a double bed and a cardboard carton for a lamp table. It was their room and they were with their Daddy; they didn't mind the lack of furniture. Slowly we built up a stash of toys so they would not have to carry as much back and forth.

Huntley would wake me up on Sunday mornings by coming into my room and just standing there. I would wake up, dimly knowing my little boy was there looking at me. He'd grin, then go back to their room to play with his sister. It became a ritual. Then I would get some coffee and sit in bed. Soon they'd be climbing all over me and we'd all be rolling around the bed, tussling, howling with laughter.

When I was with them, my attention was on them—not on trying to save a marriage. This truth felt oddly tragic: That this was better for them than when their father had been so preoccupied.

I started dating and was pleased, amazed to encounter so many fine, bright, good-looking women in their 30s. It seemed to me that they should be happily married. When I thought about it, I felt sorrow for our generation.

A Friday evening:

I was buying a pack of cigarettes at a store on El Camino Real in Santa Clara, trying to argue myself out of picking the woman up for our scheduled date. I'd gone to her house on time and there was no answer, although a stereo was blasting. Puzzled, I'd gone for the cigarettes.

I got in the car.

"Just drive home, Smith," said the Brain.

"I want a little lovin'," said the Baby.

"I gotta get laid," said the Bod.

Oh, well. It was two against one.

I went back and this time she answered the door. I gasped. She was wearing a see-through white blouse and a see-through halfcup bra, plus a skirt that opened to her waist when she walked. She had two degrees, was bright, professional, came from a fine family background, and all this lady wanted was what I wanted. After a dinner she didn't eat, we sped to my place.

I hugged her, kissed her.

"You gonna ram it straight up me?" she purred.

My brain leapt. This was just what the Bod had wanted—a lovely, bright, soft-porn queen. But . . .

"You got it, honey," I purred.

"What else you want, Scott?"

"C'mon, I'm going to show you."

"No—I want you to tell me."

"You do?"

"You can have your fantasies with me. Anything."

In the morning, she wore just my new red orlon sweater, and sang an imitation Joan Baez in the kitchen. The Brain said I should ask her to leave now. I couldn't stand Baez anyway, especially a flat imitation.

The Bod—was it me?—said "Now!" It slid up behind her and she stopped singing, her body starting to wiggle as she bent forward, elbows on the top of the dishwasher.

"Ohgawdscott!"

And there I stood, the Bod happy, the Brain staring out across the Pacific to Monterey, wondering if I would have dinner at the Tinnery that night.

In the spring of 1984, the City of San Jose hit an unprecedented crisis. It had gone out on a limb with its investments and suddenly discovered that it had made big mistakes—and could hold its losses to $60 million.

San Jose had a new city manager, Jerry Newfarmer, who assured me he would be candid with me and a reporter, Jan Shaw. He said he'd tell us anything we wanted to know. I asked him to have lunch with us—on the record.

The lunch, in the dining room at the Sainte Claire Hilton, was excruciating for all of us. Newfarmer was under intense fire. Shaw had to dig deep to get more information than the daily was getting. And I had to judge the situation clearly enough to have a sense of both truth and justice.

I found myself believing Newfarmer's version of what had happened. It was intuitive, though reinforced by his obvious candor. I was supposed to be the hard-bitten cynical editor, and here I was believing a bureaucrat. Was I wrong? I wouldn't know for months.

The freedom wore thin within three or four months.

I wanted, sometimes desperately, to find my mate. But I knew that I was in a recuperative time. No matter how bright and beautiful the woman, no matter how hot the sex or how comfortable the morning-after, it was not yet time.

The sobriety, the job, the kids, the divorce itself—these were my priorities now. I hated the knowledge but knew I needed to accept it.

I'd sit in front of the fire and write notes to myself about acceptance. I wrote several columns about acceptance. I talked with buddies about acceptance. I had to accept things exactly as they were before they could change.

I don't know where it came from, but I found a sentence that, whenever I'd think of it, helped enormously:

God's got the world exactly as He wants it right now—it's perfect.

I was enjoying the luxury of living alone. I wondered whether I might get so comfortable living alone, that I wouldn't be able to change my lifestyle if and when I met Ms. Right.

I'd never dated freely before. When my college buddies were dating, I was married and raising a family. Later, when I was single in Washington and Tucson, I was so obsessed with alcohol—and often so drunk—that I had not really dated.

Several times during 1984, I'd think maybe I was going to get serious with someone new, only to discover that it wasn't a match and I was more comfortable alone.

Then Ginny re-entered my life.

It began late on a weeknight. I was sitting in the darkened living room, stoking the fire. The phone, beside me on the floor, rang.

That small "hi" was all I needed.

Rightness.
Renewal.

Ginny was so much me, so right intellectually and emotionally, that within hours of her first visit I considered asking her to move in. But our sex life still wasn't comfortable or fulfilling, and something else felt amiss, something familiar, yet unidentifiable.

Whatever it was, I didn't want to face it. Not then. But soon enough an answer came.

She got drunk.

She dried out and we talked about it for hours.

She got drunk again.

Gradually I came to see that something between us triggered her drinking bouts.

Loss. I saw that I had been carrying, like a heavy old bag full of pain, a deep feeling of loss.

I had lost twice, both a wife and family life, and had lost a lot of the old expectations about what a marriage, or even a relationship with a woman, could be.

The expectations had set me up for so much pain. They were expectations that, when I examined them as one now, were based upon fantasy in the first place.

Hollywood and Doris Day, television and Donna Reed, Broadway and Julie Andrews. The music sang to me still: Romance, Lifelong Loving.

As the expectations died, I felt listless, bored, depressed.

If you couldn't have the fairy tales, what was there?
Some witch in a bathrobe across from you at breakfast?
I'd undoubtedly make a mistake now,
End up with some witchy, bitchy woman
yakking about coffee prices and repairing the garage door.
I cannot trust my own choices.
Just look at the truth: Failures, losses,
and now Ginny!
She's drunk.

We need the eggs. That's all there is.

So this guy walks up to me and asks why the hell I write what I write.

He isn't the first to wonder. Dot dot dot.

I've been the editor, am now the publisher, of a business newspaper. You'd think—hell, even I would think—that Smith would try to turn out a weekly Deep Backgrounder on what's really going on out there.

"I mean," says this guy, "you got all this news going on, and you're in the middle of it, and you write about what you think when you're stuck in a traffic jam!"

The chairman of our parent company, Mike Russell, probably has a better handle than most on what's going

LIVING BUSINESS

Scott B. Smith

on out there. He and his partner, Bill Worley, are entrepreneurs, are building an institution with their own sweat and guts and, oh yes, brains.

And Russell decides he wants this guy Smith's stuff to run in some of his other newspapers. I think I know why. It's neither complimentary nor threatening. It's just fact.

Russell works very hard, wins, wins, loses, wins. He's the kind of guy who probably grinned knowingly in appreciation of the terrible, wonderful gray truth Woody Allen spoke at the close of "Annie Hall."

Woody's been through hell & bean sprouts chasing Annie and loses again. Why does he keep doing it? He needs the eggs. It's a line from an old joke and it's no joke at all.

We go to school and we get older and we accumulate. We have adequate shelter, food, clothing, family. And we keep on pushing. If we earn $30,000, it's not enough. If we earn $900,000, it's not enough.

Because it's not the money. Russell and Worley have "made it." They've got the Lear and the yacht and the Corporate Staff and more money than I would understand.

What the hell *is* a million, anyway? Ever counted a million of anything? Know what a million dollar bills would look like, laid end to end? Doesn't mean anything at all to me except some have it and I must not have wanted it bad enough to go get it.

Think about it. Aspirin please. Mike Russell wants better newspapers, better profits, Joe Montana will play again. Bob Hope is still on the road. Mozart knew he'd gotten it right and kept on writing. Even on the cross, Jesus didn't have it down pat.

Why *don't* I buy the one-way to some atoll off the Barrier Reef and hole up with a brilliant woman and just lie there?

Why do we keep going after we've achieved, after we've accumulated, after we've fought and lost and fought and won and won again?

It's human. It's the way God made us. It's our nature.

Woody closes Annie talking about the eggs, and you and I and Mike Russell and Ronald Reagan and my buddy Dick Holland who runs a house-cleaning business all know just what that line meant.

"It's still the same old story, a fight for love and glory." And someone makes millions, whatever that's worth, producing a game for our Saturday nights called Trivial Pursuit so we can compete to see who can remember who wrote that lyric. Right?

Ya see, business isn't the business of earning our shelter and acquiring enough beans to get us through another day. If it were, man would've stopped shortly after inventing fire and the wheel. Maybe God would've stopped shortly after inventing the thumb, or endless surf to inspire and frustrate the poets.

Pancho was addicted to business of tennis and Peale to the business of getting Positive and Rodgers to greater love songs. Why didn't they stop?

Why would man stop, in future centuries, at just inhabiting Mother Earth? Why wouldn't man, in future centuries, *find out* whether time exists, whether there's another dimension where to go, whether God actually laughs?

For those of us addicted to the business of business—or newspapering about business—we're not really as concerned with which accounting method the McDonald's chain uses to account for day-old hamburger.

We need the eggs. It is in our nature, way in there where we really live, to progress, to improve, to get just one more answer.

Nobody ever gets it completely right. (And perhaps nobody ever gets it completely wrong.)

It's the chase, the eggs, the process.

Sunday morning Feb. 3, 1985, I made a pot of coffee, propped up some pillows and started "The Right Stuff" on the VCR. Watching the flyboys die to fly faster, I felt as if I understood something about me, and Mike Russell, and you.

That movie isn't about flying any more than Tom Watson is about the centimeters between his heels when holing a long putt or John Sculley is about kilobytes.

Now if I could just convey that in just the right words, in just the right sentence, in just the right column, in just the right format, in just the right year . . .

The only thing I have or you have is the process our spirits are in, today. Right now. That process, no matter how painful or ecstatic, is all we have. And that is Life and we had better enjoy it. If business is what we've chosen to do it in, then that's living business, and that's what we'll call this thing I write.

The San Jose Mercury News published a long piece saying the Business Journal had made it. The story included a paragraph about my column's offbeat topics: Loving to see whales before I left for work in the morning, for example. And it noted parenthetically that I was a recovering alcoholic. I felt good about it—maybe someone would be inspired to try to stop drinking or to hire a recovering alcoholic like me.

I decided not to write about my alcoholism until the company could no longer be hurt by it. But, I hoped that someday I'd write a book about my recovery and its miracles and coincidences.

Our little newspaper was no longer so little. We had 40 employees and I worried that if a fire inspector dropped by, the city would close the clutter we called an office. I decided to move us into the heart of downtown San Jose.

The Mercury-News, one of the highly profitable stalwarts of the Knight-Ridder chain, had moved out of downtown San Jose years before, and into a suburban area where high-tech plants sprawled across the anonymously dull baylands.

I found a downtown site that seemed just right: a four-story brick building that was being renovated by a bright young architect, David Takomoto. We would lease the second floor and get our logo, in solid brass, across the front of the building.

I figured that at least $400 million would be spent in new construction within four blocks of that site in the next few years, and we could get a lease at a low rate as pioneers.

San Jose was booming. It was getting a Fairmont Hotel, several new office towers, other new hotels, a big new Convention Center. We'd be in the heart of it. But the cost of such a move would be a problem.

Mike Russell flew in and I showed him the site. We went over the costs. Sweat started pouring down my ribcage. I felt as if my good relationship with Mike was on the line.

As publisher and editor, I knew the downtown move was the right thing to do at this point in our growth. Mike agreed, but he was used to Kansas City prices. This would mean going from rent of about 67 cents a square foot per month to about $1.37—a difference of about $8,000 a month.

Mike and Bill Worley had put $1.5 million into the newspaper by then, and had every right to look for increasing profits rather than increasing rents.

"Do you know what you're doing?" Mike asked.

"I hope so."

"If we owned the building, okay. But when we're leasing—the economics are a lot more than that $8,000 a month, Scott."

He showed me that over a few years "your decision would cost us a quarter-million."

Was I losing Mike's confidence?

You've risked that before.

This could be great ammunition for anyone in the company who wanted to shoot me down in the future.

It's the right thing to do.

"Look, Mike: It's a lot of money, but it's the best deal we can find downtown. We should get the money back in increased revenue through the years. Most important, it would dramatize our commitment to downtown San Jose. Plus, it helps establish the paper, as a community institution as opposed to an unpopular daily that deserted the downtown."

Finally, back in our offices after the tour, Mike led me into my office, closed the door, stuck his face right into mine. "You jerk!" he said. His eyes were smiling.

I'd won. The eyes and inflection said it.

As I drove homeward on Route 17 that night, I realized the miracle of it all:

It doesn't matter whether I get promoted or fired in the future.
I had the faith-in-God to do what I'd felt was right, and never
even thought about picking up a drink while under pressure.
These guys have rolled their $1.5 million dice with me
at the steering wheel
—Me, a guy who was a helpless alcoholic, bound to die, back in 1977.
No matter what Mike thinks of me or does in the future,
I'll love him for this.

July 1984:

About 11 a.m. on a Tuesday, I stood praying for guidance in the shower. The window was open so that fresh air blew through the hot water and steam.

I see a face.
A woman.
Brilliant yet gentle blue eyes, going right to the heart of me.
Short brown hair, flaring slightly outward.
Good features, unusual width between the eyes.
And a wonderful feeling that she would understand me.

That face floated before me for maybe 30 seconds.

I hated the feeling. I was walking through shopping centers, walking into meetings, in church basements, going through business routines—always searching for that face.

To myself, I called her "The Face in the Shower."

I assumed she was the One. She existed, I was certain. I would meet her. I would know before she would know.

She would be a challenge or the circumstances would be a challenge, but she would be with me naturally.

Would she be married? Hooked up with someone? Would she be an alcoholic? What if she lived in Australia or Florida?

For weeks I searched in crowds for that face, that wonderful face.

The Business Journal was having a direct effect on people and companies. It was so unlike Washington, where journalists wrote for other journalists.

And now Mike Russell had hired his longtime accountant-friend, Armon L. Mills, as president of American City Business Journals, Inc.

The first time we met, Mills was on a whirlwind tour and I didn't get much of a feel for him. I sent him a perfunctory note congratulating him on his job and saying I still wanted to keep in touch with the boss, Mike.

A few weeks later, Mills flew in for a closer look at "the San Jose market," and we met for dinner at Hugo's at the Hyatt-San Jose.

Accountant or not, the guy was real; we'd be okay.

Mike had hired a man who could even manage Mike . . .

Enjoy life. She will come along.

I told me and told me. It worked sometimes.

I knew I needed to get refreshed. So, in the fall of 1984, I headed out across the Pacific again, but this time on a vacation.

Sydney, Australia
August 27, 1984:

On arrival at 6 a.m. on a Monday, I got in touch with some recovering alcoholics I'd known were there—strangers in a hemisphere I'd never visited. Their problems, and recovery, were me all over again.

Wherever I ever go, I've got instant friends.
Because of my weakness.

They gave me warmth, support, even asked me to meet with others like them—and me—in the highest levels of business and government.

I was stunned at the stature of the people I was meeting there. What the hell did they do in Australia? Just drink and sober up and then run the place?

I walked and walked, ate oysters by the dozen, bought two wool sweaters, one for me and one for my brother 'A'. I met and danced with several women but didn't try to entice any back to my room.

At 3 a.m. on my last evening, I was recruited to dance—hard, fast dancing—by a Polynesian lady who must have weighed 220. We won a dance contest.

Free and comfortable. Yet wishing for, missing, my mate.

As I waited at the airport for my Qantas flight homeward the next day, I felt a familiar tugging.

A book!
It's here, waiting for me.

I went into a newsstand I'd visited earlier. I looked at the wide displays of paperbacks, saw nothing and gave up. Chills continued up and down my spine. I turned and took one look back.

Forty feet away: Red cover, large white letters. I couldn't read the words.

That's the book.

The title sickened me. "The New Male/Female Relationship" by Herb Goldberg, Ph.D. I never, never read junk like that!

It was a thick American paperback. I sighed, paid the clerk and forced it into my briefcase. I knew I'd never read it.

I had booked myself into Maui for three days' rest after Australia.

Settling into the luxury of the Qantas business-class section for the nine-hour flight to Honolulu, I opened the briefcase and the book slid out onto the seat. After my coffee and dessert, I opened it. For laughs.

I did not put it down until we were gliding down into the Hawaii morning eight hours later.

Goldberg's book was going to be a bible for me and I knew it. He had me and my generation's marital problems pegged.

What a coincidence, finding this book,
right at this time in my life:
lonely, confused by failure, hurting.

With wit and compassion, Goldberg described the typical American relationship:

The male initiates everything, from the first date to sex to marriage. He is the "act-or." She, the "reactor," responds to his actions.

The male gets the responsibility and the guilt. He is "responsible" or "to blame" for everything, but can't figure out why. The female, a responding Cinderella for her grown-up Daddy, the male who'll provide a real-life dollhouse and real-life doll-babies, ends up feeling repressed and angry and doesn't know why.

Goldberg's prescription for a "new" way of living—of a solid, equal and real relationship—seemed fanciful to me. But, I decided his statement of the problem was wonderful. It would serve me well to reread it the next time I got into a serious relationship, to make sure I wasn't replaying the old, false tapes.

I wrote a column about the book; it seemed that important to me and my generation.

With Goldberg's guidance, I saw that my ugly image of the nagging wife was just as unrealistic as the White Picket Fence stuff. I just hadn't found a woman who was right for me.

September 1984:

We'd decided to try something different to celebrate the Business Journal's move downtown. Instead of the customary cocktail party for a select 300 leaders, we'd throw a party for everyone.

Lew Wolff and Phil Boyce both said it would be good for the downtown to create something that could draw office workers out of the towers and out into the once-so-dead streets at mid-day.

Our circulation manager, Pat Hazel, worked out the details and we announced that the San Jose Business Journal would host a "business barbeque and bash" in the Civic

Center Park on a Friday noon—bratwurst and chicken cooked over charcoal, salad, beer or Coke. Plus live music. All of it free.

It worked. Seven hundred people showed up.

Some of the downtown's street people stood on the edges blinking in disbelief. I invited them to join us, and they did.

They are me, but for the Grace of God.

The "bash" felt so right that I grabbed Pat Hazel after the first hour and said we should do this every month. Pat, fresh-faced and confident, but with streams of sweat pouring across his face, nodded agreement, then rushed back to the heat of the charcoal fires and the long lines of hungry lunchtimers. We'd just started a tradition.

The Business Journal sometimes seemed to bump and grunt, but it was moving steadily forward. And one of the most beautiful parts for me obviously wasn't as easy for others to appreciate: I was watching one of my kind get his bearings in sobriety, just as I had.

Chuck Gathard, our photographer, was not-drinking one day at a time. He had about seven months of sobriety when I hired him, sight unseen, at the suggestion of Don Keough, who'd known him for several years.

Tall, angular, Chuck's painful transformation of personality—the process so vital to longer term sobriety—seemed to be made more painful by his personality and the somewhat negative impression he was making on people.

I felt for him. Hell, I'd been there.

And as I watched Chuck grow, I saw my own growth on two levels: First, the psychological transformation I'd gone through, almost unconsciously, around the time Denise and I got married. I'd been sober a year. To stay sober, I'd had to go through enormous changes. Second, my growth now, with more time and change under my belt.

I was learning love. I knew it. When things went well for Chuck, I felt enormous joy in my chest. Sometimes it was almost overwhelming.

Two other employees came to me separately and said they felt that Chuck should be fired—he was obstinate and arrogant and a genuine pain in the ass. I said I thought he would change. I would hang onto him, talk with him.

We threw a second "bash," and 1,100 people turned out.

At one point, the head of a prominent company took me aside. "We ought to get these bums out of here," he said. I looked toward where he was pointing. There were two drunks in baggy, filthy clothes waiting in line for free beer. And a bag lady was pushing a grocery cart that held all her worldly belongings.

I nodded dimly and forgot it—until 5 a.m. the following Thursday, when I awakened in heart-pounding anger.

By the time I reached the office, I felt that I should throw out the column I'd written for that week and write what was in my heart.

I took a long walk around the downtown, debating. Did I really want to take this kind of risk? It could cost the paper a lot of money and popularity.

Back in the newsroom, I sat down at a computer and wrote. We're here by the Grace of God, I said, and anyone who thinks he or she is "better" or "cleaner" had better get grateful for what they've got.

The next week, we were getting letters and phone calls expressing agreement.

October 1984:

I'd taken Jessie and Huntley to McDonald's in Monterey, then to the Edgewater Packing Co. building on Cannery Row, for carousel rides.

Now I stood watching my children so free and happy on the merry-go-round. Through its whirling-horse images, I could see the open front door of the building.

> *Maybe the Love Of My Life will walk through that door—*
> *I'd see her through an opening in the merry-go-round.*

I burst into laughter. The woman to my right—Midwestern, vacationing with her hubby and kids—stared at me. I saw just how silly my romantic notions could get.

Or was it silly? After all, Ed Schmidt had told me that when I was really searching for something, it would be right under my nose.

I'd been getting to know a guy named Bob Keady and liked the way he kept life simple. He would call me in the early morning and announce: "I haven't had a drink today. Have you?" It had been nine years for Bob. And every day, he said, he liked to start out by talking with another recovering alcoholic.

He was from an old East Coast family, was going through a divorce. We found a lot in common, and I asked him to help me stay sober. He said okay. It would help him stay sober, too.

There was one major difference in our circumstances: Bob had found a woman, named Jody, who might just be his true mate.

Within weeks they were exceptionally close to each other, and Jody and I had found that we read a lot of the same things, had the same spiritual questions.

As we talked about my divorce, he sounded relieved that I was not holding Denise "to blame."

I'd seen that while many divorces might be avoided through hard work, there were some marriages that just weren't going to feel right to either party. No one was to blame; each had a life to lead and had better get on with it.

I'd also found through the years that when I assumed one of the parties in a divorce had caused it, I'd often been wrong—if I later got more facts. The actions which might be blamed usually were reactions to something else.

I sat against a faded blue canvas beach chair, my chest and face to the warm sun. I had taken a long walk down the beach, had returned with some large clam shells for future ashtrays and soap dishes.

I'd picked up a pair of miniature clam shells, still locked together at the center. I was struck at the perfect match of the two shells. Separate shells, yet connected forever, their lines and colors and size matching exactly. Each ridge, each shading, each imperfection—they were twins yet separate.

There in that wondrous ocean they had been growing together, at the same pace enclosing life.

Was there a woman who could match me like that? My natural mate?

A day later, while driving along Pacific Coast Highway, I saw "The Face in the Shower" again, this time for maybe five seconds. It was just as warm, beautiful, understanding. She hadn't changed. I turned off the stereo and tried to get a feel for where and when and how I'd find her.

I got no answers at all.

"Here's to the ocean!" I lifted my grapefruit juice.

Bob grinned and lifted his wine glass. "And ocean living."

Bob Kieve, President of Empire Broadcasting Co., was about to make a serious offer for a condo at a posh retreat along the coast south of my place.

I had just made an offer that day on a house by the beach—with ocean views from the den, master bedroom and bath, living room, dining room and kitchen, with decks, front and back, a skylight over an open stairway, a fireplace in the living room, and a two car garage and space for another bedroom and a bath.

"So tell me, Scott: What made you finally decide to go ahead and make your offer?"

"Threw my heart over the bar, so to speak."

"That's a funny phrase."

"Comes from Peale."

"Oh?" Bob was always like this—a childlike curiousity.

"It means . . . geez, Bob, I'd think you'd know more about Peale than I do."

"Scott, I never really studied him. Guess I should. I've known several people who've loved his books."

"Well, I've found that it works for me. If I really believe something, it will happen."

"And that's how you reached your decision about buying that house?"

"Yup."

"So what happened?"

"This condo I'm in now, I'm renting."

"Right."

"As you probably know, there's a pool and a big sauna on the project's grounds."

"Right."

Vita, Bob's companion, was honing in on what I was saying. She was quiet, yet I got the feeling that behind that mysterious face and the dark eyes there was a very warm woman.

"Well, last Saturday night, I was sitting alone in the sauna, and it was maybe midnight."

"Yeah?" I was surprised at how intently both were listening.

"I got to staring at one particularly bright star, almost straight up, and I was wondering what the hell to do about buying a house—I really liked that place down there, wanted it, but I knew it was out of my ballpark. I just couldn't afford it, yet I will not buy this condo because the owner wants far too much for it. But suddenly, staring at that star, I remembered a principle in Peale."

"Well, what happened?"

"This'll sound corny." I noticed that I was leaning forward on my elbows, intense. "I prayed, right then, at that star. Prayed that I would know the truth for me, know God's will for me about where I live and how and my finances et cetera."

"Yes?"

"You mean I'm not sounding crazy yet?"

Bob's eyes were gleaming. Gawd I loved the guy.

"I just suddenly knew that I would have whatever I envisioned and believed I would have, so . . ."

"Wait a minute: You 'knew' that?" I nodded. "How?"

"I don't know, but I knew it with absolute certainty—that whatever I would envision and believe, would be the future truth."

Bob shook his head, as if it sounded only barely plausible and yet he would have an open mind.

"So . . ." I decided to stay open and candid, and took the plunge. "I just envisioned me living in that house and being able to afford it, and being happy in it, with or without a mate."

"And then what?"

"All of a sudden I knew it would happen, really happen."

"So you got up and posted an offer on the front door at midnight?" His eyes were dancing with delight.

I chuckled, but I really wanted to tell Bob how I was feeling.

"Sure, sure . . . anyway, and the next day, I called my friend Bob Keady—one of my best friends, the friend who's in real estate—and said I thought I would make an offer.

"He suggested a real low price, much lower than I was ready to go for, and something told me to go along with it. So I did; the offer was presented to the sellers—they live over in Fresno or somewhere—this afternoon, I think."

"So you might get your answer tomorrow? Or even, if it's not good, tonight?"

"I guess so."

Shortly after they'd left, the phone rang. It was Bob Keady. I sucked in a deep breath.

"You sitting down, Scott?"

He was playing with me!

"Yup. At the dining room table."

"Your offer was presented to them in person and over the phone about 4 this afternoon. I was on one end, their agent on another end, and the sellers on another phone."

"Yeah?"

"They called back just now. Apparently, they just got the written offer and sat down and talked it over and made a decision. I love it when we get people who can make decisions quickly. Most of the sellers we deal with go real slow and delib . . .

"Yeah, Bob—just tell me!"

"There were a couple of things they rejected."

Oh well.

"They want two clauses changed."

Silence.

"You mean, they want just two things changed, but not the price?"

"That's right."

"You mean, I've got the . . ."

"Now wait a minute. Let me tell you what they want changed. They said . . ." His voice seemed years away to me.

Peale had been right!

I had been right on track. I hadn't been crazy. What I had seen was this string of events now unfolding.

Or was it just one more coincidence?

In prayer—honest gut-level talking to my Father—I had found the most practical tool of my life.

And the laughter and lightness, the joy and warmth and loving were all inside. Positive prayer and a sense of gratitude, both inside me, brought these joys to my external life.

The results, as Peale said, were almost a science.

And then came the spiritual punch line: I remembered flying over the area 10 years earlier and announcing that someday I would live along this stretch. Crazy as it sounded then, I had believed it.

Two months later, our sales manager, Don Waier, pulled together a group of guys and we moved me into the house. Now, I joked, all I had to do was pay for it.

The back deck overlooked a ravine and a state park, with the ocean about 100 yards to the right. Quickly, this deck became my spiritual home. I needed a place where I could do the most practical thing possible: prayer and meditation.

May 1985:

Short, live-wire, brown hair, crackling voice, bright brown eyes, sober more than a year. I saw her the first time at a small gathering of people recovering from alcohol.

The name was Leslie. I discovered that her license plate—on a spunky brown convertible—might be a key to her last name. And I found her finally in the phone book, dialed and got a young girl's voice—her daughter Lisa. Yes, she'd ask her mother to call me back. Even though it was 10:45 on a Sunday night.

She called back at 11, bright and curious and funny. What the hell, she said, she'd probably had dinner with worse guys than me. Wednesday would be fine. She would meet me there.

We were old friends before the entree arrived. We had begun what seemed to be a *resumed* relationship.

Just before I left on a trip back east, we wandered into a bookstore together. She suggested that I try Shirley MacLaine's "Out on a Limb."

I acceded, but I knew I'd never touch it.

June 1985:

My daughter Laura was getting married. I flew to Ohio. From there, my parents and brother and I drove to the Bethesda/Chevy Chase area for the wedding. As we arrived, I felt a nervousness I'd never known before. I would be watching my daughter get married. I would be seeing my first love, Lynn, and her husband Lyman, and her parents. I would be with Donny at last. He was doing well in his job in food-service management for Mariott. I was proud, and had missed him so . . .

I would be a curiosity to people, I figured. I could hear the comments: "He doesn't look like he almost died." "He looks successful." "He isn't wearing a gold chain around his neck like Californians are supposed to."

I expected to feel like an outsider at my own daughter's wedding.

I'd felt so terrible so often about Don, Laura and Lynn. Could I ever repay my debt to them—could I get through this weekend?

Lynn had paid many of the expenses. And if she'd ever done anything well, this was it. I'd been house-poor and divorce-poor and hadn't contributed enough. Yet I knew I had done the right thing: Laura's younger sister and brother out in California needed the healthy, solid father-base that Laura and Don had lost to the disease of alcoholism. So if my money was going to the support for the younger children, I realized, I needn't feel guilty.

My uncle, Bennett Wilson, came in from Worcester, Mass. with his wife Nancy. It was almost a family reunion. We all stayed at the Marriott in Bethesda. I saw a famous sportscaster in the lobby and bar, puffy-faced and bleary-eyed. It was the reminder I needed. No matter what I felt during the weekend, no matter how uncomfortable it got, there was one thing I could not do: pick up a drink.

Don and I got a brief chance to talk. There was one quick reference, and it was all I needed to know that he'd gotten past the "no-God" theories he had repeated in his visit to California four years earlier.

He said that he'd been reading a Bible, that he'd started to understand something about the power of prayer. I smiled, didn't need to say anything.

Thank God he's over that sophomoric phase, I thought. He's becoming a man now.

I saw Lynn for the first time in years, and told her how much I appreciated everything she'd done for the wedding and in general. It was the best amends I could make at this point—just to be gracious, grateful and available whenever anyone needed anything.

Best wishes to Fiona Irving et. al.

Went back east for a wedding and semi-family reunion, some golf in gentle Ohio rolls, and even some strolling around the old town square.

I'd suspected that the East wasn't still around, but it just hadn't occurred to this Californian that there was a strain of invincible survival in the Old East, the one I'd thought was heaven when I was 12.

My brother "A" and I, feeling 80 at 28 and 44, respectively, were helping our parents drive home to

LIVING BUSINESS

Scott B. Smith

Ohio after the wedding in Washington. To understand why the family almost got the giggles in the car, I had to recognize what we'd just been through and why the New York Times was so hilarious, yet right.

It had been a beautiful, awkward weekend and the blossoms of Old Style seemed lovely yet confusing to a Californian in 1985.

The wedding, held on the Audobon estate's grounds, was impeccably correct—rose petals and cake-cutting and a bride's white *sewn by her grandmother* for love and posterity.

But this was 1985. What were they doing? Not only did the entire party look good and repeat the Lord's Prayer, but the band played "Daddy's Little Girl" and commanded the bride to dance with her, uh, father.

Her father danced and told her his California home was hers anytime no matter what, and didn't let one welled-up tear show. Then the song was one-fourth over and he beckoned the bride's second father to cut in. She seemed to love both.

It was like that. The first father and second father got along well, and the second said with relief that he got along almost as well with his first wife's second. In fact, he got along well with his second wife's first husband's mother's second husband, too. And this was not the fast set.

A long weekend it was, yet over too soon. Soon June '85 would blossom only in someone's scrapbook.

In the car on Sunday, "A" and I sat in the back seat amid our family's drivetime reading: Wall Street Journal, Value Line, Shirley McLaine (imported by the visiting Californian), the Post (never touched), an Atlas, a Double Crostic, and the Sunday Times.

My MBA brother starting reading aloud the dozens of wedding announcements in the Times. His timing, as usual, was second only to Johnny C's.

> "Fiona Irving, a daughter of Flora Miller Biddle of New York and Michael H. Irving of Norwalk, Conn., was married yesterday to Peter Benson Wold, son of Peter B. Wold Jr., of Bottineau, N.D., and Anne Hartung of Minot, N.D. The Rev. Bruce Forbes performed the ceremony at St. Bartholomew's Episcopal Church in New York.
>
> "The bride, who will retain her name, is a doctoral candidate in art history at Columbia University, from which she received a master's degree in art history. She graduated from Barnard College. Her father is a partner in Irving & Jacob Architects in Norwalk. Her mother is president of the Whitney Museum of American Art, which was founded by the bride's great-grandmother, the late Gertrude Vanderbilt Whitney. The bride is a granddaughter of Mr. G. Macculloch Miller of Old Westbury, L.I., and the late Mrs. Miller, who was an artist and member of the architectural firm of Noel & Miller in New York, and of Mrs. E. duPont Irving of Wilmington, Del., and the late Mr. Irving.
>
> "Mr. Wold, a senior partner in the Minneapolis law firm of Wold, Jacobs & Johnson, graduated from North Dakota State University and received a law degree from the University of Minnesota. His father is chairman and president of Wold Engineering in Bottineau. The bridegroom is a grandson of Mr. Peter B. Wold, the late Mr. Wold, Mr. O.B. Benson and the late Mr. Benson, all of Bottineau. Mr. Wold was a customs inspector for the Immigration Service. Mr. Benson was a lawyer."

Back in Medina, Ohio, the gazebo in the town square was still there and Dave Jones was still president of the Old Phoenix Bank (thought it'd been bought), and Tom Rowe, who used to run the Westfield Companies, is still playing golf.

Somehow, I'd thought 1985 would be a year after '1984' and the Old East would be gone. I'd been wrong. How nice. Great institutions do survive. The Old East has, and even the Times is back to reporting the Vanderbilts.

She told me that our problem had been my ego.

Later, as she sat talking with her family during the wedding-eve dinner, I stared at her familiar profile and thought back to all the emotional effort that had gone into our attempt to save the marriage. I wondered if she had any idea of how much pain I had felt, then and later.

> *Of course she does.*
> *And it wasn't any worse than her pain.*

"Scott, pass the rolls, please." It was my mother, and my mind flipped back into the events of the dinner.

I wanted my daughter to be joyous, and to feel my love. I'd lead a toast. With my grapefruit juice.

Laura and Randy—I liked him immediately, thank God—took their vows in a garden on the old Audubon estate, and we had the reception there. It was dignified and lovely—just right.

As the party wore down, I wandered off to a quiet corner of the huge lawn and felt another miracle of sobriety.

> *I expected to be an outsider. I'm not.*
> *I was nervous. That's gone.*
> *I expected to feel too much emotion. I do, and that's fine.*
> *No big emotional deals here, Scott,*
> *You're accepting the ups and downs with equanimity.*

I remembered the consternation I had felt years before when I'd go to Bill Worthington in Tucson with my latest crisis, and Bill would quote Kipling:

> "If you can meet with Triumph and Disaster
> And treat those two imposters just the same . . ."

It was finally happening for me, just the kind of sobriety Bill Worthington had talked about.

The next day, Ann and Al and "A" and I drove back together, laughing as we never had. I'd seldom felt as at-home with us as a family group. If it hadn't been for my illness and the recovery my parents had helped force on me, I might never have felt that warmth.

On the plane back through Chicago and into San Jose, I decided to try MacLaine's book.

Boring, I thought, as I read quickly into its first chapter.

Then, magically, I couldn't stop.

16

Tuesday night, July 30, 1985:

In the old days, bars. These days, bookstores.

I had been up since 5:50 and had enjoyed—and survived—another 15-hour day. I needed time-off, a few minutes browsing in a bookstore or record store.

Since my office was in the downtown of that maze called the Silicon Valley, I lived in a little town 40 miles away, along the Pacific. I wanted the daily escape to my ocean.

I'd developed a little habit of taking off the necktie and stopping at a bookstore/coffeehouse. On this Tuesday I wanted to treat myself to at least one new novel by Walker Percy, whose "The Second Coming" I'd liked so much.

I asked the kid behind the counter if the store had any "Percy Walker," saw him blink, and corrected myself to Walker Percy. I said I especially hoped the store had one more copy of "The Second Coming." It was, I said, the best novel I'd ever read.

A small woman with a radiant face and long hair stepped forward. She'd never heard of Percy, she said. He was a novelist, was he?

I wondered who the hell she thought she was. I was talking to the clerk and hadn't said anything to her.

Short, with straight long brown hair. Fine, small features.

"Yes," I said. "He's a Southern novelist. Wonderful stuff. I was hoping to read something new by him, and to get another copy of 'The Second Coming'."

She wrote down the name of the book. Her handwriting was small and had a somehow familiar slant.

Gawd, but her face was so . . .

Embarrassed, I hurried out, bumping the doorjamb, and jumped into the the car.

As I started to turn out of the shopping center, her face still mentally before me, I had an impulse to go home and get my own "The Second Coming," underlined and annotated, dear and almost sacred to me—and bring it back to this uppity woman with the dazzling face. I wondered how she'd look if this stranger brought her a surprise like that.

South on Pacific Coast Highway. A new yellow full moon was smiling on my left.

It was a Tuesday night and normally I would have had dinner with my children. Were they missing me? No matter; I'd have dinner there the next night.

My schedule must be getting to me, I thought. Too many commitments. I was on too many boards, that was part of it. And now there was an intensifying personnel problem in the office. And the problem appeared to be one of those things you couldn't quite pinpoint and fix. Damn!

Oh, hell—the mortgage will be due this week and I had wanted to get some of that loan paid off. Damn!

> *Too much, Scott. Too much.*
> *That's why I live down here. No one finds me here.*
> *"Roll on, thou deep and dark blue Ocean, roll!"*

Then off the highway, down the winding two-lane stretch my kids called the "the country road," and up over my hill—and a howl, aloud. A big open howl at the moon's early-evening shine on the Pacific, from here to Monterey. Oh, thank you, thank you, thank you, thank you.

The moonlight was starting to sift down through the skylight in the staircase and upstairs in the living room. I felt it.

> *Uh-oh.*
> *Something's happening, something deep and wordless.*

Mentally I recorded the moment.

"Good evening, plants. I'm home now." I knew people would see how nuts I was if they were to hear me say good evening to my house plants—the publisher, the hard-nosed editor, living alone in a three-bedroom house along the beach, greeting his plants the way most men greet their wives. But I'd been reading; research showed that the plants could hear me.

Weird, this urge. What was it with me? Oh, of course: full moon.

Music. Get it started.

I loved my habits. What a treat to get home to my own place and do exactly what made me comfortable.

I fed a blank tape into the stereo, stacked two Cleo Lane records on the turntable so the stereo would tape the records while I drove back to the bookstore—if I decided to go. Then into the kitchen to make my standard drink: grapefruit juice and 7Up, half and half in a one-quart glass.

Craziest damned feeling, that urge, almost a compulsion, to drive all the way back down there, 15 miles, to give some arrogant, striking woman my precious copy of the only novel that had ever seemed to come close to describing how I'd felt, and why I'd left Denise and the kids.

That book hadn't been given to me and I had not picked it out. I'd bought it for 25 cents almost two years earlier in one of the damndest coincidences of my life. I'd been led that Saturday in 1983.

I thought about the long night of tears and pain holed up in the room in Monterey taking inventory of my mistakes, and how I had emerged the next morning, knowing I had to leave Denise. And then being drawn off the highway to the little store that sold paperbacks out of an old school bus—knowing somehow that there was something I was supposed to read. And seeing the used paperback and knowing that I was supposed to read it: "The Second Coming", about a man who had everything except a reason to live.

I'd felt led then. And this evening, standing by the stereo with moonlight streaming in, I felt led again.

Oh gawd was I still woooee-nuts? Was all of my life, past and present, just illusion? This urge obviously wasn't a good thing to succumb to. Maybe I'd just gotten so hungry for a mate—"best friend/best companion/best lover"—that I was really on a flyer, the kind that could hurt my heart and lose a beloved book in the process.

I had been learning to listen to my own common sense instead of honoring the impulses in my life. It was hard for me to trust me. I'd made mistakes with those impulses—hiring a guy, buying that tan sofa, drinking mouthwash—lots of mistakes out of impulses.

Crazy crazy crazy but I'm gonna do it.

I started singing. What the hell? Life is short. I pulled out the beatup paperback and wrote my name, phone number and address on the inside front cover.

Whooo-ee, Scotter. You're . . .

But I didn't feel nutty. My mind was hearing some internal music, a sort of joy new to me. Here I was: publisher of a good newspaper, I write every week, whether I want to or not, which is damned good for me, I've got a house on the beach, even if I can't afford it, and what the hell?, I feel like this and there are no chemical reasons to feel like this and it's Tuesday and I deserve . . .

Cleo Lane's soft truth broke through: "This is the dawning of the Age of . . ."

The record sounded just like the moment. Was there another singer alive who could do this with a voice? Cleo Lane, bless her, knew how to make that song sound just as eerie as it should be.

"*. . . harmony and understanding . . .*"

Silly song, really. I mean, what are the chances, I thought, that the Earth or mankind was making a quiet, slow change?

It was 9:51 as I drove the Chrysler back up the hill, into the Puccini moonlight, singing that silly song. Funny, I didn't feel silly at all. Puccini would take her the book. So would Byron.

Smith, when will you get over the grandiose?
And when will you stop second-guessing yourself?
Yeah, but that too is second-guessing . . .
Okay, then when will you stop playing these mindgames?

I dug a Bacharach tape out of the box on the rear floorboard, put it in the stereo.

So what if she wasn't the Face in the Shower?

The Bacharach/Hal David sound from the early 1970s—gawd, I loved it!—reminded me of my days in Washington, of national politics and presidents and the dramas I'd watched, and of Lynn and the Camelot—a real one, not some goddam Kennedy imagery—I'd walked away from.

It was okay. That was what it took for me to get where I was now, I thought. And it was better for Lynn. Better, overall, for everyone, I felt.

It takes what it takes.

I ejected the cassette, tuned in the classical station in from Monterey and relaxed with Brahms.

Twelve minutes on the highway, and then, on the busy avenue approaching the bookstore, I knew I'd better not think about what I was about to do, or I'd back off.

Just do it, Scott. You've come this far.

And it's no big deal. Keep whistling, kid.

I parked in front of the bookstore, jumped out, deciding not to think about what I was doing, and walked in.

She was there, behind the counter. She didn't see me.

There was one customer, to my left. I stepped around him, caught her eye and firmly put "The Second Coming" in her hand.

I hadn't realized just how much I'd wanted exactly what I saw: That radiant face exploding in joy and surprise. How delicious! How too-quick this is, Smith. Crazy, crazy Smith.

She gasped up at me, delight and a question on her face.

"There's a full moon," I answered, before she could ask.

I had to leave, not ruin it. She asked how to get the book back to me. I mumbled that my name and address were in the book—"and please do return it."

I almost ran out, exuberant and knowing instantly that I was not to pursue her.

The next night: Wednesday, July 31, 1985:

As usual when I'd meet Donna Wilson for dinner, I realized that I'd forgotten how sweet her face is—woman-sweet, not babyish. The distanced blue eyes across the straight nose, the wide upturn of smiling lips.

We met at a Mexican seafood place. She had news about her business, which was going very well, and we went over it during her white wine and my grapefruit and 7Up.

Over my scampi, I told her about my crazy trip back to the bookstore the evening before. She thought it was funny and dumb—and might get me involved or at least laid.

"No, no. It's not really like that."

"Oh?"

"Donna—what's that funny look on your face."

"I probably feel sort of . . ."

"Well, this woman had this spiritual sort of face. Real clean, no wrinkles and no sign of whatever negatives she's lived through."

"Was there a ring on her finger?"

"I didn't notice."

"I don't think I ought to believe you."

"Honest. And—not only did I not get her name, or even ask for it, I just ran out of there and I will not pursue the matter."

"Of course you won't, Scott—you know she'll call you!"

Damn! That was the trouble with Donna. She knew me so well, and it could be so helpful sometimes, so naked other times.

Donna Wilson was nine years younger than I, but she was probably my best advisor when it came to major things. I'd consulted her on buying a house, on writing, on my job, on commute routes, on what not to include in speeches, and on relationships.

Still, as we drove away that night—her car going home to the mountains, mine home to the sea—I thought it strange that I would even tell this story about the bookstore woman to Donna.

I do, I thought, I really do the damndest things.

August 7, 1985:

I heard the coffee maker crank up at 5:56, 14 minutes before the alarm clock would go off. The whirr of the electronically timed bean-grinder would wake me out of any dream. As usual, I was too numb to growl about waking up too early, as I always did.

A Wednesday, and there was nothing special on the schedule for today. Just a normal day—in fact, a bit quiet.

Since I had to wait another 13 minutes before the coffee maker would ring five times, signifying that the brewing was done, I turned on the shower, still full of sleep, and stepped onto the back deck to wait while the shower warmed up.

"Oh thank you, thank you!"

My first-words-of-the-day routine really felt right. To my left, dawn was cracking above the wall of the narrow canyon separating the back of my place from the state park. To my right, the surf was gentle, pinkpurple in the dawnlight.

I stepped into the hot shower and started humming. It felt so good to get six hours of sleep!

What happened took less than one second. There was no physical change. I didn't crumple in shock or leap with joy.

But I knew, knew absolutely, in that sliver of time that I should go ahead, immediately.

I was not to wait another five years. I was to start my book right away.

And I knew that Mike Russell would agree to it. And that the book would do well. People were waiting for it. Not for me, but for the feeling they'd get from it.

And I knew that I would be okay and was not to question what I felt—just do it.

Soon I was on the commute route, up the old two-lane road up the mountain toward the Summit, and opening the briefcase on the passenger seat, pulling out the microcassette recorder, and dictating:

"Wednesday, August 7, 7:34 a.m. I knew in one instant in the shower this morning that I shouldn't wait until the B.J. is more profitable, shouldn't wait until I've found the right woman, shouldn't wait until I have some real money—that I should go ahead now with a book.

"I don't feel anything except the certainty.

"I do know that it should be in the first person and should tell my story exactly the way it's happened . . ."

I snapped off the recorder and took a swig of the coffee. What was it I wanted to tell people?

We've become a machine society . . .
Yes, but that's not it.
The Establishment people hide behind "Right" stuff and miss out on the good stuff . . .
Yes, but that's not quite it.
A button-down-collar type can find God and sobriety . . .
No—that's corny although true.
No no no no no no no no no -
I have to show people
that what's happening in my life
is happening to the Western world—to a
people entering a New Time.
My details may be different,
But the evidence is coming in now:
There's a subtle revolution going on!
Yeah, but won't people think you're
just another California Kook, or
wrapped up in illusions?

Not if I can get them to see and sense
what's happened in my life.
Just the way it's been, the way it is.

I was passing Donna's driveway. Funny how it was there, at that moment, I thought. Home. Wouldn't she be excited! I pulled out the little recorder again:

"Write memo to Armon Mills and Mike Russell proposing book . . . and that I be allowed to hire a general manager . . . Tell them that I want to continue as publisher here . . . that I will continue to write the column and oversee the operation, if they want me to.

"Convert my den into a more formal place for writing.

"Lube up the typewriter, momma, Scotty's gonna write a book now!" I was almost shouting into the helpless little Sony. I was aware of the exhilaration, aware that I was alone on a little road through a redwood and fir forest, shouting and waving my arms as if I weren't driving.

And I was aware that it was perfectly okay to be like that. More dictation:

"Tell about the alcohol and the divorces! Tell about the years in Washington and touch on what LBJ was like, and how the press screwed us all . . . And really talk about my generation and all the disillusionment and disorientation. Talk about my parents' generation, with no strings, no minced words.

"Describe this life today—hell, even this moment!—and all the wonder I feel.

"Do it!, do it!

"But the point of the book—it's the point of my life today—should be the coincidences." I laughed out loud. "The coincidences!"

I had no fear of what readers would think. No one could ever think less of me than I had thought of myself nine years earlier. My bottom had given me liberation.

There was a dark moment of doubt the next day:

Why do I expect people to read about me?
Ego?

Or-
Is this 'why' I was kept alive?
And is there something in me screaming to be understood?
Is it both, perhaps?—

A message to tell, from a guy needing to be heard.
One guy in a generation undergoing a spiritual revolution.

If it's 'wrong' or 'ego', I decided, I'd just to have live with it. It was how I was, what I knew I was to do.

I thought of Mike Russell and grinned. "Got a new mission, Mike!"

I sensed that I would never forget dropping my proposal in the mailbox at Deer Park the following Friday morning. I was embarking on a long new journey and I knew it.

Four days later, I talked with Kansas City. Armon Mills told me the book proposal was "a go." And what a coincidence: The company had just hired a Kansas City lawyer-politician, Tom Shawver, to become general manager at one of the papers. He was now in training with our publisher in Milwaukee, Don Richards. I told Armon that I hoped Shawver would like California.

Within days, I was in Kansas City for a company meeting. But I'd changed: Everything in me was focused on the outline of the book.

And everywhere I looked, I saw evidence of a quiet revolution within the deeper spirit of the world around me. The Kansas City dailies now seemed full of pieces about it, from news events to a review of the new movie "Cocoon."

I was on to something new to me, and probably new to many people caught up in the humdrum of business life.

The book was becoming an obsession, and I needed to stick with my program of staying spiritually fit and thereby sober. I was working with several men who were trying to stay sober.

A couple of them were addicted to alcohol but had deeper problems. Slowly, I came to see that I could not help them: They had problems greater than alcoholism, and generally they had a hard time being honest and willing. They needed medical attention.

I needed to not-drink and be willing to be myself.

Sunday night August 18:

I had to get something by Edgar Allan Poe. I didn't know why.

I turned the car around, got back up on the highway and drove back to that favorite bookstore, not even remembering the last time I'd been there.

As I hurried through the store to the section where I knew I'd find Poe, she came straight toward me.

"Hey—aren't you the guy who? . . . That's quite a book!"

"You read it?"

"I tried to reach you. Several times."

"I've been on the road."

As we stood talking, I felt a sense of urgency.

"I don't even know your name, but maybe we ought to get together."

"Susan."

"How about dinner?"

"Uhh." Her eyes fell, then came back.

No ring. She's single but not used to dating.

"How about this Friday night?"

"I think I have something—no, I don't. No, I'm free that night. Well, okay—if I could just meet you somewhere."

I named a restaurant and insisted that she give me her name and home phone number.

"I don't, uh, normally give a stranger my number . . ."

"You'll have to trust me."

Our eyes locked in a smile. She went to the front counter and wrote them down.

I smiled, went to the rear of the store, got an Edgar Allan Poe anthology, paid for it, smiled again at her, and left.

Later, as I sat with the book, I had my first feeling that Edgar Allan Poe and Woody Allen looked strikingly alike.

Dinner was quiet, intense. By the time the entree had arrived, we'd each sketched the basics of our lives to date.

Susan had been through her own sort of bottom—four years of hell getting out of a marriage and emerging into the spiritual rightness that had put that clearness in her eyes.

As I listened, her story reminded me of what an alcoholic—or at least this alcoholic—had to go through in order to stay sober: A good education and early success. Then problems. And now the admissions of powerlessness, the turning it over to a higher power, the inventory and confessional stage, the amends, the prayers that faults would be erased, and the seeking of that Power's will rather than self-will.

After dinner, we strolled to a small park on a bluff overlooking the Pacific, sat on a bench and silently enjoyed the silvery expanse of ocean beneath the almost-full moon.

"There was a group I was in, and—well, it's strange, but some of them believed that when we come to this planet, our souls actually fly in, right past the moon." Her eyes were a silver mist.

I leaned over and kissed her lightly.

We sat for another half hour, then she got in her little car and sped away.

September 7, 1985:

I called Susan to change the time of our second dinner from 7:30 to 8:30 to allow me more time for working on the outline of the book.

She said she was quite tired. I suggested we meet some other night. She suggested we meet "but briefly." I demurred, preferring some quality/length to our next date. We agreed to try meet for brunch the next Thursday.

Half an hour later I left the computer for coffee. I stopped in the dining room for a look at the sunset—it was gathering orange around a front approaching from the Pacific.

I dropped to my knees before the table:

"Thank You for everything. Please, help me—guide me or show me a woman who will be comfortable for me—someone who'll inspire and nurture me."

The prayer was brief, intense. I went back to the computer. Half an hour later—I had been writing well, I felt, and enjoying it—the phone rang, an interruption.

It was Susan. She wanted to see me "right now, tonight." I said we'd be comfortable at my place.

I thought of the prayer.

Coincidences.

Thirty minutes later she walked in, in tan skirt, pinkish sweater. She later confessed that she'd gone out for a glass of wine with a friend and they'd talked about me.

I built a fire and we sat down and talked.

About 2, we kissed, then talked some more. It was delicious.

About 4 a.m. we marveled that time had gone so quickly, that we'd stayed up in front of that fire so long, mostly talking about our individual perspectives on a relationship with each other.

The necking had been delicate, gently powerful. I never touched her.

"Maybe you ought to stay here—in the children's room."

"I knew I would. Do you mind?"

"Not a bit."

"Do you mind that I'm not sleeping with you?"

"Just relax, and I'll relax."

Got up about 10:35, met her 15 minutes later in the kitchen. We sat in the dining room for an hour, and then Bob Keady called. I pulled Susan to me as I sat talking to him, my head against her ribcage, picking up the speed of her heartbeat.

We moved to the living room—she seemed at home in my house—and talked about music. She told me of a psychic who said she probably had been a musician at the turn of the century. I stayed quiet, later said my grandmother had been an opera singer. What a coincidence, she said—so had hers.

Slowly I realized that this was the second time I'd sensed being with an "old friend," perhaps from another life.

And I realized that I had now passed the sex phase in dating. I wanted a friend, a companion in my life and my spiritual quest.

But Susan was not "The Face in the Shower."

It gets eerie sometimes:

I'd taken the kids to dinner in Half Moon Bay. Stopped at a Quik Stop for coffee-to-go. At the light at Kelly and Highway 1, I ordered myself to slow down. There might be a large deer on the road, I told myself.

Two miles north of Davenport, 35 minutes later, a large deer walked too slowly before my headlights. I braked to a stop and watched the animal amble into the fields to my left.

I had the sense I had either known, and that knowing had saved my life, or my thought had somehow created the situation. Either way, it proved my sensing to me.

For months to come, I was struck by that simple example of what I felt certain was occasional precognition.

The truth is out there.
Just learn how to plug in.

Monday night I couldn't reach Susan. Finally, at 11:20 p.m., the phone rang and it was her. She said she had wanted to tell me something:

"I'm not used to receiving from a man—I've always been on the giving end. I suppose it's different because it takes away the safety of being in control. I decided not to run away from it just because it is new for me. It's unusual for me to be receiving, and I almost feel selfish or something, but I decided to stick with it and go ahead and feel it."

I said okay.

Here I was, carrying an ocean house with a great view. . .

And Bill Worley told me he wanted to give me the same advice he'd been giving his partner Mike Russell: "If it floats, flies, fucks or has a view—rent it."

I'd been passing through the main terminal of the San Jose Airport.

Two strangers stopped me—one to congratulate me on writing what he thought were good columns, the other to ask if I was the man he'd heard one night telling about drinking Scope mouthwash . . .

The corporate president, Armon Mills, came to town again.

Mills was my age, had been a managing partner with a major CPA firm. Pure Midwestern. Honest as Abe. He wasn't an accountant. He was a manager—one of the best I'd ever know.

I'd gritted my teeth about the prospect of explaining what made me tick—such things as hanging out with a bunch of sober alkies, relying on God but not going to church.

From our very first dinner at Hugo's in San Jose a year earlier, we'd understood each other.

I couldn't figure how anyone could manage Mike, or Bill—plus the rather explosive personality of Jim Taszarek overseeing sales operations in all papers and Don Keough running the editorial end.

Time and again I watched, bemused and amazed, as Armon quietly would get the job done, and the fights straightened out.

The marvel was, Armon Mills was a genius at keeping Mike Russell at some level of understanding and calmness with the equally high-energy people Russell had hired. They were all so explosive.

And Mike Russell had hired Mills to do just that—to manage Russell, in effect.

What was it Bill Worley kept saying? He wouldn't be Up There without Mikey, as he called him—and Mikey wouldn't be Up There without Bill. I wondered if either could keep the company growing and healthy without Mills to keep us all Up There, by holding us down to earth.

Later, I wrote a column about a manager who'd rather win than fight. I didn't name him: it might have looked as though I was praising my boss.

I got the feeling that whenever I asked God for help, the same things happened:

—Instead of some cosmic messages, I usually heard what I needed to hear from another recovering alcoholic. God didn't send me thunderbolts now—he sent me people. Usually people with gnarled faces and sparkling clear eyes.

—In the same vein, I noticed that whenever I asked for help, someone would pop up, right out of the blue, who needed help from me.

Coincidences.

And as I thought about it, I saw that when someone else needed help from me, it got me out of thinking about me—which was usually the perfect prescription, no matter my ailment.

I was wandering around a cluttered little bookstore in San Francisco and discovered the book "Psychic Exploration" by Dr. Edgar Mitchell, the astronaut with multiple degrees who walked on the moon and came back to explore inner space.

I decided not to buy the book then. Maybe later, when I've got time for 'consciousness' and all that stuff, I thought—right now I'm still trying just to be conscious of my own actions.

Driving home 30 minutes later, I felt I'd made a mistake.

And a familiar feeling swept through me.

Something's going on here.

BEYOND RECOVERY

17

I stood on the front deck, not quite seeing the ocean and coastline before me. What I saw was that the nature of the book might have to change at the beginning of Chapter 17. My fist banged down onto the wooden railing in frustration.

There was just no way that the book could describe the miracle of my recovery without getting into the subtle, yet dramatic, events unfolding now. It would have been so easy to just tell about the bottom and then the recovery—so simple, so predictable. But it wouldn't be an honest account of what recovery had brought to me.

Blood trickled down my hand. I'd hit the railing too hard. I went inside to wash my hand. I'd have time yet to decide whether to risk writing about the stuff that some would label too-far-out.

I'd just spent six hours in a Monterey auditorium with more than a thousand people who were incurably addicted to the drug alcohol. Each of us was sober, most of us feeling joyous and grateful.

I thought of all the centuries when there was no known answer for alcoholism.

In all previous history, perhaps more people died of alcoholism than died of plagues or wars. Alcoholism, regardless of how they labeled or perceived it, had been assumed. And the historians had all but ignored it. I wondered how many of the great figures in history—in politics, the arts, religion—had been alcoholics.

Yet here we were, dealing successfully with a seemingly hopeless physical disease, being answered so widely now with spiritual solutions—not church but spirit.

It was getting so I saw almost everything in my life in a spiritual light. Yet, I was coming to believe that no matter what spiritual path I explored, no matter how "enlightened" or otherwise I might become, the most crucial, central fact about my spiritual growth was: I have not had a drink today. I could not experience spiritual growth, nor even the presence of God, if my mind and body were distorted by a drug.

Further, staying sober was a reprieve each day from the dark, insane side of my own ego. In order to have that reprieve, I had to maintain a spiritual condition of willingness. Willingness was the door to everything important to me.

I got many, many chances to talk with other alcoholics, and sometimes they asked me to speak before a group. I'd tell my story, and it helped me to recall in detail just how dark the days in Tucson and Allentown had been. It was harder to describe the hole in me during the Washington years, the hideous inadequacy and anxiety.

I could laugh about all of it. But I needed the simple act of talking about it, bringing up the details. That made me certain that I did not want to pick up that first drink again.

We called it keeping the memory green—motivation by triggering memories, and knowing that it could happen again.

Alcohol was always awaiting our return, insidious and deadly.

When asked to speak to newcomers, I'd try to cover the basics:

- I'm a grateful alcoholic. Even grateful to have the disease. It put me on my knees, where I could grow.
- I have a biochemical condition which was pronounced a disease by the American Medical Association in 1954. It is a clinically identifiable, progressive disease, terminal unless arrested.
- My physical disease is answered, one day at a time, by spiritual conditioning.
- Most other alcoholics I've met grew up feeling much the way I did—desperately insecure, inadequate.

Low self esteem is the common trait of alcoholics.

Alcohol worked, in that it made me feel adequate. It became my best friend, my best tool. Then it failed me and threatened my physical existence.

I had relied upon alcohol to meet my emotional problems. Actually, it just covered those problems. Later, when imminent death forced me to push the alcohol away, those personality problems were still there, and had to be dealt with.

• The only answer for me is the process I went through to gain and maintain sobriety: Admission that I am powerless, then recognition that God can handle it, then turning my life over to Him, then confession, willingness to clean up my act, making amends, meditation and prayer, and giving to others what has been given to me.

• Church couldn't handle me and my bottle. Nor could shrinks. But this process worked. It worked because it drew me to people with who had licked or were licking similar problems and because it caused me to find a God I could understand.

• I have seen that God is doing for me what I cannot do for myself.

• Finally, I very seldom harbor my old feelings of insecurity and inadequacy and alone-ness. I do have God, and somehow connected to Him, an inner me who's loving me.

• Prayer has become the most practical thing I have ever had in my life. I now know I am powerless in this world. That recognition was the big one. With prayer I plug into the power that creates all the goodness in me and around me.

• What I'd thought was bad news—being an alcoholic— was great news. It took 15 years in a slowmotion nightmare to learn such paradoxes, the stuff that puts this grin in my heart today.

I've gone from silver spoon, size small, on up through youthful success back on down to emotional and physical bankruptcy—death in spirit and almost in body, and then up into this joy today.

• I realize that I didn't do it. That's the next paradox. "Take charge of your life," and you may find afterward that the great "I" did maybe 10 percent.

Once I saw that, I got damned near obsessed trying to be with the One who did it for me, and the closer I get, the farther I have to go. And the more I look for him, the more I see your faces.

When I look back, I see patterns:

• I was disillusioned by a church where I could not feel God. I found Him, but not in the church. No, I started to feel Him and get results—either that or the damndest coincidences—when it seemed I had no feelings left. It didn't happen in the church, or through theology. It happened through people like Ed Schmidt.

• I was disillusioned about a country that couldn't keep its promises.

I have a lot of confusion still about Vietnam and my years around the Johnson and Nixon White Houses. But I am no longer disillusioned about the United States. The old girl's the greatest thing going, strong enough even to harbor the "intellectuals" who think themselves smarter than the country or its people.

I was disillusioned about the white picket fence—about the love and family life I thought was promised me by Hollywood and Broadway. After male/female relationships got so confused and after I experienced a lot of failure—but four great kids—I've finally got a shot at real love.

All in all, I was let down by almost every institution I'd been told to trust, including the Great American Cocktail Hour, which both saved and ruined me.

So here I am, living at the ocean, considered "successful", healthy, and truly free, and living a life of meaning.

Furthermore, everywhere I go I'm finding cadres of my generation who are doing the same—replacing their disillusionment with new meanings, new hope. And we've either discarded or started rebuilding just about every one of those institutions.

Today I can try to put into my business life, and into every other aspect of my life, what I've learned through a series of gifts—extraordinary to me, yet widespread among my contemporaries.

You see, this whole generation coming into its own in this country is full of men and women who've needed to develop new ways to put meaning into life. Whole new worlds are opening up.

—And I have seen that this works best if I don't pick up that first drink . . .

I could only stay sober by keeping in fit spiritual condition. I knew that in my bones. Sober alcoholics had been saying it for years before me. It certainly was the truth in my life.

In order to maintain my spiritual balance, I had to be grateful and willing.

Willingness. The key. When I didn't feel it, I'd pray for it—to be willing to be willing. It always worked.

And whenever I was willing to do what felt Right, the results would flow so naturally it was like a science.

> *Spiritual principles producing material results!*

And gratitude. It had the full power of prayer. It could help produce willingness.

Every "negative" had a flipside Positive. God recognizes the Positives.

If I would just be willing, it would keep getting better.

Willing to do what felt Right. And to not do what felt wrong.

Willing to sit down regularly with my fellow alcoholics. Willing to help whenever asked. Willing to do for others what others had done for me.

If I spent the rest of my lifetime trying to help others, I couldn't repay what had been given me. Images of Ed Schmidt and Harry Phillips and Bill Worthington and Bil Wilkins, and Luke and Boyd at my door . . .

What a gift, my alcoholism!

If I had not been an alcoholic, I would not have had to get on my knees. If I hadn't gotten to my knees, I would not have found this true high.

In order to keep it, I had to give it away.

In order to give it away, I had to know or do what was Right.

If I did what was Right, I felt good about me, about the world.

Happiness was a by-product.

My brother "A" and I were, in his words, "doing up 18 in Carmel"—playing golf, in my words, at Rancho Canada, a sprawling big course along the Carmel River Valley.

We were tied going into the 17th, both uproariously high in our mock competition. "A" was now 28, super-single, about to become a vice president of Management Horizons, the hot young retail-distribution marketing firm in Columbus, Ohio. He was on one of his twice-a-year vacations at my place. The bet was for dinner that night at Rappa's, a seafood place at the end of the wharf in Monterey.

It was 6-ish on a September evening. We had the course almost to ourselves. The fairways were now a deep green carpet, the shadows long, the air ocean-fresh.

From the slightly elevated tee, we'd both gotten good drives down the middle of the 17th fairway, and I was driving the cart. Above the noise of the wind and the cart, we were almost screaming in our boyish joy of two brothers just playing.

"You couldn't beat your old brother with a putter and a bribe-"

"You haven't seen the bribe yet-"

"Probably one of your rejects-" I gunned the cart.

"Well, you seem to be doing okay—Susan seems nice!"

"Too old for you, 'A'."

I saw something move on the fairway in front of me.

"Love that salmon and pasta! You'll blow your approach shot, Scott. You'll blow it! I can just taste that salmon now-"

It was a gopher's face, edging up out of a tiny hole in the fairway. The cart was flying down the grade—too fast to swing out of the gopher's way.

I angled slightly right, just as the gopher started to step in that direction.

Thud.

"Awshit!"

"You jus-"

"I know. It was a gopher." I turned and looked. The gopher was a freeze frame, its head still standing up out of his ground, looking stoic and ever so dead.

In my previous years, it would have been a simple, dumb accident—too bad but not upsetting. But now I sensed that something was disturbed within me.

"Don't let it get to you, Scott. It was just a gopher—a dumb gopher, that's all."

I wanted to tell him that the gopher was just as much a creature of God and Nature as we. But instant intuition said not to try to explain it.

I bogeyed the hole, but so did he. I beat him by a stroke on the 18th green and he bought the dinner.

Five nights later I awoke in a sweat, the gopher's image spread across my dream-vision.

I was changing again. Getting "softer," and I loved it.

As time moved and the book began to take shape, Donna suggested I would have to be careful to establish and maintain my own credibility.

I'd told people that I was an alcoholic. Therefore, many readers might doubt the psychic or spiritual experiences I would report. We laughed as I acknowledged that people might say, "Smith's interesting, sure, but not very rational . . ."

I felt I had credibility in the community. In my civic and professional life in the Silicon Valley, no one, as far as I knew, had questioned my judgement or ability because I was an alcoholic, though many people knew about it, and I made no attempt either to hide or broadcast my illness and recovery.

I was on the boards of major organizations—the San Jose Symphony, the County Arts Council, the Civic Light Opera, Junior Achievement, O'Connor Hospital's foundation, the city's Convention and Tourist Bureau, the Board of Advisors of the Leavey School of Business at Santa Clara University.

I'd gotten so extended that I had to turn people down to help other boards or projects, even though I did not feel justified in saying "no" to anything worthwhile.

But I knew Donna was right about credibility in the book.

People might take my word for what was happening in business—whether in fact I knew or not. They'd tend to think I 'knew,' because of my job and experience and contacts. But would they take my word about my own experiences? Would it all seem just 'coincidences' or 'illusions'?

I could picture someone whispering: "Oh well, he's a bit strange—and he is an alcoholic, you know."

Yet I'd been reading about other peoples' experiences. I trusted that my experience was strikingly similar to that of many more respected people, whether they had ailments or not.

Shirley MacLaine's books had become popular. She'd had out-of-body experience, and extensive past-life regression.

Richard Bach wrote about out-of-body experiences.

I'd finally read the book "Psychic Exploration" and felt moved by the experience of Dr. Edgar Mitchell, the sixth American to walk on the moon. He had degrees from Carnegie and M.I.T., had all the left-brained success in flying and science you could name. Yet Mitchell had left the space program to study psychic phenomena and consciousness. He said it was a frontier in which science was barely in diapers.

The list of those willing to discuss psychic phenomena was impressive—great minds from Albert Einstein and Carl Jung to Henry David Thoreau and even Peter Sellers. As I read and listened, the list got longer, more impressive.

How many others, I wondered, had telepathic or past-life or out-of-body experiences? How many had declined to go public with their personal truth for fear of being considered strange?

I also knew that some people might attribute my experiences, or my reactions to those experiences, to some sort of "mid-age crisis." I was 45. And I was, in fact, in a re-evaluation of what I'd been and where I wanted to go. Writing felt so natural . . .

One night as I listened to Sinatra's jump version of the song "Mack the Knife," alone and dancing to the music, I said to myself:

"To hell with what any one thinks or says. This is me and that's all I have. The important part is just to know myself and try to be myself—and to tell about myself."

If it helped someone somewhere, it would help me, too.

My growing interest in—belief in?—reincarnation was disturbing to some of my more fundamentalist Christian friends. It bothered me that they lightly dismissed the evidence that Jesus' references to reincarnation apparently were ordered erased from the New Testament at the Ecumenical Council of Constantinople in the year 543 A.D.

I also was intrigued that some very intelligent people seemed satisfied with the traditional "church answers" to questions I'd never thought were fully answered by the traditional Western churches.

Poverty . . . early or untimely death . . . Hitler . . . wars . . . "bad luck" . . . disease . . . famine . . . The churches had never quite given me an explanation that was consistent with my sense of a loving, all-positive God. Why would so many people go through such undeserved pain or tragedy?

Reincarnation explained such "tragedy" in life in a way that made it not only rational but also acceptable. It suggested that each soul chose such experiences in order to learn lessons of the soul. That made sense to me, both emotionally and intellectually.

For example: My father had died at age 28 for no apparent reason except that medical science didn't know that patients should get out of bed soon after surgery. He'd had gall bladder surgery, been kept in bed, developed a blood clot and it had killed him.

The story of it had plagued me. Why him, God? Why leave me fatherless, God? Why steal my mother's husband? Why why why why?

Reincarnation told me that he must have had his own destiny to work through, that the death was not tragic unless perceived that way by others. It told me he still exists and that I probably have known him many times in many ways, and undoubtedly will know him again, in some other dimension or back here on Planet Earth.

It outraged me sometimes to wonder if the church had erased such thoughts about reincarnation from what was passed along of Jesus' teachings. There was evidence the church had seen reincarnation as a threat to its growing political and economic base, before and after 543 A.D.

I thought of Jesus now as "the senior guy" in spirit development.

And I saw things that were still in the New Testament—which I'd started reading again—that indicated the "church" hadn't erased everything after all, back in 543 A.D. It was frustrating to know that if I spent my days as a student of the subject, I probably wouldn't find empirical proof of what Jesus had really said. And I certainly wasn't a student of it.

If it was true that the churches had edited his teachings, in effect, it was to me an outrage. But somehow I knew that it must also be one of those perceived negatives that can become an enormous positive: In my case, this made me go out in search of answers, and my answers, whether reincarnation or something else, might mean more to me.

And ultimately, I felt, as Mathew had said, whatever I believed and prayed for would be true for me.

My mind kept wandering back to the visual impression I'd had of a woman and Scott: Two whirling discs in space, each a gentle, organic engine with chunky gearteeth, each spinning fast in space, slowly edging closer to each other in the void, then meeting and meshing. As if they had come from the same mechanism at some previous time.

Was I just imagining?
Or was the image somehow true?

Suppose, I thought, that it was real—then a lot of other images might be true, and it would be sadly true that I'm seldom conscious of true reality.

Was the material world, as I'd sensed back when I was 2, just some sort of stage where we acted things out?

And if I ever really shared these thoughts with others, would they dismiss them figuring I was an alcoholic who had continued to hallucinate after he'd stopped drinking, or had substituted fantasy for booze?

To me, the truth seemed clear: Spiritual realms exist, prayer works.

I know that, regardless of what anyone thinks. I know it.

Much of the appeal of belief in the occult seemed to be to those who felt left out of mainstream values and traditional beliefs—people who needed to find something to believe in. Did I fit the latter category?

I didn't know. But I did know that something was happening in my life and in the lives of people I knew. My intuition was telling my brain: Explore and examine. Listen. Answers will come.

I'd picked up a record album at a music store in Carmel Valley.

Ben, the owner, might not be everybody's "nice guy," but I found him bright and fun and fascinating—and good counsel on music. He'd sung in the opera and had a law degree: he'd had gone to great schools.

When I got home I put it on, sat in the leather chair in the living room, listening and waiting for a fresh pot of coffee to brew.

Tony Bennett's All-Time Greatest Hits. I'd bought it for one song.

For once in my life,
I have someone who needs me . . .

Something had changed since that night when Mr. B. sang it to me at the Shoreham. Maybe God had become that "someone" in my life, and "someone I've needed so long."

That's it. That's right, I thought: I'd spent all those years thinking "the right woman" would fill that void in me, that horrible hole in my gut.

It wasn't a woman at all! What a burden to have put my deepest hopes on those women whose eyes, and lives, I had entered so eagerly.

If I found a mirror-image of me in a female—my other half, as the people around my little town might say—she'd have as many problems and faults and foibles as I have. And that is not the Savior Woman I'd cried to find.

I had been unable, for years, to know any of this because either I wasn't ready for the knowlege, or had covered it over in booze.

I was enjoying my aloneness and my writing and soaking up the sun and green hills and beach. On a Monday night I drove to the music store and treated myself to five records: Tchaikovsky's Sixth Symphony, Shostakovich's Piano Concerto No. 1 and his Fifth Symphony, and Prokofiev's First and Fifth Symphonies. And I bought good blank tapes so I could immediately make recordings for the car.

Then I noticed something: When I wanted to work hard on writing and be alone, I wanted classical music. Shostakovich, Tchaikovsky, Mozart, Beethoven.

When I had been so involved in developing meditational progress, I'd bought orchestrated music about space and the imagination—scores for "Close Encounters," "Star Wars" and "E.T." And I had played a lot of Andreas Vollenweider's mysterious music.

Life's risks make one grateful for details

There's only one way to say it: Straight, and in specifics.

It's Tuesday night. I've been on the highway. When I got home, I put some kona beans in the grinder and am brewing half a pot of coffee. Its aroma is filling the kitchen and stairs landing now. I've lived alone for 2½ years and can indulge not only in the aroma but also in "my" music now.

Let me go back a week: On that Tuesday afternoon, I came flying back into the office after lunch, my head full of digital, left-brained stuff. I was trying to leave for New York the next day.

LIVING BUSINESS

Scott B. Smith

A cohort stopped me in our lobby to introduce a woman who's been doing a lot for a charity I admire.

I fell out of the digital mode for an instant. We spoke for maybe two minutes, max. An hour later, sweaty and shaking like age 14, I phoned her. Yes, we'd have lunch. Oh yes.

I got on five planes in the succeeding days and felt safe all the way from San Jose to New York, Washington and back.

I got back, and had a most remarkable lunch with Her.

It feels—or normally would feel—risky to write about that. But at least I can . . . I taped a string of favorite old songs, then mailed the cassette to Her. That's an ohmygawd for this kid, age 45.

Then, tonight, I headed north up Pacific Coast Highway. I usually drive about 55 miles each way on Tuesday nights to take my kids, ages 6 and almost-5, to a pancake place in Half Moon Bay for dinner.

There was heavy fog on the winding two-lane road. Traffic was light and cautious; most of us wore headlights in the 5 p.m. mists.

A pair of brights slammed up behind me, pushing, pushing. I turned the stereo down, grit my teeth and lightly touched the brakes to try to get the guy to back off. He was not backing off.

After maybe 10 miles of his brights just 15 feet off my trunk, he whipped around me, in fog, across a double yellow line. He was driving a bright yellow Chevy pickup. He chose to press on and also pass the car in front of me.

He was flying in blindness, maybe 70 miles an hour. There was an oncoming car. It swerved. He swerved, cut in sharply on the car ahead of me. No accident. He zoomed away. I tried not to wish him poorly.

An hour later, the kids safely beside me, I saw a highway patrol officer and told her about the yellow Chevy pickup, just in case the driver was still around.

Dropped the kids back at their mother's at 7:15, and headed back southward. The fog was an ominous wall. I held the speed to maybe 30. So did others.

Cranked up the stereo and tried to relax with the drive. Put on Barbra's version of "Being Alive," a song which I had included in the tape for Her—the risk I'd chosen to take, and one which felt scary at the time.

Flashing red and blue and yellow lights in the distance. Brakes, down window, cut the music.

A heavy-duty flashlight attached to a fog-shrouded officer waved me into the lane for oncoming traffic. I crept along, and saw the carcass in the road.

A man's feet stuck out from the plastic bag. Had it been 25 years since I'd covered fatal accidents as a young reporter, since I had helped the police scrape a family off the concrete on Highway 22 in Pennsylvania?

I saw the mangled sedan the man had died in: It looked big, gray business-like, but now half its original length.

There was another officer in the roadway. I asked if it was a single fatality—"so far," he said "Bad week on this road."

I got about two miles before I gagged. I stuffed it, kept going. But just as I did, a pair of headlights raced up behind and around my car, passing blind in the fog just after passing a fatality.

It wasn't the bright yellow pickup. That guy was probably on a barstool somewhere, warming up for his late-night drive back to wherever he came from.

I toned up the stereo again, and bellowed out with Barbra.

"Being Alive!"

I am thrilled that I have taken a little risk in the past week. I am grateful I saw my kids tonight. They're coming to my house this weekend. Grateful their mother is happy, has a risk of her own now. Grateful my favorite classical station, KBOQ in Monterey, is playing joy in the fog tonight. Grateful for a typewriter and the smell of coffee. Grateful for business problems and successes.

And since I choose to live at the ocean, grateful to hear that surf. It roars when there's heavy fog. As if to celebrate life and its own endlessness.

It surprised me that I gagged out there on the road. I'm a newspaper guy, toughened long ago to that stuff. I am pleased I gagged, and if I have a nightmare tonight that'll be OK too. I'm not so toughened after all.

Surprised, too, because I have spent a lot of energy over the last couple of years in considerations of death and life beyond it.

That plastic bag held someone's employee, someone's father, someone's lover, someone's son. Whatever follows life, he's there. Four hours ago, he was here.

But the yellow pickup's still out there . . .

The kona coffee gives a heady zip. My son Huntley drew the canyon picture of Mickey Mouse smiling out from a 5-by-7 oak frame atop the disk drive here in the den, where I can hear the surf rolling in, rolling, rolling in.

I'm glad I took the risk last week and today. Glad even if She decides I'm a cornpone who never got past Cole Porter.

Grateful too that Cole Porter didn't honor his fears and decide to stay in law school instead of writing his heart's music.

Grateful for today. Just today.

And business is just fine, thank you, just fine.

When I had been dating heavily, I had bought pop stuff.

And back when I had first broken up with Denise and was hurting so much, I'd bought a lot of Sinatra.

We seek that which will enhance the seeking.

Agnieszka Winkler and I met for lunch at the Decathalon Club. Business was great and she wanted to know what I thought about Art Lund, the man who'd entered her life via Rotary and, in part, through me.

When I mentioned, for the third lunch in a row, Shirley MacLaine's stuff, Agnieszka showed only a casual, polite interest. I was frustrated. I just knew she'd be coming along one of these days. I saw it happening in so many faces now. And, as a very bright and successful executive, she was sort of a gauge, I felt, of what was happening.

The book was well under way now. My "writing days," usually two a week, were full of music and emotion, highs and swearing and storming between den and living room, to re-live the past, and describe it.

I'd felt for several years that there had been "two me's." One was the crazed alcoholic, the other the sober Smith. The more I wrote about the alcoholic, the more I felt "him" as "me," as an extension of emotions and problems I was still trying to deal with.

I told myself one morning: "I've got alcoholism, not alcoholwasm." I'd left the bottle behind but could still carry the burdens, the wreckage of my past and the dread of the future—or I could work, daily, on spiritual answers to those emotional problems.

I didn't yet know that my spirit was hard at work on the physical/emotional me.

18

I hadn't expected it.

During the early sobriety, and then during the hell of a "sober divorce" and the turmoil of getting the Business Journal on its feet, I had thought my reward would be the days when I could stay at home and write.

But as the writing progressed, I watched a series of changes unfold within me, and knew that more work and more progress lay ahead—and greater rewards. All an inside job.

It felt somehow "ungrateful" to think there could be vital personal growth that could be loosely labeled "Beyond Recovery." But there it was, happening within me, evident all around me. It presented an immediate problem. The spiritual results, inside me, might seem esoteric to many—especially to those who regarded anything beyond the tangible, material world to be the useless conjecture of a hyper-imagination.

But what I was finding was stunning: The changes within were the most practical tools I'd ever found. Nothing previously matched the practical power of prayer and meditation—and discovery—in my day-to-day living.

November 1985:

I'd gone back to Allentown for an overnight visit.

Harry Phillips had changed. He was heavier. He was happily married. And he'd given up his computer analysis work because he felt called to do God's work. Now he took me to the third floor of a charitable institution and introduced me to his friends: The long-term, seriously disabled. Harry was working as a nurse's aide, changing sheets and cheering up people who had no limbs or perhaps little hope.

There was a banter among them, and an esprit that I'd never felt. I left feeling higher than any booze had ever gotten me.

Ed Schmidt had not changed. The same Santa Claus eyes, the same stub of a cigar.

But I was disappointed: After two hours, he hadn't once advised me "jus' don't fuggin drink." I told him I'd come all the way from the West just to hear him say it, and he grinned—"that's what you needed then," he said. It was that simple.

I had breakfast with Roy Heffelfinger, managing editor now of the Morning Call. It felt warm to see this quiet man, very active in a Christian church, a man who'd quietly tried to help me when I was down 'n out—God, I loved him.

He'd been rewarded, I felt. Long ago, he said, he'd been given a chance to buy a little stock in the Allentown newspaper. It had been small, but a stretch. Years later, the company had been acquired. Much to Roy's shock, he and his wife had become financially comfortable. "It was like a gift."

I asked whether he felt that his history of giving and the stock were related or whether it was "just a coincidence." His eyes lit up in joy, and that look was his answer.

En route westward, I met in Pittsburgh with Paul Everett, son-in-law of Norman Vincent Peale. He was enthusiastically managing a program of prayer breakfasts for business people, and it was spreading across the country. I asked whether he saw new doors opening, saw the old institutions being replaced by a new level of spirituality in the land. His answer: "Absolutely!"

West Coast, Midwest, East Coast: Because I had experienced the change in me, I now saw it everywhere.

I couldn't help but wonder what would happen next in my life.

Friday, November 29, 1985:

Seat 26A, United Flight 139, O'Hare to San Jose: I was in the smoking section, almost alone. I pulled the leather writing pad out of my briefcase and started an outline on a yellow legal pad.

I left about two inches of blank space between each of the headings: "What's going on"; "Sales"; "Facts"; "Profits"; "Decisions."

The cabin was light with the morning sun. We banked to our right and climbed to 35,000 feet. My shoulder and neck felt warm and I realized I had not felt sunshine in about 10 days.

I'd covered some emotionally important ground on this trip: A publishers' meeting in Kansas City, then three days in the Washington area with Don and Laura and her husband Randy, plus old Star friends, then on to Allentown and Pittsburgh. And then to Medina for a family Thanksgiving.

The big downer in the eight days was the knowledge that Joe, the Allentown broker who'd advised me so wisely not to work during my early recovery, and then had suggested that I read "How to Be Your Own Best Friend," had contracted cancer of the lungs and died. And the "other Harry"—the one who'd wanted me to advise him even when he had far more sobriety—had gotten cancer of the brain and died.

"They died sober, Scott," Harry Phillips told me. We nodded. There wasn't anything more to say.

I'd also visited an old family friend, Jo Jo McClellan, in the hospital on Thanksgiving Day, and sensed she was ready to die—but it had felt right; she was ready.

Was I starting to see death in a new light?

Now it seemed as if I should be emotionally and physically drained. Instead, I felt calm, rested, ready for something.

I would not have wanted to admit it to anyone I could think of—not even Leslie Downs—but an uninvited "astrological reading" had been leading into me into a realization, whether the astrology had any validity itself or not, and I certainly doubted it.

Before I'd left, I'd listened to my tape of Marge Waier's unsolicited astrological reading about me once more. And in it (whether the reading was accurate or not about my future), was a truth, an overwhelming wonderful truth about my life-to-date:

I had always had my mother's love.

Funny, how truths can arrive. I knew it would bother my mother if she knew how I'd finally heard the right thing, under the premise of someone reading my life through the stars.

I also knew just how sad or silly it might sound to her if she knew that over the years I had not felt "fulfilled" with her love, that I had felt that there hadn't been enough. But that was the truth. (I'd also worried that somehow she thought she had "caused" my alcoholism. It would be the normal family-member's reaction, in any family—to think somehow they had been responsible.)

Yes!, I had always had my mother's love. Ann just hadn't known how to verbalize it, or to show it physically as much as I'd apparently needed.

I thought about it again: Who could shut her own son off from the whole family when he was down, out and dying? Only a mother who had the love and the guts to know that he needed his bottom.

My heart sang for her—joy that I was sober, joy that we'd had such a fine Thanksgiving together. And, oh yes yes yes, joy for me, for the whole family, for her husband Al, whom I loved more each day now.

Ann had loved me—loves me now. It had taken this much work and pain, this many years, for her sick son to see it.

And, as with most of the truer things I was finding in my life, there were paradoxes imbedded in the rock:

1. I'd been slow, obtuse. But now, finally, I was gaining the knowledge of her love through a process that was carrying my consciousness far beyond anything she might think "true" or "real."

2. She might someday read my book, and I'd have to write about this. I felt embarrassed, and knew that it could make her uncomfortable to read this and know that others might also read this.

I decided to skip the work in my briefcase and to read instead. This needed to be a restful flight, after all the emotions of the trip plus the preceding two weeks—six hours with the dentist, surgery on my eyelid, breaking away from Susan, trying to stay afloat in corporate politics, finding a new editor for the San Jose Business Journal, and working on my first book.

I closed my eyes. I immediately had a calm feeling, a peaceful knowing that if I'd just wait for a moment, I would be able to see something . . .

I shrugged it off, reached for MacLaine's "Dancing in the Light" and sipped on coffee.

The MacLaine book, I thought, would be exactly right for the moment—her final chapters, starting now with her visit to New Mexico.

The captain came on the intercom to say that passengers on the left side could look down and see a 707 refueling an Air Force tanker. I looked and marveled at the flea-and-fly display below us.

Then, to the right and slightly higher than our westbound airliner, I saw a commercial jet, perhaps the same size as our 727, streaking eastward, leaving a straight white contrail. The speed of the aircraft—going the opposite direction—plus the white trail was inspiring, floating in the deep blue of the high altitude.

Are people like that, I wondered—our spirits, beautiful and free and streaking through time, so far above the day-to-day rituals?

I shook it off and got up and walked back to the bathroom. The peacefulness continued although I was physically and mentally 'of this world' again.

Back in my seat, I closed my eyes for a moment.

I saw my real self.

My face—me but strikingly cleaner, clearer.

I opened my eyes and the face was still there.

I could see on two levels, in two ways, at once. I could see the backs of the aircraft seats, and could see the face of me simultaneously.

There was nothing strange or alien or frightening about it; it seemed natural and right.

> *It is my face, somehow younger and minus some of the timescars, yet current. It is the real, down-deep me: smiling and joyous.*

I couldn't see the body, just the face.

I examined it: There, no more than three feet away, was my face, but without the lines and without the scars of my past life. The eyes were loving me!

So which was the real me—the Scott sitting on the plane or the Scott looking at him?

> *Both, Scott. Both are here right now and both are true: the physical and the spirit . . .*

There was a flicker of doubt. I did some mental checking: No, my eyes weren't closed. I wasn't dreaming. I looked out the window and saw clouds below us and brilliant blue sky above us. And I saw the face—my face—as if it were just outside the airplane window.

My pulse felt normal. I'd presumably had the same, normal oxygen supply as everyone else on the plane. I had not drunk a lot of coffee nor had any abnormal physical experiences in the preceding hours or days. No alcohol, drugs, not even aspirin.

Then I sensed how cynical I had become through the years. Here I was having a deeply wonderful experience and something in me—the trained observer—wanted to disprove the experience—account for it rationally—because it was not "normal."

I explored my feelings. The amazement I felt was at knowing with absolute clarity that inside I am free and joyous. I saw how restless a spirit I'd become. It was as if my very Being needed rest. And I was just 45! Young, too young, to feel that I had already done too much.

I had no doubt that I was desperate to rest my physical mind and body—yet also no doubt that my spirit was that younger, joyous face.

My brain had become so loaded with all the living I was doing that the cranial circuits never got a chance to close down and relax. I'd been so caught up in the day-to-minute-to-second handling of business, writing, friends and children, the house and finances, my health and . . . it was just too much.

My work was satisfying enough. But it was too much; I would have to let down, maybe get away.

Suddenly I remembered the 17-year-old brunette from San Mateo who'd been vacationing with her family at Maui a year earlier—so lovely and natural and relaxed. She'd been attractive to me physically and on a higher, more spiritual level. I hadn't said a word to her, but I remembered thinking, "How refreshing!" What the hell was I doing remembering her at a moment like this? I hadn't thought of her once since Maui.

So there I was—the inside of me joyous, younger, wholesome, and the outside tense, caught-up.

Yet I knew that this was exactly the way it was supposed to be. And I had a book screaming at me to write it. There wouldn't be any vacations for another year.

The alcoholism, the fear of death, the painful need for love, the torture of the messed-up families I'd created—I could see now how it all served to train and test my spirit.

It fit into a process of tough yet lasting lessons.

No wonder I had been expressing gratitude for my alcoholism. My inner me already knew that it was a gift—a condition that would help me, force me, to get down on my knees, to examine my life, to change.

No wonder I'd immediately recognized truths in coincidences along the way—the one in June, 1978, for example, when I'd known absolutely that the little book was right when it had said we are here because our souls are in training.

Oh my! All those little 'coincidences' along the way . . .

Then, still sitting by the airplane window, looking around, I began to get a series of impressions of the people in my life, and what they meant:

Mike Russell and Bill Worley were granting the time and salary to let me do the writing I "had to do." Bless them!

Mike had come along at exactly the right time and I could "see" clearly that he knew it, and could see that he too had a larger purpose.

Again I marveled at the magical "coincidence" of the timing of the creation of the Business Journal.

And along had come Armon, and now Tom Shawver, our general manager, to keep the paper profitable while I did some writing that might, just might, help somebody.

I saw my mother's strength and courage as part of my recovery.

I saw my wives and what had happened. Lynn and much later Denise had, for their own reasons, long before I'd left either, chosen not to join me in my searching. Had I known that all along, but had been afraid to acknowledge it, because to do so would shatter the illusions we'd tried to maintain?

We'd had love and good times, and had become the parents of four delightful people. It was okay, all of it.

I'm fortunate, I thought, that the wife and mother figure I chose in 1978 was Denise.

I saw clearly how Denise had "coincidentally" gotten a job in Tucson, had told a friend before she left that she "knew" she would marry a recruiter there. Maybe she knew me before she ever got to Tucson, and went there to conceive Jessie and Huntley. There were, after all, very strong mystical experiences connected with the conception of each.

Was she, for example, an old friend from another time? The facts were far too "coincidental" to ignore.

My mind was reeling, yet I was calm and joyful.

What if Jessie really was my father Don reincarnate? I'd always sensed something so familiar and knowing in those wise blue eyes. My mother had spotted something, had said Jessie was the only child to carry Don's looks and personna. And I could not forget that a third spirit had been present at the exact moment that Denise and I knew we were creating a baby.

The impressions continued to flash by me, each a clear vision. There was no shred of doubt about the validity of what I was sensing.

I saw my brother "A" as a dear old friend.

H.R. had been my teacher and father. And yes, he had been there in the car in 1980, and later on the 6th green on that July 4th in 1980. He wasn't around now because he knew I didn't need him now.

Remember what he said to me: "Now will you stop worrying about Time"?

And when, in 1982 in San Carlos I'd "seen" H.R. with my father—was that real? Yes. I'd slipped into Other Time. And was that third person with his back to me—was that in fact me? I still didn't know, but it seemed important that I felt that question during this moment of clarity. I didn't know why.

As my thoughts traveled, I saw a current acquaintance as a gargoyle of himself, and I understood: He was misshapen now, his wonderful spirit trapped in his tragedy of drugs and homosexuality. What I was physically seeing was a caricature drawn by his torment. And there would be nothing I or anyone else could do—he had to work through his own bottom, find his own answers.

I knew that we are all one, yet separate and alone. We are pieces of the same huge, pulsating beauty that is God, but each of us is growing in his own way, going through his or her own individual shortening of the distance from the light in our spirits.

Reincarnation made absolute sense.

That, perhaps, there was a clue to the youthful, rested feeling I had on this flight: I'd started accepting the tenets of reincarnation. This acceptance relieved the urgency; I didn't have to get everything "right" today, nor even in this lifetime. And that was exactly how it was 'supposed' to be.

So slow down and enjoy the ride, Scott.

What was Susan to me? Was it right to break us up? What was she?

Donna had suggested that Susan was a teacher. That was certainly true. And there were ways in which I was teaching Susan. Yet, were we meant to be lovers, or even mates?

On that crazy July evening when I returned to the bookstore, I so clearly—oh yes, clearly—recognized her and knew I should go get her. I had taken her my book with love and trust, even though I didn't know her name.

Was that why I'd chosen to live in my little town? Because Susan had lived in that little town, had known and loved it so? Had I—or God—put me there so I would find her? Was that to be our home together? Or did we have some unfinished business to settle and I simply needed to find her and get it straightened out before I moved on?

And what of Donna? What was she in my life? And had I moved there to be near her?

Donna's fear of a sexual relationship for us made sense to me. Was she, then, just a deep and lasting friend? She'd feared that sex with me would be "incest." Maybe she was right.

It was confusing and I was not getting any answers.

> *Don't doubt this experience, Scott. We know about so many invisible things—radio waves and X-rays and television images, all zooming through the air. Don't doubt these impressions because they aren't tangible.*

It all fits, I thought. All my life, I've said that time either doesn't exist or doesn't matter. It had been so frustrating—I'd been obsessed with something I sensed didn't really count. Einstein wasn't enough for me, his evidence was just intellectual. I had needed this non-intellectual, internal knowing.

No wonder time doesn't matter, I thought, and no wonder even Jesus apparently spoke about reincarnation—it's obvious, Scott, obvious. Like your finger in front of your nose.

My finger! All my life I've been saying that what I felt inside was more real to me than my own flesh. I was right! If what I truly am is a spirit, not a body per se, then what I *feel* is what "is."

So God is everyone and everywhere, I thought. And I am part of Him.

> *Just be open, Scott.*
> *There is so much to learn,*
> *and nothing to fear or resist.*

Almost reluctantly, yet knowing it would help me get further along this path of vision, I finally picked up the MacLaine book. I was on page 310. MacLaine's effects on me—or rather, the effects of the spirituality I shared with her—had become almost instantaneous as I'd come to know her style and message.

Part of me was saying, "I shouldn't be reading this." This stemmed, I knew, from my backgrounding in the Episcopal and Lutheran churches and the reliance upon intellect I learned in Medina, Ohio. My mother, like most of the Bennett family, put intellect above spirit, or tried to. It felt safer, I guessed.

The concept of reincarnation felt so right to me! It made at least as much sense as the theology I had been taught. What the hell was so right about the thoughts or expectations (or lack of expectations) of a group of people in a small town in Ohio in the mid-20th Century? Even a group of people I happened to love and respect so much?

I felt enormously free in questioning their positions. I did it without rebellion but sensing that I'd gone further than they, and that my own impressions were more to be trusted—at least by me—than theirs. They were my elders, not gods.

I dove into the MacLaine book. Within two hours, I reached the section where she sees her own Higher Self. I threw the book onto the seat beside me and laughed joyously aloud.

Coincidences . . .

In the days after the flight back, I continued to absorb the implications of my experiences on the plane, and they continued to make sense. Then, on a December Sunday, I gave myself a present—a quiet drive down the coast to Nepenthe, the restaurant in Big Sur. Some "down time."

I enjoyed my own surprise at the brunch I ate there on the terrace—the vegetarian salad, orange juice, coffee and crackers. I didn't even think of ordering the Tanquerey that once was so much a part of Nepenthe for me. This was not the Scott Smith I'd known and not quite liked or respected all those years.

I watched a wrapped-tight couple meander through the gift shop, each in display-window clothes, "perfect for California." They were a sad sight, and I knew that deep down inside, each was desperately lonely. And I thought I knew because I had been like that for so much of my life.

May they find their bottom!
Pass the bottoms, please, so my friends here
can have theirs and then move along.

On days when I needed to be in San Jose, but wanted to be back at home writing the book, I carried a tape recorder and notepad in the car. The changes and realizations within were arriving so fast now that I couldn't leave them out of the book. So the text started reading a bit like a spiritual diary instead of my history. Yet I felt I had no choice but to continue—if the "diary aspect" bothered some readers, they'd have to accept it.

I couldn't let the book end until my readers got a chance to see some of what I was seeing, because I felt it was all the natural sequence of spiritual "events" that had begun back when I asked for help in not-drinking one day at a time, and obviously indicative of the change now sweeping through my generation.

I was seeing that because of my weakness, I had opened up to a new consciousness. There was no doubt in me that something very significant was happening in mankind's history. I'd started calling it "The Revolution of Spirit".

It felt esoteric even to say it. And I was not, after all, just writing esoterica. I was writing about lives that I and Denise and Lynn and others had lived and felt.

It was true that the moment had come with Denise when I'd had to save my very self, protect my sobriety. Otherwise, I couldn't be a father, or a writer or even alive. But what of all the pain, tears and sheer hard work that had gone into the long months of trying to save a marriage? I could not write the whole story.

I knew I would have to swallow and adopt two principles, even if I came out looking like a bastard: First, the book covered an inventory of my life, not theirs. I would have to trust readers to realize that divorces seldom occur because of only one person's needs or actions. And, secondly, I'd have to trust readers to sense that I had felt too much, not too little.

And even if I couldn't tell the whole story, the truth was the truth: There hadn't been an A-plus marriage there in the first place. You cannot restore something that did not exist.

19

A Revolution of Spirit.

I was seeing it everywhere. And I was coming to my own understanding of some of the background of the changes sweeping over us.

The founding of Alcoholics Anonymous in 1935—mankind's first effective answer to the disease that I have—came during the same period when man was developing the science of psychiatry.

The success of A.A., more than any other group or program, had led to a massive self-help movement which stressed internal processes to help people feel better about themselves by solving problems of body, mind, heart or soul.

Norman Vincent Peale had been the greatest single force, after A.A. had started what seemed to be essentially one big process. His first big book had come out just as A.A. was gaining national effectiveness—the early 1950s. Both A.A. and Peale were spiritual in nature—both based, in fact, on the message of Jesus. The A.A. steps stripped away the ritual and politics of the generic, tradition-burdened church.

In roughly the same period, man discovered atomic power and developed the ability to extinguish himself—which could force peacefulness among the super powers, allowing man a new chance.

Now mankind, led mostly by Americans, I thought, is edging into an era of enormous change, an era when man begins to understand that there is a scientific, cause-and-effect nature to the events in his life, both individually and collectively.

People everywhere are beginning see themselves not as evolved animals but as evolving spirits.

A bridge in time-
Go on! Cross it.

A winter morning, 1986:

In a dream—or was it a vision on the verge of sleep?—I had seen tall forms that were the aunts and uncles and friends who had died. Their spirits seemed so powerful, so vibrant, there was just no way that the death of those bodies could have snuffed out their spirits.

I sat up in bed, wondering how anyone could think they knew more than Jesus, who'd gotten life's principles so right.

I thought of one member of the older generation who vehemently argued that "visions" or meditational "tripping" were creatures of the imagination and therefore the brain. Thus she distrusted anything which could not be tangibly or logically proven.

And I saw her intellectual trap: She felt that "the mind plays tricks on you"—yet relied on her own mind, keen as it was, to disprove what others thought or sensed might be truer than anything tangibly provable.

What a waste! But, I thought, that's how she needed to be, for her own reasons.

I'd been reading a copy of "A Vision of the Aquarian Age" which the author, George Trevelyan, had given Mike Russell. And there I saw an answer to some of the "intellectual" cynics and spiritual skeptics I was encountering—the people who told me that 'life after death' was "wishful thinking," that we would walk on into oblivion.

Trevelyan wrote:

"To those who believe in the extinction of consciousness after death, and who demand proof of survival . . .

"Can you produce for me one shred of real evidence that you are extinguished? I challenge you to demonstrate that your position is anything but sheer supposition.

"An immense body of circumstantial evidence is now available for any mind prepared to consider it openly, without prejudice.

"This evidence provides increasingly more basis to conclude that the soul continues, very much alive. There is no similar evidence to bear witness to its extinction."

So *faith* is the first issue. Always. In everything.

Perhaps, I suspected, there will be "proof" of the soul and of life after-life, but until then, I could get nowhere unless, in every situation, I began with faith.

Without my alcoholism, I might not have had to learn faith.

Today, I could see, a quiet, usually unspoken faith was my underlying assumption in my dealings with job, writing, children, women, money and friends, even physical safety.

There was more, far more, to learn. And I was learning. But faith was the beginning.

The faith had to be personal and nurtured. And the best way to have that experience, for me, was by prayer and meditation.

In addition, there were things I could read that might prod my intuitive understanding.

Another book Mike had given me was called "Agartha" by Meredith Lady Young. She was, she said, a "channel" for a spirit who wanted to tell us about ourselves and our situation. I was skeptical until I started reading. Pieces of it felt far more "right" to me than the traditional things I'd heard all my life.

And I realized something so obvious: Whether it was the Bible or some Eastern treatise, there were always books which became popular because people everywhere were searching for intuitive confirmations of their own internal personal truth.

As I looked at the nature of what I was learning, I saw that in my 20s and early 30s, I'd had perhaps one or two important discoveries per year about my own existence. In my late 30s, as I began to get some sobriety, the discoveries had started accelerating. And now, in my mid-40s, the pace was rapidly advancing.

And the more I found out, the more questions I had. The world, the universe, the Creation, was opening up—it was just a matter of how open I wanted to be. The more open, the faster the discoveries came. It felt as if God or my own Higher Self was doling out insights and knowledge to the conscious me at a pace equal to my willingness and ability to absorb.

Things weren't always rosy. Denise and I still had problems at times. Our divorce had been final and our dealings cordial. Yet once in a while, one of us would show the old anger.

One day when she showed it I thought I was cracking.

Winter sunlight poured in through the bedroom door. I held my face to the sun begging God: "please help me!—I want my love—whoever, whatever she is—and my kids close to me. I can't keep going like this. I am just so tired, Father, of trying to be strong and go it alone. Oh God, please please help."

I gagged, got back onto the bed, tried to swallow some coffee and light a cigarette—to somehow push the lump back down.

There was a tightness in my chest. Not the same old band across it that I'd hated so in the drinking days, but still, an uncomfortable tightness.

In the old days, I would have anesthesized it with a bottle. Now, I knew, the answers were inside me.

Tears. Maybe I'd be better-off if I could really cry.

Leave it to God, Scott. Everything will work out perfectly
if you will just leave it to God.

Donna and I sat in the living room talking before dinner. It was my turn to cook: Lamb chops on the grill, spinach salad, kaiser rolls, chocolate cake a la mode.

She referred again to the experience she'd had with her father, an experience *after* he died some nine years ago.

It happened in her sleep, she said. But it was too real to be a dream; it just felt "way outside the norm for what a dream feels like."

As she described it, I got a strange feeling. Part of it was intuitive, and part was remembering something from a book by a man who'd claimed to have gone out of his body many times and to have visited a garden.

Donna said that several years earlier, her father had just died. She was in bed, and then she was suddenly walking in a garden with him.

The garden seemed a bit pristine to her—flowers, grass, paths of hard dark dirt or maybe asphalt. The sky was bright, perhaps bright blue.

In this garden walk, shortly after his death, her father was about 25 years old. The age didn't surprise her, although she hadn't known him when he was 25. In fact it felt "natural" to her.

He was wearing a blue coat. She didn't think she'd ever seen that coat in his lifetime, although she might have seen it in pictures.

He explained that "this" was where he'd gone after his body died. He said he had been in some shock just after his physical death, and he had felt disoriented. But friends were helping him and soon he would go "on."

"He was fine, and he wanted me to know it," Donna said. She was not incredulous or amazed about it, at the time or now.

"You sound as though you're describing some routine chat with Robin or David or some other friend," I told her.

"That's how it felt—so normal. It wasn't dramatic and I wasn't afraid or stunned. I didn't have what we'd consider a normal reaction to something as jolting as a stroll with someone who'd died a week or two previously."

I put more logs on the fire. The ocean was calm, so the small waves lapping onto the shore could be heard. Donna broke the silence.

"Then he visited my son Jesse."

"Huh?"

"Yes." She nodded. "Jesse came out of his room one morning and said he had just seen his grandfather. David and I were still married then, and David asked him about it.

"Jesse said that Grandpa said he was just fine and everything was okay."

Donna said she gave this a lot of credence because Jesse was not normally over-imaginative and he had never before spoken of anything like this.

In fact, she added, it became more real to her over the years since, because the boy never reported anything like that again.

After dinner, I got out "Journeys Out of the Body," by Robert Monroe. I read several bits aloud, and we discussed the phenomena Monroe reported. Donna had never heard of Monroe, or his book.

Then I asked her to be specific about the garden, where she and her father had walked and talked. I asked if there were any structures. She thought, then nodded: "There were some Gazebo-like things, rounded on the top."

I asked if she'd seen anyone else there. Again she thought and then said that she didn't remember anyone, at least close by.

I read from Monroe (page 80, "Journeys Out of the Body", 1977 Anchor Press edition). He was describing what he'd experienced when he had left his body and gone to an area he had labeled Locale II, where there were people and entities not unlike those in the physical world.

"On one visit, I ended up in a parklike surrounding, with carefully tended flowers, trees, and grass, much like a large mall with paths crisscrossing the area."

Donna interrupted: "Yes! That's it exactly."

"There were benches along the paths, and there were hundreds of men and women strolling by, or sitting on the benches. Some were quite calm, others a little apprehensive, and many had a dazed or shocked look of disorientation. They appeared uncertain, unknowing of what to do or what was to take place next.

"Somehow I knew that this was a meeting place, where newly arrived waited for friends or relatives. From this Place of Meeting, these friends would take each newcomer to the proper place where he or she 'belonged'."

Donna was excited. Her eyes had a spiritual look I hadn't seen in months.

"That is exactly how it was! And he said he had felt disoriented but he was okay now and somone would take him on wherever he was supposed to be."

I took pains to explain just why I thought Monroe's experience might be suspect. As a matter of fact, he'd detailed the reasons in his book, which actually gave him a lot more credibility, I felt.

But Donna seemed convinced. The two places were the same or very, very similar—and, to her, real.

To me, the scene seemed probable, but deep inside me was still some bit of skepticism.

I was becoming leary of two men. Each wore neat, crisp clothes, sped along speaking like a tommygun. Each acted as if we were lifelong friends.

Each apparently wanted my trust in order to accomplish his own unannounced agenda.

The longer I watched, the less I trusted.

I went through a period of revulsion. But then I saw more: Each man had his own brand and level of personal problems.

The trick for me was to avoid or ignore them—it was the only way I could stop judging or resenting them. And for me, resentment could get me drunk, and judging others would only hurt me.

Driving, Route 17, a Thursday morning:

It was raining. Both hands were on the wheel. There was a yellow Honda about 70 yards ahead of me, California tags.

There was also an image, up and to my right. It was Me!

I could still see the yellow car in front of me, still see my speedometer, behave normally. How come I could see both reality and Reality at once, while driving? It suprised me only slightly—I was too intrigued.

I stared, inside my head, at the image:

I was huddled, cowering, with see-through hands trying to hide my face. The feeling was enormous: Shame and embarrassment for my generation, a whole era full of single, middle-aged people working so hard at getting love, feeling lovable, having the courage to break up the couplings that weren't working for them.

So lost we had to find.

I was overwhelmed with compassion. For all of us, for me.

Two mornings later I was back at the desk in my den, finishing the first pot of coffee. I called Armon Mills, who was in Albany, where our people were acquiring a paper, No. 13 in the chain.

We spoke for 20 minutes and it was good. I was somehow more on track with work than I'd been in weeks.

He confirmed that Mike was so busy with pension funds—he'd been elected chairman of a huge one in the Midwest—that Bill Worley was now making the decisions about the newspapers.

I knew what Mike was up to: He had a new 'mission'.

Mike wanted to see that the huge pension funds—billions in unpublicized investment pools—were redirected toward rejuvenating American cities.

At the same time, he and Bill Worley were headed toward at least 20 business weeklies in the country within the year. American City Business Journal stock, meanwhile, had more than tripled in less than a year.

What a delight: Mike and Bill were doing well by being good.

Bob Keady was my constant steadying influence.

He and Jody came over to spend a day at the beach, and Jody finally leaned over him to say to me: "I know you're interested in these things, Scott, and I haven't told anyone about it, but I had an out-of-body thing a couple of nights ago."

"Oh?" I glanced at Bob. He had put his forehead against the blanket.

"I'd just gotten into bed and was ready to go asleep, and all of a sudden I just rose up above my body."

To hell with my nonchalance. My voice squeaked: "What happened?"

"I was several feet above it, my body, and the bed, and I just—I got scared! I was scared I wouldn't be able to come back. And right away I was back in the bed, back in my body."

"Yup. You got fear—that's what'll stop me, too. I get to feel as though I might die, and right away I have no ability to do anything like an OOB."

"That's right. It was fearful."

"When you were out—did you see anything? Or just feel it?"

She paused, looked down, and absently drew in the sand with her finger. I wondered what her doodle was. A question mark, probably.

"I guess I just felt it, but it was absolutely real, Scott. There was no doubt at all about it."

She was deadly serious.

Bob had pressed his forehead into the beach blanket, as if trying to hide his head in the sand.

Poor Bob. He was surrounded.

I decided to kid him about it. It was risky, because I didn't want to hurt or offend a best friend. But best friends, I knew, are for honesty.

"Hey Bob—you trying to hide your head in the sand?"

"All I know is, I haven't had a drink today," he grunted.

I nodded. On one level he was absolutely right. Our sobriety was the greatest spiritual answer we could get—proof, to us, of the Grace of God.

"But, yeah Bob, well—I didn't get sober so I could just hang around and be sober . . ."

Jody nodded.

Bob was silent.

Tucson, Arizona
Springtime, 1986:

I'd had dinner with Dodie Gust the evening before, and then we'd sat in her apartment for hours, talking about the progress, the paths we'd found in our sobriety and searching.

I had dictated notes this morning, and knew I would want more time to listen, to digest what was rolling out before her.

Dodie, now 58, was a newspaperwoman, a writer. I was surprised when she told me she'd once gone to see a psychic who read auras. He had told her that in a past life she had over-done religious studies and had flipped out on them. In this life, he'd said, she would study religion and yet let God show her what was right.

"That was pinpoint accuracy," she said.

Her response to the aura reader's reference to her past-life was, "I don't disbelieve anything and I'm open to whatever God reveals. But I think what He has in store is far better than anything human minds can conceive. We may get glimpses of the cosmic mystery, but it's always glimpses followed by guesses. There may be other planes to experience before we reach the Omega Point but I really don't think God is so limited that he has to recycle souls."

The paradox, to me, was that she was choosing to do all this within the Catholic Church, within the context of traditional theological study and interpretation.

She was completing a new book on the teachings of St. Paul, "As I Take Christ," and rewriting a more psychological book about the effects and lessons that human anger produced.

Now she wanted to simplify her life as much as possible so that she could break through the intellectual processes—without ignoring the human mind's learning—and get to the nub of her own existence: "To discover and do the will of God."

So Dodie was on a path similar to mine, but within the church.

After breakfast, I drove over to University Avenue and walked onto to the University of Arizona campus for the first time in many years. It was not home to me, but something in me was saying "congratulations, Scott."

The shame and horror that I felt on that campus in 1973-75 was gone. I felt wholesome, returned the smiles of people I passed.

I had tried, with some success, to make amends here in 1980. Now I knew my past was past, that there were no more amends and no more shame necessary.

I went over to the Southern Arizona health clinic where I'd been in counseling with Carolyn in 1975. No one knew anything of her. That was frustrating—I wanted her to see that her work hadn't been in vain.

I had breakfast with Bill Worthington, and although his eyes were bothering him—he couldn't drive the Porsche any more—he was healthy and just as hooked on Kipling, sobriety and the lore of the cattle business as ever. I was so fortunate that he'd played a role in my life.

Lionel Brown hadn't changed one iota, it seemed, since I'd last seen him in 1978. We met at his office, had lunch and then played 18 holes in the desert.

Later, Brownie and Artie and I sat talking for two hours in a Tucson restaurant. Artie was still providing a home to seven otherwise-hopeless dogs. Now I felt that I understood it: It was one way of giving back to God, of being integral to this life.

We laughed about the old days, the first time we'd met—I at the door with the vodka breath, soliciting charter members for the Lutheran mission church. They didn't go back to the church at all now. They felt they had a solid relationship with God without the politicking within a church.

I told them about some of the "coincidences" in my life and the experiences that fascinated me because they tended to prove to me that we survive death. Brownie suddenly cocked his head and interrupted: "I had a strange experience one time."

"Oh?" Although he lived so rationally with his left brain, I knew Brownie had a well-developed spiritual sense, could exhibit strong intuitive knowledge. "It was when I was young. I'd gotten very sick. I tell you, Scott Smith, it was as real as anything I have felt or lived through.

"Anyway—I was terribly ill. I remember that I drifted upward and then there was a sudden rushing feel like I was going through a tunnel."

I watched his face. It was straight, clean—insurance-adjuster Lionel Brown, now 59.

"I went there and then there was a river in front of me, and across the river it was wonderfully beautiful. But I was somehow told that if I went across the river and into the trees and the beauty there I could not come back to Earth, and I was supposed to go back.

"Obviously, it was 'death', there. And I have never felt afraid of 'death' ever since."

Of all people! Lionel Brown had a classic near-death experience. I asked him if he'd ever heard of Raymond Moody's book "Life After Life." He said he'd heard of it long ago, but had never read it. (Several months later, Brownie sent me a clipping: Dodie Gust had done a major story for the Tucson paper on near-death experiences—each strikingly similar to his.)

Later in the evening, I wandered into the place on Pima Street where some recovering alcoholics meet for coffee.

And there was Boyd.

"What a coincidence," I howled as I went over to him. "I really wanted to run into you while I'm in town."

"Boy, do you look better, Scott!"

The boyish grin, the bright and optimistic eyes, the straight brown hair were just the same as they were that first day in 1975 he and Luke had knocked on my front door. And he was healthy, sober, happy.

We didn't talk much about Luke.

Luke had died.

There wasn't anything to say.

I met Agnieszka Winkler over lunch at the Decathalon again.

She was happy, her eyes aglow. She and Art Lund had been married in January and it appeared that the marriage was agreeing with both.

And then, over coffee, it happened:

"Scott—I've been reading something you'd mentioned before . . ."

"Oh Agnieszka! You're starting an awakening?"

She grinned, her head bobbing in excitement.

7 a.m., a winter Tuesday, 1986:

Dawn was just the beginning. I had no idea the experience would last most of the day. The night before, as I went to sleep, I'd asked for clearer conscious insights into all of my life.

The morning's first impressions seemed radically important. I didn't have any sense that more could happen later in the day.

I put on a robe and sat outside in the chill bluepink morning. The ocean was so ordered, so flat; the waves rolled in with almost geometric certainty.

My life had been so chaotic. Now, finally, I was finding some predictability, some meaningful form in it.

Even my emotional life was getting unpredictable. Except for . . .

What about Susan?

She kept changing, hour by hour. Our relationship was chaotic. We'd parted and reunited several times, always at my apparent instigation—though she obviously knew how to trigger my actions.

Chaos. She said most of her life was chaos and it always had been.

Dear sweet Susan was smack-deep in my old routines! A similar personality, without the alcoholism. No wonder I had backed off. She was so like me!

She called about 8 that morning, her "hi" full of fear and confusion. She would be hurt yet again, she said, but wanted to see me. After 15 minutes on the phone, I said I would meet her for lunch.

I sat on the back deck in robe and pajamas, making office phone calls and soaking up the sun.

The thought began:

—Susan and I had agreed somehow—in a Before—to help each other overcome obstacles in our own growth in this life.

—Susan needed to overcome her need for chaos, and her fear of abandonment. And she needed to do it with someone who was closer to her levels of growth and potential.

—Scott needed to overcome his need for chaos, and his fear of abandonment. And he needed to do it with someone who was closer to his levels of growth and potential.

Oh my gawd . . .

I pushed my mind to take it further:

—We had each felt abandonment as children. Enormous pain.

—We had each been motivated ever since to avoid any such pain. Yet we had each walked out on marriages that hadn't been working. Had we each by "chance" set up those situations?

The lesson was clear:

—Do not create abandonment—or fear it.

—Do not create chaos—nor honor it.

—Recognize and accept what happened to me as a child, and what I later did to reconfirm chaos I'd felt as a child and anethesize the pain. Accept all of it.

—Accept myself as I am. Don't judge me. Be me.

—Look at Susan exactly as she is and make decisions about her as a separate lover, not as an "issue."

—If we aren't right for each other, don't feel guilty or responsible. It's just the way it is.

Within minutes, more realization came.

I stood leaning on the deck rail realizing that as a parent, I am a friend and guide, someone whose role for Jessie and Huntley should be that of best friend, and that we are partners, not adversaries in the old "teacher" style.

Partners. What joy.

I got some coffee and returned to the deck.

With nature's three-dimensional stage before me—the hillside, the surfline and sea—I sensed that I would not die for a long time, not until I finished learning how to "get" more of my life, and with a chance to do things right. And that would take more exploring and work and help.

Was there a mission for me?

Minutes later, I was watering and pruning the geraniums and daisy bush on that back deck. I stared into them in the morning sunlight.

They were friends to me! Did they somehow know it?

They enhanced my life, bringing more beauty to the scene I loved so much. And I enhanced their lives, helping them get a good balance of sun and water, and providing an environment in the flow of nature.

I felt my conscious self slide into the daisy somehow:

A bee is dancing on my lee side,
bringing me food, and taking food,
and the human friend is staring at me.
Does the human being
know that I too am conscious?

I stared at the daisy plant. Shock. I'd been somehow in it for an instant!

Did I, then, share some form of love with even the flowers and yes the bees on my back deck? The answer was wonderfully clear.

And I saw the cobwebs interspersed on the deck railing in a new light: I'd remove them, but I would not want to hurt their makers.

I could sense myself as just one more of the tiny creatures of nature inhabiting this magical blue marble spinning through space.

I took a shower and left.

I'd suggested a restaurant where we could eat outside. Instead, we sat inside by a window. I took the sunshine.

Susan ordered tea. Her hands were quivvering again, the way they did each time we broke up.

"I cannot keep leaving and hurting you, Susan."

"But I want you. I know that you love me!" She smiled into me. "I know that you don't want to hurt me."

"Susan, I need time, that's part of it."

"You're so . . ."

Somehow her words were tailing off. My own eyes were on her, but I was seeing something else.

It was real! My mind's eye was seeing particles blazing past me, to my sides. It was as if I was flying, zooming through Somewhere.

I checked my physical self: No, I wasn't fainting or sick or "not here."

"Susan . . ."

"And when . . ."

"Susan!," I whispered. "Something wild is happening to me. For me."

She stopped talking and looked up.

"I—I feel like I'm whizzing through space or something. I can actually see it."

She smiled, a wide, knowing grin, warm and happy. There was no alarm.

"What I see is like diving as you hit a pool of water, arms at your side and seeing bubbles fly past you."

I checked again. I could see the table and Susan and the two businessmen at the next table.

"My God, Susan. It's absolutely real. I'm flying somewhere on a different plane and I can see the particles dividing in front me as I plunge through . . . red and brown, sort of a rust color, some black or red with deep blue space beyond them . . ."

She still wore the huge wide grin.

"Am I flipping out?"

"No, Scott—you're flipping *in*."

The waiter came and left. We talked about people she'd known who had similar experiences. I barely heard her, though. I was plunging headlong through that wild beautiful rust-sparking color out there, in here.

Then: "It's gone, isn't it?"

I looked up at her from my soufflé.

"You seemed 'here' all of a sudden."

"Oh my gawd, now I see-" I stopped. Could I tell anyone? She was talking.

I was in Cheyenne, Wyo. The figure to my left was Donna Wilson, except she was in her late 20s and her hair was browner than now. And she was—what? She didn't have the "wisdom" I had come to know in her eyes and countenance.

Something—certain, but with no voice or visual sign—said the date was in the 1860s.

There was no threatening thought that I'd lost my sanity or was hallucinating. It felt safe, almost normal.

The scene was yellowish and dusty.

Then suddenly it was gone. My being seemed to scream "oh no!" I shook my head.

There it was again. Oh good! Donna was loading something, maybe a box or a bale of hay, onto something tall. I didn't see what it was but we were at railroad tracks and I later thought it was probably a freightcar.

She was husky yet thinner, maybe slightly shorter than I knew her to be in the 1980's. It was unclear whether I was husband or boyfriend; which one did not matter. I was hers and she was mine, and we loved each other, were partners, even in our work.

Something, that same clear thought-voice, said that I had been taken away, shut off from Donna's house, and said that I . . .

Yes! That I had died later in a prison in Colorado, and for a terrible crime of which I had been innocent although involved.

Strange, this mind's eye. I seemed to be able to turn it on or off right now.

Back in Cheyenne, same scene. To my right, there was a wooden two-story building. Somehow I knew that the porch roof hanging out above the first floor and the slatted sidewalk had a hidden, built-in ladder and you could reach up from the sidewalk to pull the ladder down.

Then the scene was gone again.

It had been almost a freeze-frame. Donna's arms might have been moving, but the glimpse had covered no more than a split second in time.

I felt no doubt at all that it was real. It was just there, somewhere within my mind or soul or memory.

My God, I thought, I did live before! I must have. How else could I see and feel it?

I was flooded with joy and gratitude. Overwhelmed, as if God had washed over me in a tidal wave of truth and joy and warmth.

It took a minute of eating soufflé and sipping my coffee before I felt assured that I was "normal," that I hadn't flipped out. I was sane and joyous. All I'd done was meditated, and prayed for insights.

Susan said she was enthralled by the look on my face. I continued eating, shaking my head in awe. This really was happening!

We had both intended to reinforce our breaking up again over this lunch. But not right now. It wasn't right. I'd bring it up later.

"It doesn't matter what you label it. You don't need to put some label on it," she said as I drove into the parking lot in front of her little apartment after lunch.

"But I feel almost . . ."

She put her finger on my lips to quiet me.

"No, Susan—I need to say this, just to say it to someone. I felt almost clairvoyant for that moment."

"I know, I know. But you don't need to label it."

She was right. I would, I knew, get confused if I tried to force this into mere logic. It was beyond any 'logic' borne of my day-to-day experience or anything I'd been taught.

And it was all okay. It felt wholesome, part of the whole.

I also sensed that it wasn't over yet.

"Can I use your phone?"

Donna's line was busy. I tried her business line, normally handled by an answering service. Instead, Donna answered.

"Hello, Wilson."

"Scott! I was just calling your house and, it's really strange—this is almost the only time I've answered this line!"

"That is no surprise at all. Not today. Just one of my 'coincidences'."

"Oh?"

"I'd like to come over there right now. It's important." I knew that my voice would convey the marvel and Donna would know it was urgent but not an emergency—and would say okay.

Susan, surprisingly to me, seemed undisturbed by my going to Donna's immediately. I said I'd be back in two hours.

I started to drive to Donna's, careful not to do anything that might tamper with super-conscious mood.

She looked like home to me. I held her in my arms and wanted to scream and cry at once.

"C'mon, we'll sit on the deck." She was grinning expectantly.

I settled into a chair and gazed out across the blue lines of forest ridges. It was so three-dimensional, much like the scene from my back deck. But it felt so familiar.

"Well?"

"It's still going on."

"I can tell." She nodded to herself, lookled back up at me from her soda.

"I've seen *us*, Donna."

She drew air down into her lungs with a sudden seriousness.

"We . . ."

"This wasn't supposed to begin for you yet, dear Scott."

"Huh?"

"It's okay. Just tell me what you're seeing."

I proceeded to describe the scene in Cheyenne. She kept her eyes closed and nodded occasionally. Her face seemed so delicate.

And then I remembered that most of her family was from Wyoming—another "coincidence?"

The phone broke in. She went into the kitchen. I sat thanking God, over and over.

As she came back to the deck, she asked if I knew anything about her friend Morton.

"Let me . . ." I closed my eyes. And it was there immediately.

"This may sound screwy, Donna, but I see a white-looking wall, sort of molded and rounded, about 10 or 12 inches high, and there's blood pouring down over it like a small waterfall."

She gasped. "He's got a bleeding ulcer."

"He does? Well, that's what I'm . . ."

"Do you 'know' anything?"

"Yes, very clearly." I was amazed at the clarity, the exactness, the rightness of what I sensed. I had no doubt that the information was correct. "He's got to clear up some deep guilt. It's something he did in Vietnam."

She gasped again. "Do you know what he . . ." She stopped. I opened my eyes and saw a troubled thoughtful Donna.

"Scott, he was basically a hired killer in Vietnam!"

"Somehow, I don't think you'll be able to get through to him right now, Donna. Something says he might shut it off, in spite of his good intentions."

"That's probably right. He's caught up in his business now." She sighed.

She seemed warmer, closer to me. I couldn't shrug away the image of the woman in her 20s working with me in Wyoming in the 1860s! (Something told me later her exact age had been 26.) Yet I knew that I must trust her instincts as well as mine. If we now were to be more than loving platonic friends, it would be months, maybe years, before we would know it.

To my surprise, that knowledge was acceptable to me. I was bemused that it didn't seem frustrating or unfair, and I felt no need to try to change it.

I left on schedule, returned to Susan and helped her get gas for her stranded car, then drove slowly up the coast for dinner with Jessie and Huntley. Later I drove slowly back down the coast in the dark. The clarity was gone, replaced with a sense of awe, and an odd fatigue.

Later in the evening, Dick Holland called, bursting with excitement.

Somehow I just wasn't suprised by his news: His neighbor Don had introduced Dick, through tapes, to some concepts of reincarnation, meditation and out-of-body experience. Dick said he just hadn't known . . .

And yes, Dick would read the Shirley MacLaine book I'd been urging upon him for weeks.

Meditation produced insights. And some came while I was driving. For example:

I wondered if I had deliberately become sort of a mini-public figure in the Silicon Valley for a spirit reason: By writing and talking openly and candidly, people said—was I trying to overcome my shame and humiliation? Maybe, I thought, my own Higher Self and/or God chose the public path—later to include this book—so that I would learn humility as a replacement for humiliation.

Strange, paradoxical lesson, I decided. One would expect that being sort of a public figure would feed my false pride. Instead, it seemed to have the opposite effect:

I was constantly, minute to minute, aware of where I had come from, aware that there was no way I alone had been strong enough to climb up out of the nightmare and almost certain death I'd faced.

I felt self-conscious whenever I tried to explain it, though. I was afraid people would think humility was false.

The only solution was to be myself, be honest, not worry about what others thought. And sometimes that was a tough assignment.

Over dinner with a female friend, during a business swing through the Midwest,the inevitable issue came up about my growing interest in reincarnation and the ethical implications.

"How can you say you're Christian and yet believe in these things," she asked.

"Funny about that." I drank more grapefruit-and-7Up. "It's actually increased my interest in what Jesus said."

"You've got to be kidding."

"Not at all."

"Well—it runs so contrary to . . ."

"Look." I was holding back my exasperation. Almost every time I spoke with someone who made a big deal of being Christian, I found myself feeling the same uneasiness.

"I know you don't want to look at these things. I know the Bible is all we 'should' need. "But the fact is that for me, the church, generically, and the Bible in general did not answer a lot of my questions in a way that satisfied me that my life was—well, meaningful."

"Really?" Her eyes were wide.

"There are lots of things that keep me going back to what Jesus said. For example, in the Good News for Modern Man edition of the Bible, he's quoted as saying 'there are many rooms in my father's house'. Now, I don't claim to read the New Testament a lot, but to me, that could easily be an invitation to the mind and to my own meditation. Those 'many rooms' may be other spheres, or dimensions . . ."

She was angry. It took me 10 minutes to calm her down and gracefully leave that topic. There was no room in her for anything except the kinds of Bible interpretation that had never satisfied me. Therefore, there was nothing further to say—that night or ever.

I was finding a few Bible-quoting Christians closing their minds and condemning me in a way that I thought might make even Jesus sad. I know it made me sad, until I realized that they had to learn lessons in this lifetime.

April 1986:

I felt increasingly reassured in the day-to-day routines within our ACBJ chain of papers, within my own paper, and in other aspects of my business life:

Life is good.
I've always blindly and naively
Assumed that Life would be fair.
It is more than fair to me.

No matter how many times I knew people were right when they said this guy or that guy was shooting at me, was undermining me, was trying to take away my credibility, I tried to turn the other cheek. Not out of some pious, Christ-adaptive goodness in me, but because I knew from my experience with God and alcohol that if I simply let God run the show, things would work out far better than if I might try to impose my own design.

It worked. That was nub of it: It worked.

Oh, I might lose power here, or influence there, might lose my job or my house or my whatever, but jobs and houses weren't at the core of happy, joyous, free living and inner security.

I'd really gotten proof in the preceding year. There had been a dark problem at work—a problem I'd decided I couldn't write about. I'd gotten through it without deep scars, even though it was emotionally and professionally exhausting.

Looking back even farther, I saw that the big job on a paper in Washington and a big home in the suburbs hadn't made me happy. I had, in fact, been far happier in much less "successful" times.

I'd seen it, too, in the lives of many around me.

I watched, through the months, several men and women who had made it big—millions of dollars, heaps of Designer Living. Their eyes told me the truth. Some were happy and secure. Some were tormented.

There were plumbers and Mexican laborers and unemployed people who had more joy and security in their eyes than some of the "successful" people.

On the other hand, I'd seen that Right look in Phil Boyce's eyes, and his bank would soon be approaching the $1-billion level in assets.

Regardless of 'who', it was an inside job. The money and "success" needed to be dividends.

Things material would not fix things spiritual. But spiritual work could produce material joys.

Karen Evanoff and I had stayed in touch through the months since she'd left the Business Journal to finish her degree.

Her mother Jean continued to pray, to not drink, to not have any recurrence of the cancer.

And occasionally, when I'd wonder who was my best female friend, I'd wonder if it was Karen, even though we only had dinner—and lots of laughter—perhaps once every three months.

Our friendship was a source of great joy. I knew that I should never disturb it.

I'd never had friends like Karen and Donna and Jerry and Dick and Bob Keady and Bob Kieve and . . . the list was getting longer each year now.

Each was a person to whom I could say anything. And, I felt, vice versa.

I knew that when I told them about my fears or failures, I was giving them my deepest level of love—and was getting it back as they did the same.

A far cry from the drinking friends.

A bright day in May 1986:

The warm shower almost burned my skin. I'd been on the beach for an afternoon and was about to take a nap. I was happily relaxed, no worries except the normal little ones.

And there she was. "The Face in the Shower."

Oh damn, said part of me, without knowing why.

It was not quite Elizabeth McGovern, the actress. That was my first reaction. But she had some similar features, especially in the cut of the hair, the forehead, the brilliant eyes.

Then it was gone.

She'd been standing with her left side toward me, this time in a red dress with white patterns of some sort. And once again it was an image. No words or voice. And I knew that I was shutting it off the moment my damned mind started saying "she doesn't look like Elizabth McGovern."

The rational side of me was defeating the inner real me!

But then I knew what my initial disappointment, the "oh damn" feeling, had been: She was not any woman I knew.

Elizabeth McGovern's face was as close as I could get to finding a similar facial impression within me to "The Face in the Shower."

I knew that the human brain, when it's trying to decipher something new refers in its internal memory to the closest image it holds in a category, and therefore could be labeling or categorizing something erroneously.

Had my computer-brain brought up McGovern's face simply because it seemed the closest-in-category to the face it had just seen?

It hurt that I still hadn't met the woman behind that image.

Three days later:

The image came, flickered, and then came up strong in my mind's eye:

My mother Ann was standing stiffly erect, her forearms forming straight vertical lines up her chest, the hands clenched in front of the jaw. It was a boxer's defensive posture when the opponent is attacking furiously.

Protection. That's it: self-protection.

That was her life posture. She'd been so hurt so young—just as I had been—by her father's death, and later her husband's, and by whatever else that she had learned to cover and protect her emotional self.

And she learned protection with a better device than her arms—her marvelous intellect. She could bob and weave and jab and throw a roundhouse, and seldom if ever get hit. Geezus, she was a goddam champion!

Strong to a fault.
and smart to a fault.
Is that my mother—or me?

I saw almost daily that the less often I judged myself the better I felt—and it opened me up to changing myself.

Ever since the Monterey inventory back in the fall of '83, I wondered if I had manipulated women into liking me, including Denise. Now I saw that wasn't necessarily the case.

Perhaps, I thought, my self-esteem had been so low that I had felt no woman would love me for being just me and therefore one of two things had happened: Either I felt that I'd manipulated them, or I suspected that they liked me because they thought I had position or power or money. Either attitude ruled out the simple idea that they might love me as myself.

I'd seen that my mother loved me because I was simply her son—yet on that issue, I hadn't known that I truly had her love until November's trip. Now I knew that I was a good enough guy that a woman could love me without being manipulated or enticed by "position."

I was working on the book and re-reading my notes on the yellow legal pad from my inventory in Monterey in 1983. At that time I'd written: "Assuming current relationship w/God, if I had my dream life, how would it be?"

I had listed 13 "dream-life" conditions.

Of the 13, 12 and a half had come true in less than three years—everything except "quitting cigarettes."

I noted that something else—a woman—hadn't been on the list then.

I stared at the old notes. Twelve and a half out of thirteen . . .

I was not surprised. I'd come to expect that what I wanted in my heart would happen. On God's schedule, though—never on mine.

Later, in the shower, I got down on my knees again. Before I could pray, I was hit by a truth: my lifelong feeling of inadequacy was false, like the flip side of false pride. Was it Matthew who quoted Jesus as saying, "With Him all things are possible?"

No matter what the circumstance, I am only inadequate when I am relying on my personality rather than on Spirit.

The city manager, Gerry Newfarmer, met me at Eulipia for lunch.

Time had vindicated Gerry, and his smile showed it.

On the whole, the City of San Jose was a well-managed $3-billion business. And Gerry had survived being the new city manager when it had lost that $60 million in the bond market.

I remembered the lunch at the Sainte Claire Hilton two-plus years earlier.

"So what's next for Gerry Newfarmer?"

"Just doing my thing, that's all."

I was driving home later, and turned off the stereo. Was the car always my thinktank?

Look at the intuition's record:
It's been right about 95 percent of the time.
And always ahead of the brain.

Mike Russell . . . Bill Worley . . . Armon Mills . . . Bob Kieve . . . Bob Talbott . . . Gerry Newfarmer . . . Phil Boyce . . . Lew Wolff . . .

Every time I'd trusted my hunches about these guys, I'd been on the right track.

And it was reassuring to note that the people who had an attitude of "giving it back" had done so well: Russell and Worley and Mills had grown a mini-empire in newspaper publishing; Kieve's stations were doing very well; Talbott's stores were growing; Newfarmer had survived some tough politics; Boyce's bank was about to hit the $1 billion level; Wolff had scored big and was headed into new ventures which excited him.

Or was it all just coincidence? Like the times I wanted Bacharach or Sinatra and would turn on the radio and find Bacharach or Sinatra . . .

I turned the stereo back on. Bob Kieve's mod-pop station, KARA, was playing, uncharacteristically, a song by Burt Bacharach.

20

"Life is an experience. It is not reality."
—Chuck C.
Los Angeles.

The small, seemingly unimportant coincidences rolled on like the endless waves I enjoyed so from the back deck. I watched the progression with more glee each day.

If noticed as singular events, they wouldn't seem to mean much. It was the pattern that helped me see what was really happening in my life and all around me. The whole was larger than the sum of the pieces.

At first I'd not seen them. Then, as the months of sobriety grew into years, gradually the isolated pieces had started fitting into patterns. Just as it took separate grains of sand to make a beach, it took the little events to form the more meaningful picture. You had to stand back to see the pattern.

Each set of waves, or events, brought a lesson about living, if I was alert and looked for it.

What happened to be "coincidences" seemed to have, in fact, a hidden cause. I wondered if the human spirit had the invisible, unfelt power to create or attract the events. And if so, did the "coincidences" then carry forward the circumstances necessary for the spirit's learning?

• Dick and I had dinner on a Thursday night. He was well past three years of sobriety. I suggested it was time he sponsored someone in their recovery. He agreed. One hour later, an acquaintance called from Colorado and asked Dick to sponsor him . . .

• I sat on the beach one afternoon reading the chapter on precognition in Dr. Edgar Mitchell's book. I still wondered whether precognition was "true." Later that same afternoon, I had a sense I should see Susan—hadn't seen her in a month. I called. Her car had broken down, why didn't I come over for a chat? I did. While there, her phone rang and it was a crisis. She needed a car immediately, and she needed someone who had a certain kind of knowledge. I was there, I had a car and I had exactly that knowledge.

• At a time when I thought I should doubt my own precognitive insights, I met a woman in Monterey—we'd both sat down on the same bench simultaneously to have a cigarette—who'd had a lifetime chock-full of precognition. She'd avoided a plane flight that had crashed; had a long list of similar but less dramatic precognitive experiences. She'd been that way since childhood.

• I'd been looking for more personal descriptions of out-of-body experiences, again exploring whether the phenomena were "true." I had dinner with a woman in San Jose who casually said she'd left her body "at will" during high school—"whenever I was bored." I went off to Monterey for dinner and jazz with another friend, and she started telling me how she'd been in an accident, had two major surgeries, was given morphine but didn't like its effects on her—she had floated out of her body one night . . .

• When I'd wondered about life-after-life experiences, and about death, I met a woman whose husband had died of a brain tumor. His best old friend had been weeping at the bedside when the stricken man uttered his last: "If you saw what I'm seeing, you wouldn't be crying!" He'd died right then, she said.

It wasn't much later that my conservative New England friend Lionel Brown had told me about his near-death experience, and how it had given him "certainty" that we live on.

• When a business friend called me about a family member's drinking, I explained how the intervention process works. Moments later, another friend called and casually told me about a review of a new book on intervention in that same day's San Francisco Chronicle. It probably had the information the first caller had needed . . .

• Another business friend would give things away. He told me that every time he did, he'd get some unexpected, out-of-the-blue benefit. It confirmed his feeling that giving is a lesson in his life.

It just kept happening. On and on and on and . . .

I wondered how many people chose to ignore the "coincidences" in their lives.

And the real paradox, of course, was that they probably had created some or all of them themselves, at the psychic-spiritual level.

They chose to ignore them, I guessed, because adding them up, seeing the patterns, would force them to take a deeper look at their own spiritual existence and the creative power they possessed—but often ignored. But why would people consciously ignore such "meat" in their lives?

"Modern man" had been raised in the industrial and technological revolutions. He had glorified the "rational," the left brain—at his own expense.

Events and "coincidences" could be a mindopener for so many, as could good books. Perhaps it was threatening to them.

To me, the MacLaines and Trevelyans and Mitchells of this world were front lines in the breakthrough of the Revolution of Spirit.

And I could see a role for me in helping people to start seeing. If they would see what had happened for me, maybe they'd take a closer look at their own lives.

Dick Holland was more than a "coincidence" in my life. He was an inspiration.

Alcoholic and homosexual, he had volunteered for training and became a counselor or big brother to people who had Aids. It was one way, he said, he could "give back" the goodness of his sobriety.

If I thought I was being "good" by helping someone, I'd realize how small it was compared to what Dick was doing.

Dick and Corky got a new house with an extra room, and decided they should lend the room to someone needy. Dick made a call and instantly "ran into" a German woman in her 70s who had no place to live. "Coincidence," he said with a wink. A few days after they gave the woman a free home, right along the ocean in a grove of trees, someone offered Dick and Corky a solid sum to buy out part of their business.

"Out of the blue—isn't it wonderful!," said Dick. "An' me—just a dingy in the sunshine of God's love!" He was laughing uproariously. It was infectious.

On and on and . . .

And then Bill Worley called one morning. He'd been talking with a friend from Laguna, Ca. She'd quoted this:

Coincidences
Are miracles

In which God chooses
to remain anonymous.

I asked Dick that night over sunset and fresh halibut at a Moss Beach restaurant: "Do you suppose this stuff is happening all the time, like every day, in our lives—in everyone's lives—and we or most people just aren't alert enough to realize it?"

"I thought maybe it was just us," he said. "But it feels like a lot of people—not everyone, but a lot—seem to be getting the idea, one way or another."

"Dick, I think every soul goes through crisis in this life. Ours happened to be alcoholism, but everybody gets theirs. And everyone gets to have the coincidences, the prayers answered, and the chance to see the lessons."

Dick grinned. "But maybe they get more coincidences if they're on a path of spiritual progress, not just counting their money."

During several hours at home with Mike Russell in Kansas City, he had helped the two of us into a meditative state. Afterward he said that all we'd really done was a simple form of biofeedback—monitoring the "energy" flowing into us.

Back at home, I got a clipping from my daughter Laura. The Washington Post magazine had run a piece in which she was held out as an example of someone using biofeedback to control or reduce or eliminate longtime killer headaches.

I got the feeling that I was being told something, even wrote a column about my simple uses of such techniques. I felt uninitiated, perhaps ready. I knew that I'd had some success controlling headaches—and no success at all with toothaches.

May 1986:

I recalled something from four years earlier: In the midst of my heartache, in mid-'82, there on a quiet Tuesday evening in Palo Alto had stood my friend Barbara, who had not had a drink then in nine years.

She said she'd found a new peace of mind after her first several years of sobriety. How? She'd decided to try, just try, to stop judging herself.

"You may think this is wrong or immoral, or even worse, amoral. I really don't care what you think. If I'm not going to let me judge me, I can't let you judge me.

"I just know that I am me and I live within my conscience. Beyond that, on a day-to-day basis, I try to have fun and not judge me for how I'm having it."

I hadn't thought much about that until years later, when I realized that I was less defensive about my actions. I thought of Barbara's advice and knew what a gift she'd passed along.

That piece of advice may have helped me more in the darkness of Capitola when I'd left Denise in the winter of 1983-84 than anything else: If I could do what felt Right inside, and just be willing not to judge myself, I felt better.

It made sense according to my experiences: *Let God do the judging.*

But then I got a sense that maybe even God doesn't judge . . .

It had been a hectic weekend morning with the children, phone calls from friends, breakfast making, and spilling. In the midst of the hullabaloo, as I stared out from the kitchen window at the foggy flat ocean and the fishing boats floating there:

> *God's plan is that somehow He has created many of Him.*
> *Zillions of us/Him.*
> *And as each progresses, gets past its own weaknesses of 'will'*
> *and learns how to become more like God,*
> *then God has created*
> *worlds within worlds within worlds. All within Him.*
> *And we wouldn't learn*
> *without mistakes.*

June 16, 1986:

Bill Worley, now handling more of the day-to-day policies within American City Business Journals, was at his down-home best, visiting in the publisher's office at the San Jose Business Journal. Armon Mills sat to his right. I sat across the partners' desk from Bill.

We'd been talking turkey about the San Jose paper, and the company. The company's stock was still doing very well; there were major expansion plans under way. And now we were going to talk straight about Scott B. Smith, aspiring author.

The door stayed open.

"If your book doesn't sell, Scott, we . . ."

"It'll sell, Bill."

"You sound like Mike."

He'd meant it in a jocular way. I thanked him anyway. He grinned.

"So . . . if it doesn't sell, what are you going to do? Have you thought about it?"

"No, and I don't think I'll need to."

Armon smiled. When he was relaxed, he could smile one of the sweetest smiles.

Bill rolled his fingers as if playing with some invisible musical instrument.

"Mike and I have decided that if you've got a second book in you—well, do you?"

"You bet I do. I've already started research notes for it."

"If you do, and if it sounds like a good idea to us, then we'll stick with you through two books, regardless of whether the first ever sells a single copy."

I was astounded. These guys were more than I'd ever dreamt could happen in my life.

How'd it happen?

I'd prayed. That was the only answer I had.

Late June 1986:

I sat on the back deck as the late afternoon sun slid to my right. The spider's web caught my eye, and I stared into it, entranced.

The sunlight was at just the right angle so I could see every strand the tiny creature had strewn.

The symmetry was simple and beautifully complex. And as I stared at it, I saw more and more strands.

That web, just 10 inches across, was supported by strands going to attachment points along the two vertical rails maybe three inches away. But there also were long, loping pieces that tied it to the top hand rail four feet away.

That little creature, size and weight so unbelievably small, had to have God in her.

Why did I think it was "her?"

Because, I felt, no spider could have enough brain cells or environmental schooling in its own lifetime to perform or understand this engineering on an intellectual basis. No, my friend had an intuition that carried genetic information and memory. In other words, it operates out of what we call the right brain, the intuition—and females generally do get closer to that area of truth.

But that will change, I thought. Just wait and watch . . .

Right!

Where did that 'voice' come from?

Close the eyes, listen, listen, just listen. Surf. Listen. Birds. Listen.

And then I heard the bzz of another tiny miracle: The hummingbird had come back, was hovering in mid-flight above the geraniums, maybe two feet from my face.

Scientific mathematics said that tiny bird could not fly and hover like that.

Something spoke very softly to me from within:

"Our souls are in training here." Just as that little daily book had told me.

"We must gain enough knowledge now that we gain the spirit-tools to start understanding, start recognizing the lessons in our own lives—each action, each thought, each moment—for their value to our spirit."

"That's why MacLaine's book was important to me. Or the big book on alcoholism, or Peale's 'Power of Positive Thinking.'

"Same with my love of Walker Percy and Woody Allen or Herb Goldberg, though their messages are different.

"I fit them into the pattern I draw of my experiences and I start to see.

"If I think that spider's web is intricate and beautiful—look at my life thus far!"

My mind seemed to be going into a natural conversation of some sort with the gentle voice inside me—it felt like I was communicating directly with my own Higher Self, without seeing it.

My physical, conscious being was saying:

And if there is no death, if we do live maybe hundreds of times, experiencing everything there is on this earth, this plane of life, then these books and even movies are helpful because they're part of our education in this lifetime.

I am just here to learn. That's all.

"Right."

So, I am part of God. There is no death. There may not be, in fact, any physical reality at all—it's all in the thought process, all in what this generation calls consciousness?

"There's a reason to call it that—because that's what it is. Being conscious-of, alert and aware-of. Opening up. The world had closed-off during the technological revolutions."

And the biggest single revelation, biggest revolution in mankind, that can happen now will be the worldwide individual knowledge that there is no death?

Not only that, I thought, could it be that there is no "bad," or "evil"—these things are just part of the schooling, like math problems to be solved?

Now I'm getting somewhere.

It was impossible to tell how the "conversation" took place. There had been others—this was more direct. In the old days, even just a couple of years earlier, I would have discounted this. But too many coincidences, too many wondrous things were happening. I could no longer doubt that.

something's going on here.

My brother "A" had given me a cordless, walk-around phone.

If I got too much distance and material between the portable set and the wired receiver, I got a lot of static. There was too much material garbage interfered with the movement of radiowaves—sound vibrations that formed voices, and therefore meaning.

Was this something akin to the spiritual message-waves and earthly static? Did the psychics somehow cut through that static interference and hear clearly what others, like me, only dimly perceived as "distant, unintelligible voices."

Frank Sammons called to tell me that Bob Talbott had keeled over during a walk in Carmel on Wednesday morning.

Bob's gone home. He's still around.

Minutes later, I realized that I had been writing about Bob at exactly the hour when he 'died'—the only time in the year-long process of writing this book that I'd felt compelled to write about my "Monterey inventory" of '83, and Bob Talbott's effect on me.

He'd had heart problems, but his death was a surprise. Frank kept saying he was thankful there'd been no long painful lingering.

I noted to myself that I no longer harbored the notion that a good man's death was tragic. And it didn't surprise me that at the hour when Bob's physical being fell away, I'd had such a strong compulsion to write about him.

Coincidences . . .

The book had become my life. The writing felt clean and wonderful—until I realized that I kept writing about the joys and coincidences, and was not writing about the darkest parts of my bottom back in Tucson and Allentown.

In July, I started to dig into how it had felt—faced it, threw me down into it. It was as tough as I'd thought it would be.

In order to write about how it had felt, I had to re-experience it.

It was a gift, painful even though I knew the principle involved: "No pain no gain."

There were times in the writing, long mornings with the phones unplugged, that felt like I was crawling around in the basement of my soul, no lights, nose pressed against a dirt floor, sucking it up with no certainty of ever getting back up out of it.

I had to do it.

So I wrote a column about "a writer" going through just that. It was feebly disguised—any of my friends and certainly some of my readers would know who "he" was.

But somehow I had to express the pain and the loneliness—and the joy of knowing what you only know if you've lost and come back.

It said: "The long dark stuff opens into light you wouldn't recognize unless you'd been through the long dark stuff."

I was changing.

And the realization was growing: Maybe this was my 'mission': To write about what had happened and what happened currently and in the future, to help build the bridge between the Old School and the New Age.

Ours, I decided, has been the Disoriented Generation—a generation so disillusioned that it lost any sense of structure.

Like so many in my generation, I'd been disillusioned about government. I'd rebelled in my own way. Now I saw the pendulum swinging, and I sensed that maybe somehow I could help reinforce Jeffersonian commitments to individual liberty and freedom, and to free enterprise.

Funny, I thought, that the 'liberals' who wanted to reinforce individual liberties were so often against opportunities in business.

That's starting to change, I thought. Free enterprise will get a big new swing of the pendulum as the spiritual growth spreads.

Like so many in my generation, I'd been deeply frustrated and disappointed by the church. Now, I hoped, I'd gone far beyond that and was part of a subtle change across the land—a spiritual revolution.

My bottom had led me to spiritual action, and when I did occasionally show up in a church, and listened to what Jesus was quoted as saying, I took it as a call to personal action—not a call to the front pew.

My interest in reincarnation and other "exotic ideas" was drawing me closer to understanding Jesus.

Like so many in my generation, I'd been heartbroken by my disillusionment with the White Picket Fence. Now I was seeing what it would take to make a marriage work—I, or we, finally were finding realistic possibilities, in place of the old Hollywood/Broadway/TV, Doris Day/Rock Hudson expectations.

It seemed that in other critical areas—education, health, retirement, leisure, and more—the spiritual changes were bringing new attitudes in place of the post-war promises and materialism and ultimate disillusionment.

Disoriented in the '60s and '70s, we were finally finding a new home—and it was a subtle, giant step for mankind.

July 1986:

Every day I looked forward to the end of the evening, when I would tilt my red leather chair back, put on some music by Andreas Vollenweider, and meditate.

I'd gotten so that I could put my body into a sleep condition, while my mind remained acutely alert. An "Alpha state."

On July 3, I had a visitor.

I was getting a clear 'voice'. As it began, I reached for a small pad and scribbled notes on what it said. Here they are, in part:

"You are to take care of plants. Do not get a hot tub." (I had considered it.)

"Wait and prepare for her.

"You do not need to smoke. Your nature is not to smoke."

"You have, will have, all that you need. The point is to nurture life—especially your own.

"In some sense, answers will come through your body—you are too much in your mind, too much in intellect control.

"You need sensuality in your life to experience the psychic growth you seek.

"Deep green plants, quiet music.

"Write a little poetry.

"Life can be a gentle dance—cherish it."

The 'voice' was using words, my language, but it had no physical sound. I felt it was external—some other entity.

I decided to try a conversation. I would speak aloud, then listen.

I asked "is there reincarnation?"

Instantly: "Of course!

"Stop trying so hard. You have the faculty for everything.

"I have shut your phone off temporarily for you. You forgot to do that tonight.

"Now:

"Whatever you seek, believe it and it will be.

"Be careful."

I asked what Donna Wilson meant in my life, and the answer shot back:

"Great love . . . You have resistance to her because of your shame.

"Donna has much fear. She needs your stability.

"Your fascination with Donna's house includes your (hidden) memory of an old church with similar wood. You'll see."

I was stunned by the apparent presumption that Donna and I would be more than 'old friends'. But it was quite unclear to me what "great love" meant.

Great friends? Great lovers? Married partners? "Just" spirit-partners?

I asked, "What about Denise?—Is she okay now?"

"Denise is waiting to go (on). To you, she was an old friend—just a friend. Your union was good friends. She knows it but not in our sublime sense."

I asked: "Is this whole conversation phony?"

Instantly: "Are you getting truth?"

Then came the words which were to haunt and guide me for weeks to come: I had asked, "what should I worry about?—My selfishness?"

"You've been horribly, terribly hurt.

"You must be nurtured and allow yourself to be loved.

"Your talk to alcoholics about how you grew up needing to be the 'brave little boy' was right—but you still do it.

"You're better now at loving yourself.

"You need the gentle loving companion now smiling with you."

I asked "who?"

"Look around you."

On July 7, again in the evening with the lights low, the same voice or entity was back. I didn't take notes until I sensed I should.

"Love unconditionally—don't hold it in or you won't really receive it.

"Go ahead and give intimacy and get it—on deeper physical and emotional planes.

"Drop any intellectualized form of it.

"Don't pay any heed to what others say about it or you."

I asked why my father had died and I had broken up two families.

"Of course he died. That was a working-out with your mother Ann.

"Now you have a chance to take the risk of trusting.

"You wouldn't trust (in a past life). That's why this happened. Without this (loss of father, loss of families), you wouldn't have had to find trust."

The words rang so true that at last my skepticism was evaporating.

July 8:

I sat in the chair in the "Alpha state" and felt something tugging at me somehow—up around my left shoulder and the left side of my chest.

I caught just a glimpse: A silvery, shadowy image to my left, trying to pull my spirit out of my physical body!

It was loving, friendly.

I had no fear—just shock. But I also felt instantly amused and delighted.

The "spirit body," as I saw it, eyes open, was elastic and grayish.

I wanted to go out of the physical plane, but suddenly I felt vaguely apprehensive—which instantly shut down my awareness of the entity or image to the left.

The experience had lasted maybe 45 seconds.

The next day, the next week, the next month—I never felt a flicker of doubt that it had been "real."

I no longer wondered whether these meditational experiences were imagination. Too many friends—almost everyone I knew who was actively 'seeking'—were having similar experiences.

Coincidences.

July 1986:

I'd taken Jessie and Huntley to the pancake restaurant, "Indian place," as we called it, where we'd been going regularly for 2½ years now.

We had a quiet dinner, considering that there was a 5-year-old and 7-year-old at the table. Just our normal sort of weeknight time together.

I gave Hunt a $20 bill and Jessie the check and they ran up to the counter to pay the bill. It was our routine.

I sat finishing my coffee, feeling healthy and relaxed.

"Nice job."

It was an older woman sitting alone at a booth to my left.

"I've listened and watched the whole time you've been here. You're a fine father, doing a fine job."

I smiled feebly to her: "Thank you. Thank you so much."

I got up and went to men's room, stood in front of the mirror and looked at the tears trickling down my cheeks. There is no way anyone could know what it meant to me, to be told I was a good father—which, deep down I knew—after all the failure behind me, and after being told so many times by two women I'd hurt that I was such a poor father.

"Oh thank You, thank You."

Heard a man tell a story. I laughed because it wasn't funny:

A civilized Englishman visited the islands off the Barrier Reef of Australia years ago.

The people there had a daily lifetime routine: Get up in the morning, go out in their little boats and get a few fish, eat, and then just lie on the beach all day, eat at night, make love, sleep nine hours.

The Englishman told them they should get larger boats.

"What for?," they asked.

"So you can go farther out to sea."

"What for"

"So you can catch larger fish."

"What for?"

"So you have more food, and can sell some of it."

"What for?"

"So you can make some money."

"What for?"

"So you can pay for the boats and buy new clothes."

"What for?"

"So you can get civilized and make lots more money."

"What for?"

"So you can become very successful and then you can relax on the beach every day and not have to worry."

Trouble was, I decided, the point of "work" was not the "result" as much as the process itself. We couldn't get all the lessons if we were just flopped on a beach each day. We needed business—work—for the stage of it, the platform where the lessons could be acted-out and learned.

I was sitting on one of the stone benches, staring at the fountain, a 48-cent coffee in a styrofoam cup resting on my right, and thought: I'm back in a shopping mall, just sitting, just like December 1977, when I was starting to recover.

No, not at all. What was it that friend had said that night this spring when she seemed so spiritually clear and connected?—That I had found my own truth, but I hadn't quite realized it yet, that I was in sort of a graduation phase of my life . . .

I thought of the events and "coincidences" in just the past year:

—The plane ride November 29, and what I saw! The memory of my own face as I saw it that day touched me more than any message or book could.

—I'd started to understand that I am a spirit, not a body, and that I am a part of God, with the ability everyone has to plug into His power.

—The beginnings of some deeper, more loving understanding about my mother, and about Al. And so many others.

—Meeting Susan, under such improbable circumstances, as if I'd run into a close longtime friend.

—The evening I knew there'd be a deer on the highway. It had been another confirmation of the precognitive.

—The day when I'd "seen" Donna and me in Cheyenne in the 1860s.

—The changes that had opened for me as I saw that reincarnation would explain so much. I feared death far less, felt more happily curious about what happens, who I meet, what friends say . . . all of it.

—The sense of people having roles in my life—my parents and stepfather, H.R., Laura, Don, Lynn, Jessie and Huntley, Denise, Bennett Wilson, and his sister, my aunt Jane. Bob Linder. Lionel Brown. Mike Russell, Bill Worley, Armon Mills. Bill Worthington, Dodie Gust. Ewing Philbin, Bob Keady, Ed Schmidt, Harry Phillips, Dick Holland, Jerry and Jane Kelly, Bob Kieve and Donna . . . It would be a very, very long list.

—The constantly expanding certainty that my alcoholism had been a blessing. It had put me on my knees, where I could begin my real journey.

—The "conversations" with my Higher Self.

—The flashmoment in the shower in August 1985, the knowledge that I should write the book at once, not later.

—The knowledge that I wouldn't be afraid to tell what had happened to me, for me, inside me.

Each day felt so good and was being lived with the increasing awareness that time, the monster in my old fears, is just a way of measuring movement, that change is good and not to be feared, no matter what my brain tries to tell me.

And "time" seemed to be providing progress for those I loved.

Lynn had her own title company now in Bethesda, Laura worked for her, and had bought a starter house with her husband Randy.

Don was in management with Marriot.

Denise's love-risk apparently paid off. She was planning to get remarried in 1987.

Life had gentled-out for all of us.

My own demand that I stretch myself in 360 degrees on a weekly basis was wearing me down and I knew it. I was tired and hadn't had a real vacation in 15 months. And that last one had only been five days.

Too many hats, too many responsibilities? I wasn't sure.

At work, I was slowly backing away from day-to-day operational responsibilities. We had a strong editor, and an ugly personnel situation of a year earlier had been resolved. But the Silicon Valley had been in a slump and our advertising sales volume early in 1986 had been off target. So we were playing catch-up ball, and it was hard on everyone.

In the community, my role seemed to be increasing. Half of me welcomed the chances to "give it back." Half of me said it was too much, especially while I was writing a book. I was a member of six boards of directors, and several of them deserved a lot of my time.

Through this maze of busy-ness, I was writing this book, writing the weekly column, writing editorials. And I also wanted to keep my eye on the business, see my kids, spend time with fellow alcoholics, maintain a three-bedroom beach home alone, keep up with my own reading, see friends, enjoy the beach, keep cutting new tapes for myself and others and hearing new music, and get exercise (preferably running my beach).

August 1986:

The book was almost finished.

Looking back across the abyss of almost dying, of then surviving and growing through marriage, "success", divorce and other circumstances, the truth was very clear:

There was just no way I could have done it myself. The only explanation was that I'd had unseen help.

I'd become willing, in each situation, to do things God's way. After that, I'd had the help of the universe.

There had always been hints, little signals, of what would be right for me. They were individual things, what was right for me at the time.

My intuition had told me.

Because I'd gone so far down, emotionally and spiritually and physically, I'd become willing to listen to the intuition. And willing to try to do something about the situations. Through positive thinking, I'd learned how to capitalize on the hints or instincts. Then, through positive experiences, I'd learned to expect the results.

And when I expected something in my heart, it happened.

But in the final analysis, I felt as if I'd done 10 percent, God or my Higher Self or other people or spirits had done the 90 percent.

That's how I escaped death and got sober.

That's how I risked the torture of admitting that the marriage to Denise would not work.

That's how I found the Business Journal.

That's how I started writing a book.

And that's how the next thing will happen.

I discovered a mouse living with me. Every place I'd go, the mouse would show up, whirring past me in the den or living room or bathroom.

The old me would've bought mousetraps. Now I couldn't do it. I was endeared by the chewed-up cough drop wrappers in the bathroom drawer.

Within days, I was talking to the mouse, even risked writing a column about it. What I didn't write, but felt in tidal waves, was: Since my daisy bush had consciousness as part of God—therefore, so did the mouse.

But what if it was a momma?

One day's sunset, the Fall of '86:

I got in the car, rolled back the sunroof and headed toward Monterey. Maybe I'd go to that restaurant I love and have a double shrimp cocktail for my dinner. With grapefruit juice and 7Up, of course.

I was driving south along a two-lane road through the deep-green farm lands.

Plants and insects and animals and human beings, riding the crust of this little blue planet spinning in space . . .

To my right through the sunroof, I saw a nearly full moon hung suspended in the bright yet deep evening sky.

To my left out the window, the pastel yellows and golds and reds of a delicious sunset.

The sunset, a day's end, felt promising.

My 'strength' and 'best thinking' almost
killed me years ago.
I am here because I got down on my knees.
And alcoholism put me there.
oh thank You and,

From way down inside my chest somewhere, I howled in

loud laughter, and threw back my head and boombellowed to the evening sky:

Thank You!, thank You!, thank You!
I've got all the 'problems' now
I prayed to have . . .
What a coincidence.
And oh hey, something else for You to handle:
There's this mouse living in my . . .